Roadkill

Arthur Boyt

Arthur Boyt

Roadkill Copyright © 2022 Arthur Boyt

Edited by Arthur Boyt
Cover Art by Arthur Boyt

ISBN: 9798839332683

Imprint: Independently published

Arthur Boyt

Contents

Arthur Boyt

Arthur Boyt

ACKNOWLEDGMENTS

Hellen O'Hare for giving me invaluable feedback
and Basil Kearsley for the hours spent helping to publish this book.

Preface

I have written this book because an article in the Times on my eating habits sparked radio and television appearances followed by more newspaper and magazine interest such that my wife suggested I seize the opportunity of writing a book about it. That was 16 years ago. Once started I discovered a great deal more to this subject than I had at first realised. I have learned a lot and broadened my interest in many fields; I hope that what I have selected may do the same with my readers.

Introduction

The book contains my recollections, many of which were gathered from my diaries. This prompts me to give my reader a tip: if you are not already a diarist, get a diary for this year, or use any new notebook or exercise book and start today. It will give you so much fun in later years visiting periods in your life otherwise totally lost. It will provide great interest to your grandchildren (should you have or ever acquire any) and you could use it as a basis for a book as I am now. You probably will not become famous like diarists Samuel Pepys or Anthony Wedgewood Benn, but you will be laying up for yourself, your descendants, and your relatives a treasure of days gone by. You can start as young as you like, Colin Perry was a boy living in London in the war who wrote down his daily doings. His one diary which survives is published as *Boy in the Blitz*, it is a valuable archive of that period seen through the eyes of a City office boy. He destroyed his other diaries for fear that a girlfriend would read them!

Picking up the body of some unfortunate bird or beast from beside the road, taking it home, skinning or plucking it, cooking and eating it for dinner is, for me, the most natural and normal thing to do. I have done it for the greater part of my life and for a period of about 20 years I ate almost no other meat than roadkill. Having an allotment which provided me with plenty of fresh vegetables, I spent very little money on food: just on milk, eggs and porridge oats. Let me tell you here that I never go foraging for roadkill, what I get I find on essential journeys and I never, never try to kill something with the car.

Were I also to tell you that I am a bit of a freegan and have enjoyed some delicious tit-bits and luxuries, as well as staples like bread and potatoes, by dipping in the skips and bins at the back of supermarkets, would you immediately class me as a scruffy hippy or a dropout? Why should my foraging habits alter the regard with which I am held? I look upon myself as - nay, I can boldly say I am - a respectable member of society, a pillar of the community. I may be a high priest of parsimony and a role model of economy, with that I shall not argue, but should eating roadkill make me a pariah or an odd-ball? Of course, I practise my parsimony discreetly, but I am not ashamed of lifting a bit of roadkill or dipping unobtrusively into a skip now and again. I derive a certain satisfaction from being able to cut into the body of any bird or beast without being so put off by the sight and smell of its blood and guts that I cannot proceed and eat what I intended to when starting to open the package and I am proud that I am not so snooty, or proper, or PC, that I would pass up a chance to save a penny or two of the housekeeping by dipping into a skip.

Are we now too civilised to gather windfall apples, nuts, or beech masts? In parts of Europe, apples, pears, plums, damsons and cherries are planted by the roads and people gather the free harvest very gratefully. Would we do that in the UK? A few people still go blackberrying so perhaps there is some vestige of our early vegetarian gatherer lineage surviving despite the straightjacket that civilisation seems to force us into. I know that there is a growing body of people who do stop and pick up roadkill, especially the conventional game items. There is also a growing interest in wild food, Ray Mears' book of that title and the TV series it inspired and Richard Mabey's bible on the subject, *Food for Free* are indicators of this interest. Neither of them touches on roadkill so the recipes included here should fill a gap in the subect. If you are in North America, *The edible wild* by Berglund and Bolsby is the complete cookbook and guide to edible plants on that continent.

Perhaps I should say here that I have never (yet) been ill from eating roadkill but I am not immune to getting stomach bugs because I have several times eaten buffet food, like sandwiches and scotch eggs, and been ill afterwards.

If there is anything I should like to achieve by writing this book it is that there should be a change in attitude by drivers towards the wildlife through whose territory our roads pass. We even call it *roadkill* we could never call it *carkill* because that would put the blame on us. Why should our roads be corridors of carnage? The present attitude seems to be one of couldn't care less. If an animal gets in my way, bad luck. Why should I worry about a rabbit or a cat or a dog? Because that attitude may apply equally to our fellow men. A driver who is genuinely concerned over the well-being of an animal in the road is not going to risk colliding with a human being. A habit of slowing down and being prepared when an animal is on or near the road is going to condition our driver to take the same precautionary measures when children or cyclists are about. His training to anticipate an animal's unexpected movements is going to stand him in good stead when it's a human in the equation. Saving animals' lives may save human lives. An awareness of animals both alive and dead is going to make him more aware of people and the possibility that he could kill them. Yes, I know that animals do rush across roads without warning and the arrival of silent electric cars is only going to make that worse.

I hope that, having read the book, drivers will be more aware that, at night, unseen animals in the road can come right through the windscreen and kill them as one nearly did to me; the seat belt is of no benefit in this circumstance. Reading this book could save your life!

Skull and bone collecting

My mother, being a botanist as well as having a BA in English, imparted information on trees and plants whenever the opportunity arose and encouraged my interest in natural history. In our early days, my twin brother and I had a large toy cupboard that housed our collection. It had one shelf devoted to old bird's nests in which pride of place was given to a huge jay's nest which we had managed to poke down with my mother's walking stick while on an autumn walk in Berrybushes Wood near King's Langley. We also had a cabinet specially made for us by Dodson Wiltshire, a deaf and dumb brother from our meeting in Watford. This contained our collection of butterflies and moths, and other things like Roman tesserae from the waste dumps of an archaeological dig at Verulamium. I was six when we started collecting butterflies. We always used a 'killing bottle' with ammonia, chloroform, or carbon tetrachloride (Thawpit) for swiftly despatching our specimens. One day at my infants' school, 'Brodick' in Woodland Drive, a boy brought in a garden tiger moth pinned through its thorax to a piece of card with its wings pinned out. It was unimaginably beautiful, but it was still alive! It squirmed to and fro, crucified under our very eyes. I was traumatised by the cruelty and protested that it should be killed or released. Whenever I saw that boy in later life, that image forced its way into my consciousness, to me he was always a torturer.

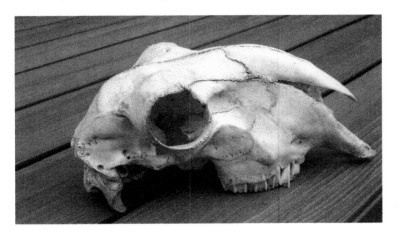

Sheep's skull, © Arthur Boyt

The cupboard also contained some skulls. One of them, a huge sheep's skull, had had to be packed into the luggage for our return by train from a holiday in Devon when I was nine. On one day during that holiday, my father, who was a solicitor and who enjoyed cycling and a game of cricket, asked us twins, very much to our surprise, if he could join us on one of our before-breakfast expeditions exploring the shoreline and muddy creeks around Salcombe harbour. It was fun having him with us, getting our feet wet and slithering about on slippery rocks and seaweed, he had never accompanied us on any of our expeditions before. Unfortunately, his bowel clock forced him to go behind a bush for a while and made us late for breakfast at the guest-house.

Going back to his first day at work the next week and two days after my tenth birthday, he had a heart attack on the train on his way to his office in Southampton Row, in London my sister Naomi was with him in the carriage as well as a brother from our meeting, Roston Shaw. They called the guard and laid him out on the seat. No one tried external heart massage in those days or mouth-to-mouth resuscitation. The guard threw a message from the window as the train passed through Wembly for an ambulance to meet the train when it stopped at Willesden. Of course by the time he reached hospital in Park Royal he was dead; he was 51. Dennis and I arrived home from school for our lunch (we called it dinner) and as we passed the kitchen window we were surprised to see mum sitting in the kitchen with several brethren around her. We heard Naomi give a scream (What was she doing at home at this time of day?), "*I'll tell them, I'll tell them*," we heard her shout. She burst out of the back door and putting her arms around both of us, led us into the back garden."*On the train to London this morning,*" she began rather breathlessly, "*Daddy had a heart attack and has gone to be with the Lord Jesus.*" We knew without asking that this meant he had died. "*He was reading the paper one minute and gave a little cough and collapsed.*" The news was too big for us to take in and we said nothing. We went into the kitchen which was full of sympathetic sisters fussing around. Dinner was served and then mum said that we would not have to go to school in the afternoon. We thought this was great and went round to our friend Maurice Mendham's house, which was the Stamford Arms in Nascot Road, to see his pigeons. His mum wanted to know why we were not at school and was aghast when we told her we had the afternoon off because our dad had died. But I digress.

To get back to the cupboard with skulls: there was also the skull of a mute swan in the cupboard, which we had found dead on the bank of the river Avon below the Clifton suspension bridge while we were on holiday with daddy's sister, Auntie Annie, in Bristol. The head had required a lot of twisting and pulling to remove. My Uncle Stanley, who was an analytical chemist, instead of telling us off for bringing such a thing home, provided an old saucepan for us to boil the head until the meat fell off. It then turned into a glistening white specimen and took pride of place in a little corner of our own

London's Natural History Museum and showed us how to turn a rotten animal's head into a clean skull specimen.

First roadkill experience

"*Den*," I shouted, "*where are you?*" I had to share with my twin brother the horror and excitement of a gruesome discovery. "*I'm upstairs,*" came the equally spirited reply. "*Quick! I've found a dead cat.*" A thunder of feet down four flights of stairs, a thud and a crash and he burst through the swing door into the kitchen. "*Where is it?*" "*It's in Langley Road, come on, I'll show you.*" He wrestled his bike, a 24in-wheel Vindec, from the bike shed, we dashed down the passage beside the house and out into the road. I grabbed my bike, a 26in-wheel Raleigh that I had bought for £2 from Trevor Watkins who lived opposite us in the big house on the corner of The Avenue and Alexander Road (his father was a grumpy old man with one leg shorter than the other and who had once been Mayor of Watford), I leapt onto my bike and the two of us tore off to where I had just found this dead cat. The cat lay in the gutter right outside the house belonging to Percy Bolton, then Headmaster of Watford Grammar School for Boys. The cat was black with a bit of white underneath, but what caught our attention was that one eye had been squeezed right out of its socket and lay grotesquely on its cheek like a black and white marble with white and red strings leading into the sunken empty socket. While part of me was repulsed, another part was mesmerised. I didn't dare touch it. I just prodded it and turned it over with my foot. It was strangely stiff and its fur was matted. It was no longer a cat; its violent death had transformed it into an untouchable phenomenon, but it fascinated me. I couldn't pick it up, but I didn't like to leave it. Little did I realise then, at the age of 8 or 9, that I should, in years to come, not only pick up such a disgusting specimen but readily stop to examine and collect any number of animals that, just like this one, had been killed on the road.

First badger

Once we had bicycles, at or before the age of 9, Dennis and I were stretching our wings and getting around the countryside on bikes; one trip was the 8 or 9 miles to Denham aerodrome to - with a bit of luck - watch a few light aircraft take off and land. On the Denham bypass, I found a dead badger on the grass verge. I did not dream of taking it home and so left it there at the base of a tree. Returning a month or so later I visited the spot and found it had become a skeleton. I had become interested in bones and skulls so I meticulously collected up every bone from the tangle of skin, hair and grass, and took it home with me. The skull was the loveliest thing I had ever seen. The outstanding feature of the badger skull is that the lower jaw and the skull are hinged and cannot be dislocated.

Badger, © Arthur Boyt

It looks very savage with its prominent canines and it has the largest molar in the upper jaw of any animal of its size, which it uses for crushing roots and bones. The skull has a prominent ridge running from just behind the eyes to the neck, the sagittal crest, to which the huge masseter muscles are attached that gives it such a powerful bite. I was enthralled by this wonderful specimen and it became the star of my already growing collection. Roadkill specimens are not just opportunities for a free meal, they also present a unique package of bones for the avid bone student and collector (I have picked up skulls from Finland to Cape of Good Hope and from Saskatchewan to Sydney). Unfortunately, I did not collect the feet bones of this badger into four separate bags and so never managed to reassemble this jumble of odd-shaped bones into a complete badger's skeleton as had been my intention. But I did put the vertebrae onto a cord in the right order that I kept for many years. The badger's scapula or shoulder blade is very distinctive in that it is rectangular. Don't ask how many badger skulls I have today.

First roadkill dissection

When I got my three-speed Raleigh tourer which cost me £22 in 1953 (it was not the green top-of-the-range model, as used by the police, with an automatic switch from dynamo to battery whenever you stopped, but the black version which you had to manually switch from dynamo to batteries) and Dennis had his blue, single-speed Rudge, he and I. at the age of 13, decided to cycle the 111 miles to Norwich where our sister, Naomi, and her family lived. Den felt we should get into training and led me for many a mile to acquire the desired stamina. We were good at cross-country running, but a 20-minute race is no preparation for an eleven-hour cycle marathon. Several 70-mile rides later and we were ready for the adventure. Because my bike was heavier, Den carried the panniers on his bike and I rode it occasionally. My recollection of roadkill on that ride was a great spotted woodpecker in its wonderful black, white and red livery and a house sparrow that had been hit by a car but not killed. One of its eyes was swollen and it wasn't able to fly. We offered it bits of our sandwiches and nursed it in the hopes it would recover quickly, but after 20 minutes it seemed no better so we put it well away from the road and left it to the attention of its family who were anxiously chirping in the surrounding trees.

While we were staying in Norwich we met up with some friends for a ride into the country. On one of these expeditions, we encountered a dead rabbit. We never then dreamed of eating such a specimen. I suggested dissecting it, but we had no knife. I found a piece of broken glass that served as a scalpel. I cut into it while one of our friends, Roy Norman, who was doing biology at school, told us what was what. The first thing the incision revealed was the caecum or blind gut, a convoluted green bag occupying more than half of the space in the rabbit's abdomen. Then there was a coil of tangled tubes attached to the animal's backbone. When I had sorted this out we could see a pale bag, which was the stomach, with dark red slabs of liver draped beside it. Then there was the small intestine, duodenum, jejunum and ileum, from the stomach to the caecum which was a dead-end branch to the gut. The last part was the colon running into the rectum before the gut disappeared into the pelvis. There were droppings lined up in the rectum waiting to be voided. Above the liver was a sheet of tissue, the diaphragm, that separated the lungs from the guts. The diaphragm, which controls its breathing, is a unique feature of the Class Mammalia to which we and the rabbit belong. In the chest cavity the lungs were pale pink and frothy and between them was the heart. The two kidneys were fixed to the back, one a little nearer the front than the other. I then put the guts back in and we buried it; I wiped my hands on the grass but they were smelly all afternoon.

First roadkill meal

Turning points in life often come without warning. Our response to a trivial event may well alter the rest of our lives. Often it is just a readiness for adventure that makes us push open a door and explore what lies beyond. So it was with my brother and me. We were cycling back to Watford from a holiday with our cousins in Cranleigh about 1954 when we came across a pheasant lying beside the road in Windsor Great Park. We stopped to examine it. It was a hen pheasant and it was dead. It was beautiful, every feather a kaleidoscope of browns and buffs and black. It seemed such a shame to leave it there and besides, being a 'royal' pheasant, it was not just any old pheasant, this one belonged to the Queen and, if we took it home and ate it, we should be dining at the Queen's expense! There wasn't an inch of space in either of our bulging panniers (ex-army canvas bags), so we fixed it under the straps of one of the carriers and got going. We hadn't gone far when the pheasant slithered off onto the road as though it preferred to stay in the royal park. A more secure job and a watchful eye ensured it remained with us for the rest of the journey.

Arriving at our home in Canterbury Road near the Junction in Watford, we pushed through the gates, ran round to the back and, bursting through the scullery door, yelled, "*Mum, look what we've got!*" Mum was thankful that we had arrived home safely and, after we had examined it in every detail and were wondering if it was possible to eat it, she said, "*What do you want to do with it?*" "*Can we have it for dinner?*" we asked hopefully and to our amazement and delight she said, "*I don't see why not if you pluck it and gut it, I'll cook it and we'll have it for dinner tomorrow*". The plucking was a lot more difficult than we had imagined: the flight pinions only came out one at a time and if you did not have a good grip on them they could slice your fingers. The feathers all managed to get everywhere in the kitchen as well. If you tried to pull out too many feathers at once you ripped off the skin with them.

When at last the feathers were all off, Mum showed us how to hold the bird over the gas ring and singe off some hairs, which seemed to be growing all over it. This filled the kitchen with the pungent pong of burning hair. Getting the guts out also presented unforeseen problems: the breastbone seemed to come down almost to the vent and there was hardly room to get your hand in. Once I had squeezed my fingers into its tummy the guts were cold, wet and slimy. I got a grip on them and withdrew my hand. They came out quite readily all green and brown like a long slimy worm. Pushing my hand in again and feeling around there was this hard slippery ball which I thought was its heart, but when I got it out, Mum said it was the gizzard. "*Shall I show you how to prepare that for eating?"* she asked. *"It is a bag of stones surrounded by muscle. The muscle squeezes the stones together and they grind up the food as it passes through. It is a sort of stomach with teeth. The stones are all kept in this very tough bag and you have to separate the muscle from the bag".* So saying she took the gizzard and with a sharp knife cut carefully through the muscle until we could see the greenish-white bag inside. Gripping the cut muscle as best she could with her knobbly arthritic fingers she began to peel it away and suddenly the bag popped out leaving two neat lumps of hard muscle.

We cut open the bag and spread out the little bits of sand and grit and some partly ground-up grains of barley all mixed up with some slimy green stuff. What a bizarre device birds have for chewing their food! Some sloppy purple/brown slabs had come out with the gizzard. Mum said this was the liver. It was OK to eat and unlike a mammal's liver did not have a gall bladder of which she warned us to be wary. Further groping in the carcass and I found the heart and the lungs which came out altogether when I forced my fingers down behind them and drew them out. The heart was a sort of acorn-shaped red muscle with white streaks of fat on and the lungs were pink frothy-looking lobes firmly attached to the heart. Surprisingly there was not much blood running about, but there were some dark red clots that slithered about and stuck to things. Then it had this sort of bulge at the bottom of the neck that felt as if it was full of grain. *"That is the crop,"* said Mum, *"you have to remove it with its contents."* So one of us cut through the neck skin and peeled it away from this loose thin bag, which was semi-transparent, and you could see grains of wheat or something inside it. It tore as we were getting it off and yes, it was full of grains of barley and a few small snails. *"That is where it keeps the food before it goes into the gizzard,"* said Mum. *"A bird needs to pick up food as quickly as possible so that it can get away to safety if it has to and it can then go on stoking food into its gizzard."*

Mum said not to cook the head, so we cut it off with secateurs and a knife. This left the neck sticking out so we cut that off too. *"The neck, heart, gizzard and liver are called the giblets,"* said Mum. *"We cook these separately and make stock from it which is a nutritious watery soup that can be used for adding to a stew or casserole and for making gravy."* In this way we learned some of the rudiments of cookery as well as the elements of anatomy; the pheasant was becoming something of a schoolbook as well as a stimulus to learning! Mum put the bird onto a greased baking tray with some potatoes and some lumps of lard on top and popped it in the oven. It was not long before sizzling noises were heard from the oven and a mouth-watering smell began to tickle our nostrils. Mum made the most of our interest and while the cooking was progressing she got us to scrape the carrots and prepare the Brussels sprouts. At last, all was ready - but not quite, we watched in anticipation as the steaming bird, almost pulsating with delicious smells, was removed from the oven; but it had to stand for 10 minutes or so before the carving could commence. We sniffed eagerly at the hot and steaming carcass before us. My elder brother John was given the job of carving it. He was never very dexterous and therefore received a good deal of advice and criticism as the slices of brown and white meat slithered onto our plates. Somehow or another the bird was taken apart and distributed to the waiting circle of plates, John 'gave thanks' and the meal could begin. My! How we relished that bird! For the first time in our lives, we wanted to think about the flavour of the meat set before us. It didn't taste like chicken and was certainly nothing like beef or lamb. We enjoyed it. Little did we realise that we had opened a door in our lives and for both of us it was the beginning of a lifetime of harvesting roadkill.

To stuff or to eat

About that time John gave me a book on taxidermy, entitled *Taxidermy* by Leon L Pray. The first specimen I mounted was a stoat which I had found hanging on a gamekeeper's gibbet. It looked pretty good when I had done it and I set it up in what was to have been a glass case but never got round to putting in the glass! I next got a cormorant; there had been a photo in the Daily Mail of it sitting on a Private Fishing sign. I soon heard that it had been shot, so I cycled the ten miles to Water End on the river Gade and collected it. I mounted it with a wire frame of the wrong gauge and so it always remained a bit floppy; it was never mounted in a case with or without glass. Then I was given a jackdaw by our friend Eddie Wakefield who said he had found it dead. I soon found it had been shot by an air rifle. Anyway, I stuffed it and mounted it as though it was alighting on a branch with its wings up in the air because I could not get it to look natural with its wings folded. None of these morsels appealed to me as something that could be eaten. I should have been aghast at the suggestion that I could eat them. Regular game was OK but to go beyond that I did not even contemplate.

In the summer holidays after that find in Windsor Great Park, Den and I cycled to Norwich again to stay with Naomi and Leslie and their family. As we toiled across the endless undulations of East Anglia, we again came across a dead pheasant, and once again it was eagerly picked up. We were not quite sure what to do with it. My sister might like to cook it for the family or I might have a go at stuffing it. When we arrived we suggested it could be eaten, Naomi was a little apprehensive, "*Will it make us ill?*", she asked. We told her that Mum had cooked one for us so she let us pluck it and, after a good roast in her Rayburn, it proved to be very tasty.

A week later we set out on our bikes soon after seven o'clock for the return journey home. A few miles out of Norwich on the A11 we saw something big and buff lying in the road. As we approached, it materialised into a huge rabbit, no, it was too big and the wrong colour for a rabbit, it must be a hare. What a beautiful animal! We had never seen a hare at close quarters before. Such powerful hind legs, such long ears tipped in black and such a lovely coat, all mottled brown and black and yellow. But most wonderful of all, its huge glistening eyes seemed to be watching our every move, though the body that carried them was dead. It seemed so tragic that a creature so lovely should be swatted down like a bluebottle on the road; left like a discarded cigarette packet by a couldn't-care-less motorist. It added to the weight we had to carry for the next 100 miles, but it had to come with us. When we got home Mum offered to make a stew of the hare, so I skinned it and kept the head to stuff. The hare was good eating, though the meat was a bit coarse and took a bit of chewing; perhaps it should have been left to hang a bit or perhaps cooked a bit longer. Anyway, it was another success. My stuffing and mounting of the head were not so successful as I never did get round to getting the right sort of eyes, without which it never came back to life

Brown hare roadkill in France, © Arthur Boyt

Our cycle trips to Norwich thereafter were always occasions for salvaging good meat from the highway. There was always a pheasant or two, sometimes a hare and occasionally a red-legged partridge. Rabbits were somewhat of a rarity at that time as this was just after the myxomatosis outbreak in the '50s. Should I have been worried that I might have been inadvertently poisoning my sister's family? Well, I knew enough about animal biology to know what was muscle and what was guts and that it was sensible to keep gut and stomach contents away from meat. I also knew that the bile contained in the gall bladder was very acrid and tainted any meat it got onto. So the gall bladder had to be located where it lies against one of the lobes of the liver. It has to be carefully excised without squirting the yellow juice about. Bile is strongly alkaline and after the death of an animal, it quickly begins to leak out and make the surrounding liver turn yellow. If these patches of the liver are not removed they will taste quite bitter, but they are not poisonous. The bladder also needs care in removing, but no disaster would follow the spillage of its contents as it would wash off easily and anyway, would do you no harm.

Badger's liver and enlarged gall bladder, © Arthur Boyt

Witnessing death

The first time I saw an animal killed on the road occurred on a journey by coach from Uxbridge to Cheltenham that my diary tells me was on Friday the 5th of April, 1957. Den and I were going with our friend, Ian Cheshire, for a week watching birds on the island of Skokholm off the coast of Pembrokeshire. We got up at 6 a.m. and caught the 351 bus from Watford to Uxbridge bus station where we changed to a Royal Blue coach, a Bristol, with a very distinct livery of dark blue with a cream-coloured area around the windows and chrome grab rails over the rear end for accessing a streamlined luggage compartment on the roof. Unlike coaches of today, it was a 'half-cab' with the driver in a compartment by himself who could be communicated with only with difficulty via a stiff, sliding window. We went out of Uxbridge on the A40. The coach groaned and whined, rarely getting above 40 mph. We sat at the front and if we stood up and craned our necks we could see the speedometer; occasionally on the open road, we would hit 50 mph! The engine roared, the wind whistled and the whole vehicle vibrated in sympathy. We went through Oxford and Witney and then, somewhere near Burford, looking down the road ahead I saw a pheasant step from the verge. There was a car approaching from the other direction, we gasped and held our breath, was this bird going to be run over under our very eyes? The cock pheasant, resplendent in his coat of many colours, strutted with a proud and stately mien across the highway. He was heading straight into the path of the oncoming car, but, alarmed by the roaring coach bearing down on him, the haughty bird began to run and sprang into the air, but it was too late, the car caught him and amid a burst of feathers he cannoned off the front mudguard and with a whirr of wings tumbled down onto the grass verge. Our driver braked hard and both coach and car came to a stop. The driver of the car opened his door and was getting out to collect his dinner, when our driver quickly swung himself out of his cab, ran across the road and grabbed the still fluttering bird. He went round to the back of the coach with his struggling prey, we saw him open the boot and heard it slam shut. The driver returned dusting feathers off his hands and, with a grin of triumph and satisfaction, climbed back into his cab. It dawned on us that the bird had not been put in the boot for medical treatment.

Hominid history of eating meat

Civilised man has come a long way from his vegetarian *Australopithecan* ancestors. Let us have a look at some of the landmarks in his history. It is generally believed that one of our early ancestors (*Homo habilis*) began making and using stone tools 2.5 million years ago (at the start of what is known as the

Stone Age) to begin to change his diet and eat meat. These tools were sharp-edged hand axes believed to be for penetrating carcasses and cutting skin from meat and meat from bone. It seems that our earliest hominid forebears hacked their way into carcasses, fresh or rotten, and ate the meat raw without the benefit of fire.

One and a half million years later, it was up to a new species, *H. erectus,* to begin using fire; there is a new theory that cooking roots and tubers makes more carbohydrates available and that allowed an increase in the size of the brain. *H. erectus* and another species, *H. heidelbergensis*, began using spears about 400,000 years ago which suggests that they now went after the animals they used to scavenge. So it seems that early man had scavenged carcasses for more than 2 million years before he started hunting them. The point I am making here is that our ancestors had a very long history of eating meat that had been killed by something other than themselves; which is exactly what roadkill is to us. Neanderthal man (*H. sapiens neanderthalensis*) who lived between 300,000 and 28,000 years ago was also a hunter. *H. sapiens sapiens* (modern man) appeared about 160,000 years ago and carried forward the use of fire from his ancestors.

Modern man took his stone spears into North America across the Bering land bridge when he first entered that country about 10 – 15,000 years ago and the country's megafauna immediately began to disappear. With his 4-inch Clovis spear point, the early immigrants ate and eradicated the mastodon, mammoth, horse, tapir, camel, ground sloth and giant beaver, while later hunters with 2-inch Folsom point spears did away with the ancient bison (*Bison antiquus*). I should imagine that these people only killed to eat and were not in the business of killing for fun as are their modern counterparts who call the business 'sport'. But if early man exterminated the megafauna of his time with stone spears, how much more has modern man with his gun been able to exterminate. The incredibly abundant passenger pigeon, the eskimo curlew, the dodo, the great auk, the Labrador duck to name but a few, and all the other species that used to be over-aboundingly abundant have been exterminated or reduced to tiny surviving populations: the whooping crane, the trumpeter and whistling swans, the oystercatcher, the willet, the eider, cormorants, gannets and many, many more. If not taken for food, feathers, or oil, they were torn up and used as bait for fishing, but most of all they were shot for the fun of it, killed and left to rot. This same lust for killing exists in the so-called 'sporting' community of today.

Here in Cornwall, the declining numbers of golden plover, snipe and woodcock are sought out by the modern-day counterparts of our exterminating ancestors and are shot for the fun of it. When I pressed Natural England, the body set up to conserve wild places and the creatures that occupy them, to put an end to the exterminating of these three species, they refused to do anything about it but instead upheld the right of these killers to carry on their destruction of these wonderful birds even on a Site of Special Scientific Interest (SSSI) because they are on the list of quarry species, the official list of species that may be shot.

The Royal Society for the Protection of Birds (RSPB) acquired its royal charter in the reign of Edward VII, who was well known as one of the world's most prolific pheasant shooters. Imagine the conversation when the society approached him for his patronage in 1907. SPB delegate, *"If it please your Majesty, we should be highly honoured if you would be the patron of our Society for the Protection of Birds."* King Edward VII, *"And what do you propose to do about the shooting?"* SPB delegate, tugging at his forelock, *"Anything you say, your Majesty, anything you say." "You are not going to ban it are you?." "Oh no, your Majesty, certainly not, we will take a neutral stance on the subject, your Majesty, we won't be for it or against it."* And that is their position to this day. The response of the society to information that snipe are being shot on their last breeding grounds in Cornwall and numbers are rapidly declining, is *"we have no evidence that shooting is the cause of the decline".* English Nature (EN) carried out a risk assessment and found that so few breeding birds were left that it did not matter if they got shot! So, according to EN and RSPB, its OK to go on shooting them until some wealthy 'sportsman' bags the last one!

But how do I know about this history of man's destruction of the other animals on the planet? Well, it is contained in a volume that makes very painful reading. *Sea of Slaughter* by Farley Mowat catalogues the whole horrible history of man's destruction of every bird, mammal or fish out of which he can make a penny, can have 'sport' with, or thinks it competes with his activities. This book should be on the curriculum of every school in the world and should be read by anyone wishing to buy a sporting gun. Where it deals with whaling, it records how a moratorium was achieved for a time but when it ended whaling was resumed by Norway and Japan. The Japanese say that whales eat fish, are reducing their fish stocks, and therefore must be killed. They say they are killing them for research, but 1000 minke whales are being taken *per annum*, as well as fin, sei, Bryde's, humpback and sperm whales, no scientific papers are being written, and, guess what, the meat ends up on the open market. Why do the Japanese people allow their whaling industry to carry on bringing their whole nation into disrepute by persisting in this cruel (and totally unnecessary) activity? But then do we in the UK have a leg to stand on? Even the Icelandic government in responding to criticism of its recent resumption of killing whales claimed that our hunting of deer with dogs is no less cruel than their killing of whales with harpoons. How many thousands marched in support of the Countryside Alliance to be allowed to kill deer, foxes and hares in the cruel ways they have for the past 100 years or so? These 'sportsmen' have weakened the stand we in Britain are taking against cruelty to animals the world over. And despite the passing of the Hunting Act some hunts brazenly continue hunting illegally while purportedly following a trail laid by a hunt member.

The Canadian government is still following a programme of exterminating the Harp seal – because it is purported to be destroying fish stocks. 'Brave' men enter their breeding areas and club, shoot or by other means incapacitate the defenceless cubs. In 2001, a report by an independent team of veterinarians found that in 42 percent of the cases they studied, there was not enough evidence to even guarantee unconsciousness at the time of skinning, so that almost half the cubs they skinned were not only alive but were conscious! The Canadian government subsidised these activities by more than they were even worth. No, it is man that is destroying the fish stocks, but that man needs something on which to lay the blame. Having decimated all the sea mammals, what can he blame now? Global warming! This new concept that anthropogenic global warming is almost past the tipping point and if we don't act at once we are all doomed. The failure of seabirds to raise any young on North Sea coasts for years has been put down to global warming – they say the plankton have died out or gone to cooler waters or been replaced by 'less nutritive species'- no one mentions the thousands of tons of fish and sand eels that were being sucked out of the sea and used as fuel in power stations in Denmark. I myself saw skips that had contained ground-up sand eels outside a power station there. Al Gore and the Intergovernmental Panel on Climate Change (IPCC) like Chicken Licken cry "*The sky is falling*" and the world joins in, dashing around putting up massive wind turbines costing £billions (the money coming from the likes of you and me straight into the pockets of the rich), useless (when the wind is not blowing) except for making the rich richer and fulfilling senseless EU targets. But while man continues to kill, torture, rape and enslave his own species what hope is there for him showing respect to mere creatures? Oh, dear! We seem to have gotten away from the diet of our early ancestors, so let's go back to it.

During the long, long period of early human history, when a dead animal was found or a kill made, the whole animal was on the table as it were, it was not packaged in polythene bags and handed out to a queue of Neanderthals waiting at the cave mouth. All the interesting contents of the body were present in every kill and were, I am sure, regarded as special treats. Not having been present with a Neanderthal family at mealtime, I cannot say for sure, but I am pretty certain they would not have thrown out the giblets because they were different from 'real' meat. Nor would they have fed only on the best end of neck of a hairy mammoth because they preferred it to the liver and kidneys. Heads and brains too were all part of the nutritive package that they opened every time they skinned their prey. Eating roadkill restores to modern man the opportunity to enjoy these primeval experiences. For instance, why do we baulk at eating eyeballs in Europe? You don't see a bowl of eyes on the butcher's display counter, do you? Eyes somehow fill many people with a sense of revulsion as if they were eating the animal's soul. Don't be daft, eyes can't see inside you as they go round your mouth and slither down the oesophagus into the stomach. I am sure that the chemical compounds present in a rabbit's retina are as vital to the chemistry of sight in *H. sapiens* and that eating them can only be good for our vision. I will admit that the gelatinous lens in the eye, which turns into a hard white ball when cooked, ends up on the side of my plate – is that being squeamish?

I know that heart, liver, kidney and tongue can be obtained from a real butcher (if you can find one) and sweetbreads if you are lucky, but how much nicer to have the opportunity to enjoy a little taste of these culinary delicacies every time you open your meat package. Blood, another highly nutritive ingredient, not entirely off the menu today, would have been a valued commodity, much as it is with certain African tribes today who even tap it from living animals. They, like their ancestors, cannot afford to have religious hang-ups about eating (or drinking) it. If our ancestors killed something big like a mammoth or found the remains of a carnivore's kill, they did not have a freezer to keep it in, in the summer it would have begun to decay before they could eat their way through it. I bet they did not have an official going round stamping things with an 'eat by' date. We feed pigs with rotten food and then we eat them. Perhaps it is because of the smelly stuff they eat that they taste so nice.

Everything in the shops has a 'Sell-by' date nowadays, or a 'Best-before' date and some people throw out food when it has passed the latter as if it were no longer fit for human consumption. I once came across a stack of dated freezer contents put out for the dustman as I cycled into work in London. I had a job loading it all into my saddlebag before going on my way! Three-quarters of the human population is starving and the other quarter throws away the good food they have because it has crossed some arbitrary threshold and they think it has become inedible. I once ate some meat I had put into the freezer 11 years before!

It was perfectly OK and I had no gastronomic repercussions. And we can cook the stuff and kill all the bacteria anyway. Besides, we need to encounter bacteria in our early lives or we do not develop any resistance or immunity to their activities when they do get inside us. The more we sterilise our surroundings the more susceptible we make ourselves to germs when they do get a foothold on us.

What a race of spoilt fusspots we have become. *"I don't like it,"* is the cry we hear from overfed children when something new (not a sweet) is put in front of them. Many don't know what real hunger is and can afford to turn up their noses at anything that's not sweet or covered in chocolate. I grew up in the war when food and sweets were rationed. If you didn't eat what was provided at mealtimes you didn't get anything else. Of course, kids would rather have a Kit-Kat or a beef burger when offered broccoli or turnips to eat. But we carry that over into adult life. I met someone recently who said they did not like cheese. *"What sort of cheese don't you like?"* I asked. *"Any cheese"*, came the reply. *"When did you last try some?"* *"I haven't tried any since I was a child,"* he replied. *"Well, you might like it now that you have grown up,"* I countered. *"I don't think so,"* he said. *"Why not?"* I asked, *"You haven't even tried some. What about a baked potato filled with delicious runny Camembert, or a piece of toast bubbling with scrumptious cheddar?"* Of course, he had never even envisaged such a treat let alone tasted such a thing. I was surprised he was not still wearing rompers.

Most of our fussy attitudes to what we like and what we think we cannot eat are all in the mind, and this brings me back to roadkill, which I must confess I had got away from again for a moment. The idea of eating roadkill is disgusting to some and so they cannot bring themselves to eat it. It is possible to make yourself sick by thinking that something you are eating or have just eaten will make you sick. It is a threshold, which we have to step over in our minds before we can enjoy the variety of wildlife on the roadkill menu. But were we to think sensibly about it we should prefer to have our food garnered from the roadside. I mean, take a rabbit, for example, it has grown up eating grass and wildflowers, the epitome of an organic existence, would you not rather eat that than beef from a bullock that may have been standing all winter in its own excrement, fed on heavily fertilised fodder, supplemented with growth hormones and injected with antibiotics? Do not get me wrong, I am not saying we should not eat regular farm produce, but if we are happy with all the things that do go on in the processes of modern farming then it is absurd and unreasonable to reject as inedible the natural and truly organic produce that gets killed on the road. Also, the fact that the items on the roadkill menu were killed accidentally should allay the sensitivities of those who do not eat meat because they do not approve of either the way animals are intensively farmed, or their losing their lives to feed us, or the manner of their killing. Such vegetarians may allow themselves to enjoy meat with a clear conscience. I have no mandate for trying to convert anybody to eating roadkill, I am merely trying to show that eating roadkill is beneficial, both nutritionally and economically, and is not the bizarre behaviour of some weirdo who probably also practices witchcraft and necromancy. I don't spill out the entrails and conduct an augury to prognosticate my destiny every time I gut a bit of roadkill. But it does seem a shame to me that large packages of high-quality food are available on our roads and are ignored by the public at large but which would benefit both the diet and the budget of all, and more particularly, those whose finances are under pressure. After all, it is meat, and meat costs money.

I went on a tv show once with Vanessa Feltz. There were two girls on the programme who seemed proud that they had credit card debts of over £10,000 but who did not leap at my suggestion that they should start eating roadkill as a sensible way of reducing that debt. Don't believe those people who say that roadkill has been scraped up with a shovel and will have tyre marks on or be mixed with gravel. I have eaten animals that have had one end squashed but the other end is OK. But mostly you cannot tell whether it has been run over or just hit until you open it up. But then we humans are not as rational as befits the place we put ourselves into at the head of creation, or at the top of the evolutionary tree. As long as mankind maintains its compulsion for the juggernaut of road transport, the sacrifice of wildlife that trespasses onto the hallowed ground will continue and with it the availability of good meals for free. Picking up roadkill is so much more civilised. And besides, it is carrying out a public service; clearing up what could become a public nuisance. I think parliamentary candidates should have themselves photographed picking up roadkill to show how public-spirited and parsimonious they are.

There is also the matter of clearing up the carnage on the roads. A deer, a moose or a camel lying on the highway can cause a serious accident by other drivers running into it and some of these have resulted in people being killed. But people seem quite happy to knock down even a big animal and drive on as if it was not their responsibility. Under the Road Traffic Act 1988 in Britain, if you hit a dog on the road causing it injury or death, you must give your own and/or the vehicle owner's name and address, and the registration number of the vehicle to anyone having reasonable grounds for requiring them. Failing that, you must report the accident to the police within 24 hours. This requirement also applies to accidents involving cattle, horses, asses, mules, pigs, sheep, and goats; (but not cats and poultry). Deer, moose and bears have to be reported in the US, but why should not deer in the UK, or badgers, foxes, otters? Why should not drivers be required to attend to whatever it is they have run into, instead of going on as if nothing had happened when an animal is lying there possibly suffering? I suppose I should not expect humans to be so concerned about animals when a number of them regard it as OK to knock people down and drive off. We rightly despise hit-and-run drivers, but it seems it is OK to be a hit-and-run driver as far as animals are concerned. If people were to pick up the animals they killed it would save the council having to send someone out to do it. It stands to reason, if everyone were on the lookout for the Sunday joint, the roads would be a lot tidier, and potentially fatal accidents might thereby be prevented.

People are always asking me, *"How do you know if it is fresh?"* Well, why do you need to know if it is fresh? If rotten flesh were capable of killing off the human race, we would not be here now. But it is easy to tell how long an animal has been dead: 1) Is it still warm? 2) Is it stiff with *rigor mortis?* 3) Has it begun to go green? 4) Do the fur or feathers slip when you go to pick it up? Items 1) and 2) are OK, 3) is just OK, but 4) is best left where it is. I recently ate a pheasant that had been in the fridge for about 6 weeks. It didn't smell at all and was delicious. Why be revolted by the idea of the animal you are going to eat having been found dead on the roadside when you are quite happy to eat chickens that have spent the whole of their 10-week lives scratching in their own droppings. And do I need to mention the cramped conditions in which sows are farrowed, or the conditions in which calves are reared, or the immense journeys some animals are subjected to in the days before they die? No, No, let's not mention it. What is important to today's housewife is: how much does it cost and is it a special offer? The fact that roadkill comes in its own natural wrapper does not alter the fact that it is, in many cases, better than the meat rolled out on the conveyor belt of intensive farming.

While researching this book, I have come across several people or groups who indulge in eating roadkill. The Wildroots Collective in western North Carolina found a dead grey fox by the roadside. They skinned, gutted it and then roasted it on a spit over a fire pit for a couple of hours. Some watched while four or five feasted on the fox. Members of the group now eat roadkill nearly every day, they have a good supply put away in a freezer and have tried dozens of different species of animals found dead beside the road. In his book *The revolution will not be microwaved*, Sandor Ellix Katz makes the case for eating roadkill in the name of sustainability and he talks at length about this N Carolina collective which has now become a centre of information on evaluating, skinning and cooking roadkill as well as turning the hides to good use.

A forty-four-year-old man from Bournemouth, Jonathon McGowan, was reported in August 2009 to have had a life similar to my own. He became interested in taxidermy at age 14 and now claims to eat almost solely roadkill meat arguing that it is cheaper and healthier than 'barbarically' farmed beef, pork and lamb. He too has served his friends with roadkill and they said they didn't realise it could be so delicious.

The Australian philosopher and animal rights author, Peter Singer, said he was opposed to killing animals for food, but if an animal has been killed in an accident why not eat it? Finally, and sensationally, animal-rights campaigners tend to give roadkill the green light as it is meat that hasn't come courtesy of the 'barbaric' meat industry. People for the Ethical Treatment of Animals (PETA) wrote a tongue-in-cheek article urging non-vegetarians to 'kick their unhealthy meat addictions', describing roadkill as 'meat without murder' and suggesting that 'die-hard meat-eaters can help clear their consciences—and the streets—by eating roadkill.'

Living off the road

Badger

Badger used to be one of the commonest roadkill animals in the South West. After the DEFRA cull of 2013, they are not often seen as roadkill. A high presence as roadkill means a healthy population.

Badger © Arthur Boyt

The bird-ringer's badger

This craze for collecting and my interest in bird identification led me to take up bird-song recording as a hobby in my thirties. This in turn led me to want to take up bird ringing, No, not wringing their necks, but clipping aluminium rings onto their legs by which they can be identified if ever they are caught or found again. This is a research procedure that has been in operation for just over 100 years to shed light on the movements and longevity of birds. It is operated by the British Trust for Ornithology (BTO) which then had its offices at Tring in Hertfordshire. I had begun my ringing apprenticeship in May of 1976 with a group under Chris Mead, who was not only the Director of BTO but was a world authority on migration and birds in general and a television and radio personality to boot. The group began their operations at dawn and trapped birds for a few hours before the public was out and about and then spent some hours checking 90 or so nest boxes and ringing the young (known as pulli) when they were about to leave the nest. I attended these operations on three or four occasions and even got to ring five tree sparrow pulli (*Passer montanus*). I contacted Chris again in the following year about the possibilities for carrying on with the ringing apprenticeship and he told me to be at Steppes Hill near Ivinghoe Beacon on the Chiltern scarp at 4.30 a.m. Given the early start, I needed to eat and get to bed early.

The next day the alarm dragged my spinning head from the pillow at 3.15 a.m., but the expectation and excitement of the adventure before me galvanized my limbs into leaping from bed and preparing my usual breakfast of porridge, a packet omelette and toast. Empty roads enabled my Austin Maxi to get me the 15 miles to Steppes Hill in 20 minutes and I arrived at 4.45 a.m. It was just getting light but no one was there. I wandered about for an hour and a half watching birds, fallow deer and hares until a car arrived and a large man with unruly grey hair and a bushy red beard got out, it was Chris. With a guy named Jeremy, we put up a long mist net some 7feet (>2m) high. We caught only seven birds including: a bullfinch which was so entangled the net had to be cut to release it, a willow warbler, two chaffinches and a wren. Each bird was put head first into a little funnel of paper, weighed, various measurements made of its vital statistics and a ring crimped around the tarsus of one leg; it was then released.

The closest I got to ringing a bird was being allowed to hold one. Even holding a bird is a skill, which has to be learned; the head is held between the index and the middle finger and the legs between the 3rd finger and the little finger. This prevents the bird from struggling without holding it in a way that would cause damage to it. With no birds about we soon gave up and, mid-morning, I drove home and cycled the 8 miles to my allotment.

Back at home I mowed the lawn with my lovely Shank's mowing machine and had a pot of tea. This old machine was not your cheap chain-driven job, it was driven by gears encased in an aluminium gearcase. Everything was adjustable, the angle of the handle, the tightness of the blade, and the height of the cut; all could be done with the fingers, no need for a tool case to accompany you around the lawn. And how much did this prestigious machine cost me? Ten bob, or in modern parlance, 50p! And for that price, it was delivered to the door. I bought it off a rag-and-bone man, no, not an old man pushing a hand cart and shouting "*Rag - Bone*", nor one driving a horse and cart as they would in days of yore, but a man driving an open lorry and continuously ringing a bell; a novel development in the scrap-metal industry. I went out to see what the noise was and spotted this wonderful thing on its way to the scrap yard. What an opportunity! A few moments haggling and he had a ten bob note in his pocket and I had an example of British engineering at its best. In the '60s and '70s, everyone was chucking out their manual lawnmowers and going for powered models and innovations like the Flymo.

With the arrival of mowers that don't have to be pushed around the lawn, the art of mowing by human power has, along with the art of making fire, been almost lost in the civilized world. It is more than an art form, it is a trade or profession to which one needs to be apprenticed. The length and thickness of the grass and sogginess of the substrate have to be considered and settings adjusted on the machine before any operation can begin. If the grass is thick the machine must be going at speed before the blades are lowered to bite into the grass and maximum pushing power is maintained until the cut is complete or the blades become clogged. The mowings in the grass box must be pressed down or emptied to prevent obstruction of the free throw of grass into the box. If the ground is wet, you are advised to wear running spikes, though golf or cricket spikes are nearly as good, but if none of the above is available your old football boots from your schooldays can be recommissioned and pressed into action. Plimsolls would slither and slide around on a wet lawn and quickly make it look like a wart hog's massage parlour. What people don't realise when they proudly ride or steer their flashy motorized mowers around is the opportunity they are squandering for a whole-body workout, a cardiovascular therapy session, and a small delay in the exhaustion of the planet's finite buried energy supply.

OK, OK! I'll relent, for arthritic octogenarians with an acre to cut you probably need a motor mower - but then why not let the grass grow? Let it become - as I have allowed so much of mine to become - a haven for small mammals: field voles, bank voles, wood mice, common shrews, pygmy shrews, and if you are lucky, yellow-necked mice. This will attract owls at night that will hoot romantically around you. Wildflowers, butterflies, weasels and stoats will create for you pleasures you never dreamed of. You may even become eligible for grants from English Nature or the Rodent Protection Society! If you are in N America, then gophers, groundhogs, and ground squirrels could add to your day's interest and amusement without occasioning you any anxiety or irritation. What efforts and expense we go to, to deny ourselves these simple pleasures and hinder our being a benefactor to life on the planet, rather than an exterminator.

I cooked a duck that had failed to make a safe transit of the highway that week and ate half the breast with spuds, corn, leeks and Brussels sprouts. I was just about to phone Chris Mead when the phone rang, it was Chris himself, *"Tomorrow, Steppes Hill at 4.30a.m."* This meant getting to bed early. The alarm woke me at 3.15, but I fell back into sleep's welcome embrace until at 3.30 the electric light wormed its way into my consciousness and I had to get up. I quickly ate my porridge, omelette and toast and the Maxi quickly ate the miles to Steppes Hill. Chris and Jeremy were already there. A few more arrived some of whom, like me, only handled the birds and did not actually put rings on. We put up two long nets and caught lots of birds, some 14 species including a pair of lesser whitethroats, and marsh tit, whitethroat and linnet. After they had been weighed and measured, I was allowed to handle some and remeasure the wing and tarsus to see if I got it right. I bought a pair of ringing pliers for £2 in the hope that one day I might actually be able to put rings on birds. While engaged in this esoteric pursuit, I ferreted through the bushes and found a cardboard-topped Express milk bottle from the 1940s and Wow! a Codd's bottle which, upon cleaning proved to be a Benskin's bottle from the Watford brewery - a real treasure for a born-and-bred Watfordian bottle-collector; and which was possibly 70 years old. We dismantled the nets and adjourned to Ringshall coppice to check bird boxes and to ring any suitable fledglings. We stopped for lunch and I ate my duck sandwiches. It was then that I noticed a dead animal on the roof of the hut we used in the wood. It proved to be a dead badger *(Meles meles)* Tim had found by the road and had thrown up there two weeks before with a view to obtaining its skull at some time in the future. It was green and distended. I reckoned it could be eaten and asked if I might have it to take it home for eating. Permission was granted so I took it home with me.

It was not until three days later that I was able to start skinning the badger which smelled really bad, it had gone a bit greener and was bloated so its legs were all splayed out like a long-dead horse on a World War I battlefield. I began by making the long incision from neck to vent. and peeled the skin back. When I cut through into the body cavity there was a rush of escaping gas and I was engulfed in a foul pong. I suppose anyone else would have said it was revolting, but I could see a lot of dinners in this hairy wrapper despite it showing evidence of being well past its sell-by date. I wanted to see how they turned out. I didn't have time to finish it, as I had to go to the dentist.

The next day I finished skinning the badger. Boy! What a whiff! The pong had an acrid, nauseating quality that seemed to stick inside your nostrils so that you smelled it everywhere you went. I cut through the neck muscles at the base of the skull and worked the blade into the joint of the skull with the first cervical vertebra and took off the head. I fried some onions in the pressure cooker, popped the head in with them, shook it all around for a few minutes and then added water and brought it up to pressure for a good half hour. The smell from the cooker was pretty awful! Cooled the cooker under the tap to avoid filling the house with this highly aromatic steam, added spuds, and gave it another 10 mins. But when I came to eat it, it was delicious, gamey, rich and sweet. What a pleasant surprise! I do like eating badger heads, a head is such an interesting thing to eat. There are five different tastes and textures to savour and they are not all presented in neat slices, you have to excavate and dissect them out. The badger has more muscle on its head than any other British mammal of comparable size. The reason for this is that the badger's jaw cannot be disarticulated; it has developed a hinge at the joint and however hard it bites it cannot put the jaw out of joint, and so can develop a huge muscle to empower the bite. This muscle, the masseter muscle, originates on a bony ridge on the top of the skull, the sagittal crest (which is another unique feature), and is inserted on the mandible or lower jaw. There is a pair of large molars on each side of the jaw that act like a pestle and mortar or like a hammer and anvil. Pressure or force applied to a bone causes added bone growth or ossification at the pressure point. This can be seen on the sagittal crest and around the molars where the pressure is applied and can be used to estimate the age of the animal. Careful delving with a pointed knife between the jaws will be rewarded with the salivary glands, a pleasure that very few meat-eaters will have the sense and spirit of adventure to sample (from any animal). I bet they contain many rare elements and vitamins essential to our well-being. They are situated under the tongue and against the jawbone and are a real delicacy. Then close by is the tongue - almost a meal in itself and with a subtle flavour all its own. Funnily enough, this has somewhat the same taste and texture as any animal's tongue but with a special badger flavour. The fourth item on this special menu is the eyes, they make interesting eating and I am sure that the chemicals present are just what we need to keep our eyes in good order. Lastly, there is the brain. There are two ways to get at the brain unless the skull was broken in the encounter with a vehicle, in which case it is all open for your picking at it. If the skull is undamaged and you want to preserve it intact then you have to go in by the hole that the spinal chord came out of, it is known as the *foramen magnum*. Despite its Latin name this hole is small so you have to use the handle of a teaspoon for your excavations. Poke it in, sweep it around and fetch it out. Lick off what you have got and go in again. This forces you to take your time and enjoy the delicacy to its full potential. The spoon will not reach all the brain material, so pour in some clean water, shake it all about and pour it into a cup. Do this a few times and you have a cup of brain suspension, with lumps. Brain eaters are rewarded with a rich sweet flavour and a smooth creamy consistency.

If you don't want to keep the skull to add to your collection then it is possible to give the skull a good whack with a hammer. In short, a badger's skull is a feast in itself and at the end you have (with perhaps a little further boiling and picking with a knife and scrubbing with a toothbrush) a trophy that is both aesthetic and educative - you can regale your guests with its unique structure (as detailed above). You may become a badger skull expert yourself and be able to show people the increased ossification with age and the excrescences (I've long wanted to use that word) of bone produced in response to the pressure on the aforementioned molars and the increasing height of the sagittal crest with age. Oh, what pleasure and self-improvement we deny ourselves by confining our gustatory experiences to beef burgers, chicken breasts, pork chops, and rashers of bacon!

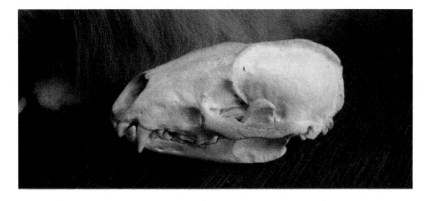

Badger's skull, © Arthur Boyt

Three days later the sacrum or pelvis was on my plate with something rather special from around that area which I have heard referred to in North America as Rocky Mountain oysters, these were its testicles and they were delicious. Also, male badgers, along with many other species, have a bone that female badgers don't have, it is called the *baculum* or *os penis* and is said to have aphrodisiac powers, a hypothesis I have never put to the test. A term in native Alaska cultures - oosik - is used to describe the bacula of walruses, seals, sea lions and polar bears. Sometimes as long as 60 cm (24 in), fossilized bacula are often polished and used as a handle for knives and other tools. I have acquired quite a collection of bacula over the years and, one day, I happened to visit the Phallological Museum in Reykjavik in Iceland. Yes, you are right, it is a museum of knobs and willies. There, among all the amazing specimens, I saw a specimen labelled as belonging to a badger but it was, in fact, a polar bear's! The museum thanked me for pointing out the error.

Now, I am ready to admit that that badger stank somewhat while being cooked. There were a lot of meals stashed away in the freezer from that animal and so every time a frozen item was defrosted and cooked, that distinctive aroma filled the house. I have had many badgers since, none quite so powerful as that one, but as I tend to leave badgers until they smell so much they should be buried, they are likewise notable for their ability to attract the attention and wrinkle the nose of anyone visiting while the cooking is being done. However, it is not only badger that has the distinction of being able to do that, but one evening, Sue cooked some boil-in-the-bag kippers that had been vacuum-sealed. They were a special offer as they had reached their sell-by date. They were neither roadkill nor were they fished out of a bin; Sue had *actually* paid for them. When she was cooking them, the stench reached me in the office upstairs before she did with a request that I come and smell the fish to see if they were all right. They looked all right and certainly reeked a bit, but as she said they had been in the fridge for only about a week after the day she bought them, I reckoned they would not do us much harm however badly they smelled. By the time they were cooked, I had been just about gassed out from upstairs and Sue had decided to have something else instead. When I cut the bags open, the smell nearly took my scalp off and I served two of them up with no small measure of apprehension. There were four of them but I felt two would be quite sufficient for my dietary needs. They tasted OK, just a bit strong perhaps, but otherwise quite pleasant. They hadn't dissolved into slime at all and even broke up into lumps and flakes just like the proper job. After dinner, I took the extra two down the track in the dark to our gateway onto the moor and threw them out for the foxes and crows and ravens to enjoy. Now, when I say 'In the dark' I mean it. When there is no moon in this part of the world it takes some time for the eyes to accustom themselves to the conditions. I nearly fell through the cattle grid because I just did not see it. There is a bridge over a stream outside our gate, dammed on the upstream side to form a pool. I wanted to rinse out the saucepan before carrying the smelly thing back to the house so stepped across the bridge to dip the pan when, in the darkness, I stepped right into the pool -Whoops! - right in over the top of my boot! I was late getting to bed that night and by 1.30 a.m. the powerful savour of kipper had come through in my goodnight drink of 'medicine' (urine). My apprehension that I should have unimaginable after-effects never materialised and I got to sleep at once and awoke in the morning with no internal eruptions or gripping pangs of colic.

The Borrowdale badger

The Original Mountain Marathon (OMM), which used to be known as the Karrimor International Mountain Marathon (KIMM), has been held once a year in some wild and mountainous area in Britain since 1968. It is an orienteering race, with the competitors being divided into different classes. The race is run in pairs with teams starting at one-minute intervals and involves carrying camping and cooking equipment for an overnight stop in a remote site. No GPS is allowed, only a compass and a map. On the last weekend of October 2008, it was held in Borrowdale in the English Lake District three miles to the north of England's highest peak, Scafell Pike, 978 m (3209 ft). I had entered with Mark Sedge (38), ex-Parachute Regiment, and a friend of 26 years. This was my 21st entry for the race but it was only Mark's 2nd attempt and we were competing in the Short Score class which involved visiting as many control sites marked on the map as possible in 5 hours on the Saturday and 4 hours on the Sunday with points awarded for the number and remoteness of controls visited and any minute over your time allowance costing 2 points.

There had been considerable flooding in the preceding week and it had been touch and go whether competitors could have *actually* reached the event. We registered at the event centre at Seathwaite Farm on the Friday and had a good night in Keswick in a B&B, Babbling Brook, which was much to be recommended. On the way to the event in Borrowdale on Saturday morning, there was a dead badger obstructing the road with traffic going around it. We stopped and I heaved it off the road. Dreadful weather was forecast and there was a good bit of wind but no rain when we lined up to go through the start procedure. At the start, I felt comfortable in a thin thermal top, an O-suit top and anorak with thin thermal leggings, boxer shorts and running shorts. We spent 15 mins deciding which controls to visit and took a route from Seathwaite Farm up Styhead Gill towards Sprinkling Tarn. It came on to rain and the wind increased. It was not exactly a picnic as we forced our way up against the stinging rain. After nearly an hour, in which we had covered only two miles but climbed over 1000 ft, we came to a tarn which I mistook for Sprinkling Tarn, this made me turn back and up the hill until I realised my mistake in five mins or so. We returned to the tarn which was being whipped by the squalls tearing across it. I began to feel decidedly chilly. Having got too hot in years gone by when dressed up for wet weather, I failed to reckon with the wind-chill factor and did not have enough on to keep warm this time. We continued steeply upwards into the crags and the cloud. I got blown over a rock and managed to gash my knee but did not realise it was badly cut. We ate our first ration of malt loaf honey sandwich (to be taken every hour) and drank from a stream. Now we had to locate the control we were aiming for and stopped to study the map. Suddenly I found myself shaking uncontrollably. I could not hold the map still enough to read. I had become hypothermic. I decided to put on more warm clothes, but this was easier said than done. Standing on the maps to stop them blowing away and held by Mark to stop me being blown over, I struggled into a sweater and leggings while the rain lashed at my unprotected body. Now really cold, I tried to run to warm up and in a few moments began to pass out; I thought it might even be curtains. I quickly got my head down to the ground and the swooning passed. Mark, who later told me I had gone dead white, got me into the lee of a rock and tried to warm me before half-supporting, half-dragging me off down the hill whence we had come. We knew the game was over, we had to retire. However, after 10 mins or so I felt much better and we ran on down passing people still on their way up and joining a growing band of people like us eager to get off the hill. Channels that had been dry on our way up had now become raging torrents. The hill had assumed a new dynamism of cascading white water and the track back to the start had become a river.

Hot tea and soup awaited us at the event HQ, where we were given a free meal ticket. We hurried to the car to get out of our wet things. Mark then pushed the car out through the muddy car park. He would not even let me go back and redeem my free meal ticket! Wisely he made me drive out on roads quickly becoming impassable. On our way out, there was the badger. We stopped of course to pick it up and then for a coffee at an M6 service station. We arrived at our friend's, Adam and Rachel Brierley's, house in Horwich for a hot shower and a slap-up meal. I treated the knee injury with urine and closed the wound with steri-strips. We listened amazed to radio and television as the events unfolding on the hills whence we had come became the leading news item of the day. The reports of 1700 people lost on the hills and a huge rescue effort including helicopters searching for missing people were entirely erroneous. A helicopter airlifted a lady who had fallen into a torrent and been washed injured onto an island along with her partner and rescuers.

Mountain rescue teams brought in two competitors with broken ankles, one with a broken leg and some cases of hypothermia, but no search was requested or carried out for missing persons. All teams unaccounted for, reported back safely on the Sunday.

The day after I got home I opened the badger and found it had been run over perhaps a few times. Its back legs were broken and guts and meat were all mashed together. I skinned enough to get the front quarters, the head, the heart and one of the back legs; the rest went out for the ravens to feast on. I tried frying small steaks in butter and onions. It tasted a treat but was somewhat tough. The rest I made into a casserole.

I once found a dead badger that had been in an accident before. As I dissected the carcass I found that the hip had been dislocated and the badger appeared to have lived some time in that condition. The leg joint was displaced and had been bearing on flesh that had developed a certain cartilaginous surface. I should imagine the badger had limped badly and could well have been in pain.

Deer

Road accidents in which deer are involved are known as Deer-Vehicle-Collisions (DVC) and they are a growing hazard on roads through countryside where deer are present. The deer come off worst, being injured or killed. Damage to vehicles varies from slight through serious to complete write-offs. However, many drivers and their passengers are injured and even killed. The Dorset Daily Echo published an amazing account by Martin Lea of a man being knocked down while moving a dead deer off the road: *Marketing manager Mr. Jones, 34, of Chapelhay, Weymouth, was on his way home from work in Dorchester and stopped to help an elderly couple whose car had hit a deer on the A352 at Whitcombe. He moved the animal but was hit by a car as he crossed the road and was thrown about 20 metres, landing on a verge. Seconds later another car ran over his leg as he lay injured. The driver of that car did not stop and police are still appealing for the driver to come forward. Mr. Jones suffered a badly broken leg, a broken arm and fractures to his collarbone, pelvis, ribs and vertebrae.* What hope is there for more consideration for animals on the road if they do this to people?

However, a collision with an animal can sometimes be fatal, as Sharon Hoblyn knows only too well - her husband was killed as a result of a deer crossing in front of his motorbike. "*He had just gone onto the A38 when a deer jumped out over the hedge. He clipped the deer trying to avoid it and went onto the hard shoulder. A lorry came along and must have clipped the deer as well -*

it took the same route across the lanes and smacked into the back of my husband. It took him 100 yards up the road - he was killed instantly," she recalls. This emphasizes the importance of not swerving when there is other traffic on the road. Motorcycles are particularly at risk as they are so exposed to direct contact with any animals involved in the collision. In fact, a couple on a motorcycle were both killed on a minor road in Cornwall a few miles from where I am writing these words. But a car does not always save you as Leslie Kingham, 50, a meat inspector, died after a deer was hurled through his windscreen. The deer had just been struck by another car after leaping onto the A37 near Glastonbury, Somerset. Another instance of someone being killed when a deer crashed through their windscreen was reported by Bob Jolliffe in The Sun on 28th November 2006. *A 38-year-old man from Watford, Hertfordshire, lost his life when a fallow deer buck was in collision with a southbound Saab car on the A35 at Beckley Common in the New Forest, just north of the East Close Hotel on Sunday, November 26. The large animal was catapulted into an oncoming Ford Focus C-Max being driven by the Watford man. Part of the creature smashed through the windscreen of the Ford, colliding with the driver and causing massive injuries. Also inside the Ford were the man's partner and their two children, aged six years and 18 months. The accident is similar to one further north on the same road but closer to Lyndhurst in October 1995. Then, 41-year-old teacher Rachel Drake died when a deer was hit by an oncoming Rover car. The deer was thrown into the air and landed on Miss Drake's Renault 5.*

The Wiltshire Gazette and Herald reported the death of a moped rider who ran into a deer in November 2007. David Pomfrey, 61, was driving from Devizes to Pewsey when he hit the deer. He refused to go to hospital and resumed work the following week. The deer had broken legs and was put down. Although he only had bruising and a black eye to show for it, he died a week later from a ruptured spleen. Ironically Mr. Pomfrey was a follower of the Pewsey Hunt.

In his books, *'The original roadkill cookbook'* (1985) and *'The international roadkill cookbook'* (1994), B.R. 'Buck' Peterson advises on how to get your own free meals from the highway by shopping with your own 'shopping cart'. He makes it sound easy, not just possible, to 'purchase' the meal of your choice provided you have the right kind of vehicle. Well, I have twice driven 9000 miles journeys in North America and never knowingly 'purchased' more than one small bird. Boy! I could have gone hungry! He does mention that the average cost of deer-car encounters is (in 1985) $350, most of which, he says, could be reclaimed on insurance. That seems a very low figure to me and I have found some figures that are much more realistic for the UK. Wilson and Langbein report that the real cost of a non-injury collision in a rural location is estimated to be £2,060 and if someone has to attend to kill an injured animal and remove and cremate the carcass the cost can rise by £35 - £300. Over 250 personal injury collisions occur every year in Britain and in 2003 at least 10 people were killed involving collisions with deer. Where human injury occurs, the cost of a slight injury is £18,840 and for a serious injury: £184,040. The annual cost of car repairs alone is estimated to exceed £11M. I am sure Buck Peterson is only joking (a joke that wears a bit thin after only three or four pages in his books) but I am sure there are twits out there who would have a go. He writes, *"If you can't be a deerslayer, you should have your keys taken from you! With their habit of stopping and staring at headlights, all you have to do is aim your motorized missile towards their lunch bucket and bingo, Bambi bites the dust!"* It would be a bit ironic were they to set out to make some roadkill and end up on a mortuary slab themselves! I know that most N American vehicles look as though they are built for ram-raiding, but a bull moose is a darn sight bigger and heavier than anything we get on our side of the Atlantic. In fact, in the US there are more than a million vehicle accidents with deer per annum, resulting in 29,000 human injuries and 211 fatalities and a cost of $1.1 billion in repair costs annually. I hope all these people were not out looking for dinner. Even in Israel, a country with few large wild animals, there were five fatal accidents between 1995 and 1999, cattle, horses, camels and donkeys being the major cause of the accidents. In the UK, the Highways Agency reports that deer are involved in between 42,000 and 74,000 deer-vehicle collisions (DVC) p.a. With 450 human injuries and quite a few deaths. I do not think that either the highway authorities, the police, or the insurance world would welcome people going out looking for dinner with their 'shopping trolleys'.

Fallow deer

It is Thursday, August the 11th 1988, a shape fills the office doorway, I glance up from my work to see a familiar figure with a large grin step into the room. The tall, fat-free Michael Richardson, wearing a light-green shirt with sleeves rolled tightly up above his elbows, pedals his way to my desk. I say *"pedals his way"* because his legs do not work like ordinary people's but, as he spends so many hours of his waking life on his bicycle, his legs appear to be pushing pedals around even when he is walking. He is a regular early morning visitor to my office and usually bears a little note indicating the whereabouts of some tasty morsel he has spotted or secreted from view on his long ride into work from Stopsely to Borehamwood. I call it long but, although the 15-mile direct route may seem long to some it is not long enough for him, so to get the distance he needs he goes on a long circuitous route via places like High Wycombe or Berkhamstead as he had that morning. The reason for this excessive mileage is not just that he is in training for a 12-hour time trial (as he is) but that he has for some years been the cyclist who cycles more miles than anyone else in the year and, as a consequence (or reward) cycle-equipment manufacturers sponsor him with their best equipment. *"Fresh venison at Ivinghoe Beacon"*, he announces as he puts the note down in front of me. A little sketch map shows the Dunstable - Ivinghoe road and the Ashridge turn with an 'x' at the foot of the beacon with the legend: Fresh venison. Mike is no great naturalist but I do not doubt his accuracy in this instance.

Fallow deer, © Arthur Boyt

He once told me he had a kingfisher for me on the Wheathamstead road just outside St Albans. I kept trying to think what it was he had mistaken it for as

I cycled home that way. It was a kingfisher! The river Ver passes under the road there and the bird had taken to flying over the road rather than under to its cost. Another time he reported a 'small duck' that turned out to be a dabchick; I should never have believed him had he told me there was a dead dabchick by the roadside, they never come onto the road and hardly ever get out of the water, but however it got there, dabchick it was. If he could not identify the specimen he would refer to it as *Raricus notknownum*. One of these, which he thought might be a black squirrel or a long-haired black rat, turned out to be a wet grey squirrel. I should never have cycled the 10 miles extra going home via Hadley if I had known that was what it was. The kingfisher and dabchick never made it to the table. They were stored in the freezer to be stuffed and as a result are still there waiting for me to have some 'spare' time, something I never seem to have nowadays.

That evening I set out in my Austin Maxi for Ivinghoe and sure enough there by the road exactly where indicated in Mike's sketch is the body of a fallow doe *(Cervus elaphus)*. My nose tells me it has been there for more than two or three days and, as I bend over it, I see the belly is a bit green. I have parked nearby, but it is too heavy to lift and carry over to the car. Does weigh 35 to 56kg, so I reverse into the undergrowth to get closer. With difficulty, I manage to heave it over the bumper and into the back of the car. With the deer safely stowed, I head homewards towards Ringshall. Suddenly I come across car trimmings littering the road and a large fallow buck on the verge. Wow! I jam on the breaks, pull off the road and dash back to inspect this huge and wonderful animal. It is very warm so must have only just been killed. Its pale buff coat is dappled with white spots and it has a fine spread of antlers still in velvet. It has such a beautiful face, so calm and serene. It is such a shame that so majestic an animal should be mown down by some unthinking, inattentive motorist speeding through what is essentially a deer park, save that these animals are truly wild. I reverse up against it, up goes the tailgate and I try to get it aboard but it is very heavy, bucks weigh 46 to 93kg. The deer already in the car is blocking the way. It is too heavy for me. What do I say if the police happen by? But by straddling its body and hooking my arms under its middle I manage with an almighty heave to get the hindquarters up onto the car, I then heave the forelegs up, move it all in a bit, and, finally, force the head and antlers in; a car full of venison. I have a great sense of relief at getting it into the car unobserved, not that I am doing anything illegal, mind you, just that people might take some convincing that I am not a poacher. But what worries me now is that I cannot take this home and expect to get it all butchered before it spoils, so I turn back and head for the home of my good friend Peter Pratt who keeps an excellent little butcher's shop in Houghton Regis; he'll hang one of them for me in his cold store.

Welcomed, as always, despite the rather late hour, I listen with a sense of despair as Peter tells me he cannot store them because regulations forbid the mixing in one room of unskinned, ungralloched corpses with dressed carcasses ready for butchering. His lovely daughter, Sarah, persuades me to stay for a meal and, while enjoying this, the phone rings. It is Basil, who lodges with me and who has guessed where I might chance to be. He has just received a call from my cousin, Duane Henderson, well, he's actually my cousin's grandson - his great-grandmother, Mary, was my mother's elder sister and she had emigrated to Canada in 1910 at the age of 18 to marry a man 20 years her senior to whom she had been engaged for four years. She married Malcolm Prince Cavenagh in Winnipeg on the 10th of March when the thermometer was standing at 73°F (23°C) (they had global warming in those days too). She moved from a three-storey detached house, Atherfield, in Argyll Road, Barnet to a log cabin in Freemont, Saskatchewan, quite some change of accommodation! Well, to come back to the present, Basil tells me that Duane, who has been cycling in France, arrived back at Newhaven this morning and, while cycling back to Watford, has broken down at Horsham. One crank has worked loose and he has been forced to stop. (The moment there is the least movement in a crank you must stop and tighten the cotter pin). A kind and sympathetic lady has taken him in and is offering him a night's accommodation. He does not want to stay the night and is anxious to be rescued. I ring the number and suggest he catches a train to London Bridge and arrange for him to ring me when he arrives there.

Thanking the Pratts for a lovely dinner, I hurry back home and tip the carcasses out onto the front lawn. The phone soon rings to let me know Duane has arrived at London Bridge and I dash off to meet him and I bring him home. After hearing a summary of his adventures in France and a discussion of why he was refusing a free night's accommodation, I ask him if he has ever skinned anything before. *"No, but I have watched my father skinning sheep a good few times on the farm in Ontario"*, he replies. *"Well, if you're interested you could try your hand at skinning and butchering a couple of deer I have just picked up. Would you like to give it a try?"* *"I wouldn't mind having a go"*, he replied, *"I don't promise I'll be any good at it, but I am willing to have a go"*. *"OK, jolly good, I'll get up early and gralloch them for you."* Duane looked puzzled. *"What does gralloch mean?"* he asked. *"Paunching, gutting, pulling their intestines out,"* I reply. With a lot of news to exchange we stay up talking before finally getting to bed at 3.30 am.

At 5.30 my alarm goes and I drag my weary body from its nice warm cocoon. The challenge of what lies before me is as good an awakener as the hot cup of tea I pour down my gullet. I winch the first of the deer carcasses up in the garage doorway and with a new scalpel blade make the first incision from the vent to the breastbone. This is the very unfresh fallow doe and, as the blade goes right through into the body cavity, the escape of noxious gaseous decomposition products banish any remaining sleepiness and make me turn away to gulp fresh air. I roll up my sleeves and thrust both hands through the opening to grab the gas-filled coils of intestines and pull them through to start them cascading onto the sack laid out on the floor to catch them. I reach up and cut the rectum through as close as I can to the anus. The stomach is a huge green bladder as big as a football. I wrestle this out and bring with it the dark purple slabs of liver. I cut the oesophagus and let the whole lot flop to the ground. I separate the massive liver and poke about until I locate the gall bladder nestling in one of the lobes. It has already digested its own wall and discoloured some of the adjoining liver. I cut away the gland taking care not to nick it or squirt its noxious contents over me or the meat. The bladder has to be removed next. Pulling open the incision, I can see a transparent bag hanging from near the vent. I take the bag firmly without squeezing it and cut as high as I can get the blade. I walk to the end of the road and throw it over into the railway cutting. I return for the sack of guts and send them over the fence after the bladder for the foxes to tidy up. That is one deer done.

The fresh buck is then hung up and the performance repeated. This is a pleasanter job, as there is no decomposition to pollute the atmosphere. The guts smell a bit but that is quite normal. The postman arrives with the mail and steps over the gutted body to get to the front door; he seems unperturbed. I suppose a dead deer is not half as frightening as a mad dog. It is now 7 a.m. and time to wake Duane and give him instructions. I knock on his bedroom door as I pass through it bearing a cup of tea, "*Wakey, wakey, Duane, I shall have to leave soon and need to tell you what to do with the deer.*" Duane struggles out of sleep and into a position to receive the cup of tea without spilling it. "*OK, I have gutted them both, so, while you're getting dressed, I'll get some porridge on the go.*" The porridge safely stowed away inside us, I show Duane how to set about his task. "*Here's a scalpel and some new blades are in a packet here; you are bound to break a few. Don't try and twist it like a knife in the joints, you'll only break the blade; they are quite delicate.*"

Before I begin, I warn him about the danger of getting bitten by one of the ticks that the buck has clinging to its skin. "*They can give you Lyme disease which is very nasty and can be severely debilitating or even fatal. Crush any you see as you go along and take care they don't get off onto you. They can be very tiny so keep a watch out. If one gets on you crush it between your thumbnails, and if it has managed to lock its jaws on you, you must remove it by gripping it firmly with blunt tweezers and pulling it firmly out*". I then show him the way to skin the carcass. "*Hook it up by one leg, skin the other leg and cut the skin off at the heel. We are not doing it for stuffing and mounting so you don't need to worry about the skin too much, although it would be nice to do something with the pelt of the buck. Once that leg is skinned you can cut it off and shift the hook to the pubic bone in the pelvis, or change the hook to this leg and skin the other. You can skin the whole animal and then cut it into joints, or you can take off the legs as you go along; it does make it lighter and gives you a bit more room, saves you getting a bloody ear every time you swing the body round. Skin down as far as the neck and then chop the neck off with this.*" I showed him my wicked-looking meat axe I had bought from a Chinese shop near Leicester Square."*This is very useful, it will go through anything,*" I tell him. "*Leave the head and neck to me for when I come home. I want to skin it and mount the head with the antlers as a roadkill trophy.*" Time is getting short for me but I have to take him right through the process. "*Take the front legs off at the shoulder joint and then take the shoulders off with plenty of muscle from underneath them. Once that is done put the hook in one side of the pelvis and, using the chopper, split the animal in two, right down the middle of the spinal column. You can bring in the two sides and chop off the spare ribs on the kitchen table and divide the rest into chops.*" Duane grins wickedly in anticipation or disbelief. I finish off with: "*And when you have done one, have a go at the other.*" Duane grins even more wickedly. "*Don't worry about it,*" I put in "*only do as much as you want to; anything will be most helpful.*" I am now almost late to get to the coach depot where I have to drive out and collect the Haberdashers' Aske's school children from Pinner and deliver them to their school near Elstree aerodrome. I jump on my bike and pedal furiously off down the road.

When I arrived home at 6 p.m., Duane was having a cup of tea. He looked exhausted. He had skinned both deer, jointed all of one and most of the other. The meat was safely stashed in the freezer. What a champion! Those deer kept me supplied in best venison for months and were the cause of a good many parties. Venison is very good for you too as it is lower in fat and cholesterol than beef or pork. The fine head of the buck went into the freezer, antlers and all, for the day when I had time to skin and mount it. It would make a very fine trophy. The beautiful dappled skin went in too, I might find time to do something with it in the future. Well, I did not find time to do anything with either, that is until the freezer packed up 19 years down the road; the new freezer wasn't big enough to take everything so I salted the skin and sent it to be tanned. The antlered head stayed in the freezer until I moved house again and then it was left out to rot and become just a skull with antlers. A problem is presented here which I have yet to solve: how to cook a deer's head with its antlers on. I cannot see my fallow buck getting its head into the oven let alone into a casserole, and yet the head is so satisfactory a meal. I could boil it in a pot with the antlers sticking out, I suppose. That would look quite dramatic. I could cut the meat off and allow the skull to clean naturally, or I could saw off the antlers with a bit of skull so that they could be screwed back on again.

Cycling out of Northchurch on the road to Dunstable one day and just having come out onto Northchurch Common, I could hear a car approaching behind me and at the same time, I saw two fallow deer running across the verge to cross the road ahead of me. The car roared by, the deer dashed across in front of him, the driver watched them pass safely off to his right... BAM!..... another deer had followed behind and was knocked sprawling on the road. (Advice to you as a driver: if a deer, or a pony, runs across the road ahead of you, don't watch it. Keep your eye on the road ahead, take your foot off the accelerator and begin to apply the brake, there is likely to be another which will smash up the front of your car). The car stopped and the driver got out. The deer struggled and managed to stagger to its feet, but its hind legs collapsed, pulling it down. It got up again and took a few wobbly steps before collapsing again. I arrived at the scene and watched the deer slowly and painfully putting space between it and the road. Its back legs seemed intact, but there was instability in the pelvis and I reckoned the back or pelvis was broken. This animal was doomed. I asked the driver to go to the house of the warden and tell him to come here to deal with the injured deer. I hung about watching the injured doe. Whenever it got up and tried to walk away I got in front to hinder it from going too far from the road. When it got into a small copse it lay down. No warden appeared in half an hour, so I asked a lady walking her dog to stand guard and try and keep it where it was or at least follow it. I jumped on my bike and rode to the warden's house. He told me he had been out to the spot and seen nothing. I dashed back and found the deer still where I left it with the lady and her dog on guard. The warden arrived and saw it was as I had said - incapacitated. But he had not brought his gun! At last, he returned with the rifle. He prepared his weapon and approached the stricken animal. It tried to get up, the gun spoke, the deer shook its head and flopped down dead. "*What are you going to do with it?*" I asked. "*I shall arrange to have the hunt kennels collect it*", he replied. "*Aren't you going to eat it*", I asked. "*No. Why, do you want it*" he said, expecting me to say no. "*Yes please, if that's OK*", I said to his surprise. "*Yeah, that's fine, if you want it you can have it. Just make sure you do collect it and don't leave it here.*" "*I'll go home and collect the car and pick it up in about an hour and a half. Will that be alright?*" I hid the deer under some brambles and pedalled the 15 miles home, got the Maxi going and raced out to Northchurch Common to where the deer lay hidden. It was still there. I had to drag it back to the road, retracing its last painful steps. It was not too difficult to get into the car and I soon had it home.

Within a week of writing these words, I was driving through Sussex between the venue of the British Orienteering Championships at Midhurst (where I had made two errors in my run and lost 9 minutes and come third in the men's 65+ class, losing by 8 minutes) and Littlehampton where we were staying with Sue's sister Jane, when a roe deer burst out of the hedge on the left ahead of us and ran into a field of sprouting wheat on the right. Remembering my words so recently tapped into the keyboard, I watched not the deer, but the road ahead and applied the brake in case another came out behind the first. At the precise moment I should have passed the hole in the hedge, another roe leaped out onto the road and we most certainly should have collided had I not followed my own advice to the letter. You see, I may be an avid and inveterate picker-up of roadkill, but I have no wish to kill wild animals, and least of all in the process damage or wreck my car as you will hear when a pheasant and my aunt's Rover met at 90 mph!

Roe deer

Driving back to Cornwall from an orienteering event on Salisbury Plain, I was on the A303 where it is a single carriageway road passing through some dark beech woods. Suddenly there was a roe deer *(Capreolus capreolus)* lying across the centre of the road apparently untouched. I glanced in the mirror, jammed on the brakes, and swerved to one side to avoid the deer, and slithered to a halt in the forest litter on the verge. Leaping out I rushed back, nothing was coming for a moment, I grabbed its back legs and dragged it off onto the verge, as I did so, the deer's head swung round and filled my open sandal with a gush of warm blood! Yuk! I quickly pulled from my pocket a paper serviette that I had salvaged from a restaurant meal of the past week and mopped the sticky clinging fluid from my foot and sandal. I got its head into a bag to catch any more leakages and lifted it carefully into the boot. The next morning when I came to get it out, Sue happened to chance by and gave a shocked scream when she caught sight of what was in the car, ...her car. It required a bit of diplomatic obsequiousness and assurances that not a drop of blood or body fluids had or would soil her car. I was a bit worried about the ticks I could see crawling about on the now cold body. I ferreted out an old fly-killer aerosol and gave it all a good squirt, but the wind seemed to carry it all away out of the car before it could do anything to limit the dispersal of these noxious pests.

Roe deer, © Arthur Boyt

I gralloched it and hung it with difficulty in the garage. Without a pulley, it is not easy to lift a heavy deer with one hand and pull down on a rope over a beam with the other especially when your arms and shoulders are becoming weaker by the month. One tends to hug the beast to get it up but that means blood and stomach contents staining and making one's clothing stink. Use of a stepladder enabled the job to be done and there it hung for the best part of a week, upsetting Sue every time she entered the garage. Then it began to smell and the bluebottles found it. It was time to get it into the freezer. Attacking the beast with a new scalpel blade made the job unbelievably easy. You wished to make an incision: there was an incision. Its coat almost fell off it. Hung from its hind legs and skinned forwards from the rear, the carcass needed rehanging when the second leg was due to come off. I still couldn't lift it one-handed above my shoulders - Ah, yes, I remember, use the ladder. What it is to have such short-term memory loss! But once I had taken the weight I couldn't get the meat hook to find purchase as the pelvis was disrupted and I couldn't reach the ladder because I was holding the body and it was still tied to the beam. However, a bit of poking about found some grip for the hook, and a two-handed raise had it once more hanging from the beam. Evidently, the deer had been run over more often than was indicated by its external appearance. The liver was all chopped up and the stomach contents spread fairly extensively around the body cavity. I decided not to salvage any of this tainted meat and took only the legs and shoulders, and steaks cut from the back. At the rate I eat this stuff nowadays, with a vegetarian wife, it could take me years to consume anyway. I extracted the heart (always one of my favourite dishes) and left everything else to be eaten by the buzzards, ravens, crows and foxes where I then lived on Bodmin Moor. A week later I began to notice the distinct smell of rotting meat in the garage near to where I had done the skinning. Had I left something out of the freezer? I couldn't find anything. Was it a rat that had come in and died? Unusual, but possible. I continued to encounter the smell every time I entered the garage. Surely it was overhead! I searched in some boxes in the roof sections, no sign of death. Then I knocked my head against something and breathed in the warm gagging odour of rotting flesh, it was the deer's feet left tied to the beam where I had cut them off!

Some guests arriving from the East told me of a dead deer on the road near to our home in Cornwall. I was directed to the A395 where it passes beside Wilsey Down Woods. There, sure enough, a roe deer lay half on, half off the road. The half on the road, the hindquarters, were rolled out flat. Guts were hanging from the remains of the chest cavity. It looked a bit messy. Having a TV crew coming on the morrow to make a film on roadkill, I thought they might like to film some roadkill that looked how everybody imagines roadkill to look like: mashed meat and guts, and so I picked it up. However, when the crew arrived, the reality was more than the director felt his audience would want to have displayed in their living rooms, maybe at mealtime, and so my willingness to demonstrate the lengths to which my parsimonious nature would take me were frustrated; maybe I'll have the opportunity on another occasion. Having hung it up, I could not bear to see what was edible go to waste and so I skinned the head and forequarters and put the rest out for the foxes. The roe was a buck, but one of its antlers was missing. It seemed a shame to have a skull with only one antler, so I went out to where the body had lain and paced to and fro until I spotted the missing item on the verge.

Reeve's Muntjac or Japanese barking deer

My first muntjac (*Muntiacus reevesi*) was found by the road bordering Ashridge Park in Hertfordshire north of the village of Ringshall early one Sunday morning in May 1977, but the story about what occasioned my being there began on the day before. I cycled to Ashridge and camped the night ready for early bird ringing with Chris Mead at Steppes Hill in the Chilterns in the morning. I spread a groundsheet on the Management College playing field, wriggled into my sleeping bag, and went to sleep under the stars. I woke at dawn and heard a super dawn chorus, but as I had no warm clothes, I stayed in bed. Several fallow deer wandered feeding across the field. Then at 5.05 a.m. a gleam of red appeared in the east and the sun rose and so did I. After breakfast I rode to the Bridgewater Monument and saw a spotted flycatcher building a nest, a willow warbler feeding its young, and a goldcrest flying to its nest high in a deodar, the first goldcrest's nest I had ever seen. I took the road towards Ivinghoe and, as I rode, counted seven wood warblers pumping out their wonderful, shimmering, accelerating song. Magic! Then I could see something big in the road ahead of me. What could it be? It was too small for a roe deer. Was it a dog? As I arrived at the scene I realised it was a muntjac. About the size of a border collie with a gold/brown coat and such thin legs and tiny feet. It had very short apologies for antlers and the pit of a large gland in front of the eye. From the pattern of blood on the road, it had evidently spun itself round and round in the process of dying. I got it off the road and secreted it under some bushes for collection later. I met Tim and another ringer at 9 a.m. and together we monitored 90 nest boxes. We finished at midday and they went home while I got my cooker going and had soup and tea with my badger sandwiches. I collected the muntjac and loaded it onto the carrier of the bike getting blood on everything as I did so. I cycled round to Tim's house and picked up a fallow deer's skull/head, which he had offered me and which leaked brains and maggots into my saddlebag. I must confess I did look a bit of a sight, two large panniers with a red tent rolled up on the back, with the deer rolled inside a blue bedroll lying across the carrier so that its head and front legs hung over one side and its hind legs over the other, with a skull perched on top! No wonder, in every car that drove by, heads turned and necks craned and many cars stopped down the road for a second look! One small boy called out to his mum, "*Look, look, look! A fox!*" I did not go straight home as I had plenty of time and it was a nice day, so taking a 25-mile diversion, I went first through Tring to Wendover Woods in hope of seeing firecrests which I had been told were present there. However, no firecrest so homewards via a series of lovely Buckinghamshire villages in the high rolling countryside of the Chilterns at the rim of the London Basin: St Leonards, Buckland Common, Cholesbury, Champneys and down into Northchurch. At one point I caught up to three cyclists, an elderly lady on a sit-up-and-beg bike with two girls following her. As I caught up they started riding follow-my-leader and swinging snake-like down the road using the dashed white line as a slalom with the old lady in the lead. I could not get past so I called out, "*Can anyone join in?*" To which the girl at the back turned and shouted, "*Yes - you mustn't touch a white line!*" So there we went, all four of us with me at number three, swerving down the lane through the gaps in the white line in the centre of the road - all following the old dear with skirts around her ankles (well, almost). Eventually. the girl behind me caught sight of the deer and called out, "*Joan, STOP, STOP!*" We all stopped and they examined the muntjac while I explained what it was and how I had found it by the road. I did not want them to think I had killed it. We had chatted for a few minutes when I noticed the smell emanating from the skull. I apologised and said I hoped they did not think it was me. The little girl said - so politely - "*I never thought it was anyway!*" Refreshed, cheered, and killing myself with laughter, I rode on. I weighed the bike when I got home and it was 35kg on the rear wheel and 6kg on the front.

The following evening I started to skin the muntjac. As soon as one leg was exposed I cut it off and put it in the pressure cooker. Then the phone rang, it was Chris Mead. "*Tim tells me you have a dead muntjac.*" "*Yes,*" I said, "*it is in the cooker right now*". "*I thought I ought to let you know*" he went on, "*they can have two things wrong with them and if you eat one, it can kill you!*" He went on to tell me that they may have a cyst in the flesh which if you eat it without thorough cooking, a worm will migrate through your body until it gets into the brain where it burrows about doing increasing damage which is reflected in growing madness, loss of motor control and finally death. "*There is no known cure*". He advised me to examine the meat carefully, to cook it well, and never to have it as rare steaks. I thanked him for the information and his concern for my well-being. I kept the cooker under pressure for 35 minutes before opening it to put the spuds in, another 7 mins at pressure, and a final 2 mins with the vegetables. I reckoned that was adequate to deal with any nasties. Meat does not need to be cooked to be digested, but it certainly does help deal with the parasites. When I loaded it all onto my plate it looked good and tasted super - tender, with a mild mutton flavour. Forty-five years later I am still alive, I may be a little crazier but nothing to worry about yet – at least nothing that I am aware of. I have tried to identify the parasite Chris was on about and have found that most likely it was a tapeworm *(Cestoda)* of either a species of *Echinococcus* or *Taenia*. Hydatid cysts of *E. granulosus* can form in any part of the body including the brain and larvae of *T. solium* give rise to neurocysticercosis when they form cysts in the brain. They certainly can kill you. These parasites are more commonly found in pigs, cattle, dogs, or foxes. This emphasises the point that undercooked meat whether it is roadkill or not should be avoided. In fact, neurocysticercosis can now be treated by microsurgery of the brain, but don't let that fact encourage you to eat muntjac (or pork) rare.

On a regular day at work, Mike the Bike visited my office to say there was a dead owl near Peterborough. He drew a little map to show where I might find it. As I had got nothing out of the freezer for that night I decided to go and look for it and pay a visit to the Wildfowl Trust at Welney overnight. I picked up two dead baby rabbits on the way and a hitchhiker. Just as I was telling him about how I had once taken a chap 20 miles too far because he did not watch out for his turning, I found I had gone five or six miles beyond my destination. When I returned to the location of the owl, it proved to be a month-dead black-headed gull! However, I soon picked up an injured herring gull and took that on with me. The area seemed to be an accident blackspot for wildlife for no sooner had I taken the gull on board, but I found a hare by the road whose heart was still beating, though it stopped after a few minutes. I also found 5lbs of strawberries that must have fallen off a lorry. I had a most uncomfortable night in the car at Welney and was woken by birdsong at 4 am. I had put one of the rabbits outside because it smelled, in the morning it had gone, but a fat-looking cat eyed me from a shed roof nearby. The gull was still alive. I had hoped to see some black terns at the reserve, but nothing was showing itself in the morning. I had some cat sandwiches for breakfast. I picked up a doll's house from the roadside on the way home and added pigeon and rabbit to my finds as well. Another rabbit chose to commit suicide beneath my wheels and this was duly collected to join the others.

Hedgehog

Perhaps the animal most frequently seen as roadkill on British roads used to be the hedgehog (*Erinaceus europeus*). According to a study by Royal Holloway and Bedford university reported by Lucy Siegle in the Observer, hedgehogs have the poorest road skills and were second only to rabbits on a recent mammal mortality survey. Hedgehog numbers have declined from a possible 30 million in the 1950s to less than a million in 2022, suggesting the species needs more strenuous conservation efforts. The PTES (People's Trust for Endangered Species) estimates that 1-2% of the national population are killed on our roads each year. Not many of them are picked up to be eaten.

The edibility of hedgehogs is well known, it is just the way to do it that is in question. Romanies used to cover them in clay and cook them in a camp fire. They would gut them first, stuff them with sage and onion, sew them up and then wrap them in clay and roast them. My impression that gypsies were to be regularly found sitting around a fire waiting for a hedgehog to cook was dampened when an old gypsy came to my house. I heard a voice at the back door and went to investigate – it was an old man dressed in patched old clothes, with a large purplish nose and sucking a pipe. He said his name was Nelson and he had seen me on telly. He looked like a gypsy so I asked him, "*Have you ever eaten a hedgehog?*" "*Yes I have,*" he replied and went on, "*we used to catch*

Hedgehog © Arthur Boyt

they hedgehogs by listening for snoring in places where they were likely to have hibernated." "*Have you ever cooked them by rolling them in clay and putting in a fire?*" I asked. "*No, I never done that*" he replied. "*Did they gut them before rolling them in clay?*" I ask. "*Yes, I believe they did. But I used to skin they by cutting they open down the back. That certainly got rid of the prickles, but it removed the muscular layer that operated the prickles. Another way is to singe off the spines and hair, scrape with a sharp knife and then wrap in clay and either put them into the fire or suspend the whole in the flames.*" Nelson then asked if I had any old car batteries or scrap metal. I dug out a battery and offered him a sackful of brass cartridge cases which weighed about half a hundredweight and which I had been unable to get any scrap dealer to accept. He offered to take them and go halves with me if he could sell them. My mind went back to a visit from another gypsy (or was it a diddycoid?) about 45 years ago who expressed interest in a Morris 8 chassis I had in the front garden. When I had helped him load it on his waggon he told me he did not have the money with him but would come back later to pay me. Did he ever? Not on your Nellie! Well, here I was again parting with scrap to a gypsy on the assurance that I would be paid later. Do I never learn? My wife resisted the temptation to buy his pegs and tea cloths. As a matter of fact, he did come back to settle up with me and gave me a set of old golf clubs for the brass. I do not play golf and already have two sets of clubs, so I was not greatly enriched by the transaction. He used to call occasionally and while I bought clothes pegs, tea cloths, or a broom, he would go away with a bag of frozen badger meat to share with friends. I have only eaten skinned hedgehog, it looks more like a rat or a squirrel when skinned and it tastes a bit the same. However, I have collected a sack of clay and I have three hedgehogs in the freezer waiting for the moment when I have the opportunity to have a cook-up.

Hedgehog © Arthur Boyt

One day I saw a hedgehog curled up in the road, too round to be dead, and so I stopped to examine it. As I thought, it was still alive but it had been hit by a car and its skin was split down the back so that when it curled up it pulled the skin away exposing the whole of its back. It had no other injury so I took it home, bathed its back in urine (antiseptic), and put it in a box; all it needed was to be anaesthetised so that its back could be sewn together and it would have a chance of surviving. It was still alive in the morning so I took it to the vet who took one look at it and euthanized it.

A team from the food science department at the University of Wales Institute in Cardiff has found that hedgehogs feature on some of the earliest recipes ever discovered way back to 6000BC. Hedgehogs were wrapped in grass or leaves to prevent them burning, although in that era they were obviously not roadkill! Nettles were eaten in those days as well, an item that I often use nowadays, mainly as soup. Pick them when young, or just the growing tops. Make sure you boil them or they can be rather painful! They were probably not used by early man until he had learned to use fire.

I suggest that you don't make hedgehog your first-ever roadkill meal. It is something you can try when you have more experience.

Rabbit

The rabbit (*Oryctolagus cuniculus*) is the commonest item of roadkill to be found in the UK. The counterpart of the European rabbit in N America is the Eastern cottontail (*Sylvilagus floridanus*) which holds the dubious honour of being the all-time roadkill record holder: There were 598 rabbits killed on 50 miles of a two-lane road in Boise, Idaho in 1933. The rabbit is very easy to skin, it seems they were made for the pot. A simple casserole or pie and you have a scrumptious meal for the whole family. But rabbits were not always that easy to find. They were brought to Britain by the Normans in the eleventh century, were kept in special areas known as warrens, and were the food of only the very well-off. In the 18th century it is said that one could be sentenced to death for robbing a warren and as recently as 1872 a 12-year old boy, William Towers, was sent to Wandsworth Prison for stealing two rabbits. Rabbits commanded a good price and in the 13th century, they were 3p each (£125 on comparable average earnings); a meal suitable for the table of the very rich. Now rabbits are so plentiful I pick up rabbits regularly and feed them to the cat. She will hardly eat any of the proprietary cat foods we offer but will gobble all the rabbit I can provide. So, if you are very poor and cannot afford a car, "*get on yer bike*" as Norman Tebbit would advise, and go looking for roadkill. A rabbit will provide good helpings for a family of six or give good healthy portions of meat to one person for six days.

The body of a rabbit lay beside the road as I returned from choir practice one evening in the summer. The fact that its ears were not down on the road warned me that this rabbit might not be dead – it wasn't. Although its hind legs were not working properly, they were not paralysed. I felt it was only fair to give it a chance to see if it could survive and recover. I slid it onto a garment and took it home with me. I left it in a box with some water and leaves to see if it would survive till the morning. Much to my relief it had not. Cutting it up to serve to the cat I found little wrong with it but a broken rib that had damaged a lobe of the liver. There was not a lot of bleeding in the body cavity although it had lost a little blood from its mouth. The cat and I enjoyed it.

Driving behind a car on a narrow Cornish lane I saw a baby rabbit dash out from the right-hand side verge straight under the car as far as the wheels on the left-hand side where it was bowled over and began jerking about. I stopped and walked up to it. It was on its side with front and back legs working hard. A pool of blood had already formed at its head and as it kicked it spun slowly round with a trail of blood marking a complete circle on the tarmac.

Roadkill rabbits © Arthur Boyt

Its eye stared up at me unblinking as the kicking subsided and it became still. Unlike the other predators that hazard the life of a young rabbit like this, the foxes, stoats, weasels and buzzards, this one's killer did not stop to collect its prey. However, minutes later my cat was having a paroxysm of pleasure trying to animate the little body before setting to and getting inside to the meat. A few months later and at almost the exact spot I saw a rabbit momentarily silhouetted against a car's headlights. The car went by, I stopped and jumped out, the rabbit was lying on its side, running for all it was worth. I waited until its kicks grew weaker and stopped. It reminded me of the first rabbit I saw shot. That was in a field being harvested near Cranleigh in the summer of 1956. As the reaper reduced the standing wheat to a small patch in the centre of the field, this rabbit broke from cover and was shot. It jerked and kicked for perhaps 15s with the back of its head shot away. It was dead but it went on running. I was horrified.

Will evolution in time give us a breed of rabbit that does not crossroads? Only if there is no benefit in crossing roads to that greener grass on the other side.

The skinned rabbit

I had been asked to preach the gospel in the Exclusive Brethren's meeting at Lowestoft. This meant spending the day there. I borrowed my brother Den's Dormobile, a 12-seater van with side windows, so that I could take a few young people for the visit. On our return, a rabbit dashed out from the right and disappeared beneath the front of the vehicle. There was a slight bump as the front and then the back wheels went over it. I jammed on the brakes and ran back. I was greeted by a most awful stench, the rabbit's caecum had burst its contents all over the road. For those who have never gutted a rabbit or done 'O'-level biology, the caecum is the blind gut, a large wrinkled bag full of chewed vegetable matter where an army of cellulose-digesting bacteria get on with their work and provide assimilable nutriment for the rabbit from the cellulose of plants from which we can derive no benefit, our blind gut being a rudimentary pocket known as the appendix which is liable to trap some object that causes it to become inflamed and (in the days before penicillin) burst, killing its owner, as it did my grandfather's younger sister, Blanche, in her early teens who died in terrible agony, watched by her younger brother and sister assembled by their father to witness the occasion! However, I was not thinking of my late great aunt as I held my nose and looked around for a carcass. Much to my amazement what I saw was not what I expected to see for there on the road was the skinned body of the rabbit. '*Gutted by one wheel and skinned by the other*' is how I put it to the occupants of the van as I tucked it somewhere safe where it would not get trodden on. It required only the removal of its feet and head and a wash to have it ready for the pot.

Digestion

But to return to the caecum, it is a dead-end branch to the intestine at the point where the small intestine, the ileum, becomes the large intestine, the colon. Digestion is a process which subjects ingested food to an alkali in the mouth, an acid in the stomach and then an alkali in the gut. This process breaks food down into a liquid that can be absorbed through the gut wall into the blood stream. Cellulose, the structural component of plant cells, and hence the main constituent of vegetable matter, is not readily digested by the intestinal juices of animals and birds. In some animals, however, evolution has devised a means of digesting cellulose by having a fauna of bacteria and protozoans living in their stomach and intestines to do the job for them. The rabbit is a hindgut-fermentor, unlike the ruminants (cows, deer, goats, antelopes) which are foregut-fermentors. It keeps its army of bacteria and protozoa in the caecum where they break down the plant matter so that it can be assimilated. However, the digested matter produced in the caecum cannot be assimilated by either caecum or colon through which it travels to the anus where it is voided as soft faeces or caecotrophs while the rabbit is lying up and not feeding. These soft pellets are immediately consumed by the rabbit. This enables the stomach and the small intestines to have a second go at the food and absorb the products made available by the bacteria in the caecum. This phenomenon is known as coprophagy, which in vulgar parlance means eating shit. It is also practised by hares, rodents and mountain gorillas.

Like the rabbit, the horse also has a large caecum in which the digestion of vegetable matter takes place, but the horse does not pass the matter through for a second cycle of digestion, nor does it have a four-chambered stomach like the ruminants. It is a less efficient converter of forage into energy and animal protein than the rabbit or the ruminants. In fact, it digests only half the cellulose that can be digested by a cow or sheep from the same amount of forage. It therefore has to eat twice as much grass to get the same benefit. Foals actually eat some of their mother's droppings in the first six months of life to furnish their insides with the right bacteria upon which they will depend for the rest of their lives. This is also practised by baby elephants.

The ruminants, or to give them their correct classification title, the *Ruminantia*, have a stomach that is divided into four chambers that process the food in a precise sequence. The swallowed food goes first into the rumen, which can hold food in quantity. This is an advantage for the animal to eat quickly somewhere where it is unsafe, before returning to safety to digest it. Fermentation begins in the rumen. The food is then regurgitated to the mouth as small lumps, each known as a bolus, to be chewed again to mix the bacteria thoroughly with the food and break down the cell walls. This is ruminating or chewing the cud. I have watched sheep give each bolus about 70 or 80 chews, which takes less than a minute. It is then swallowed to the reticulum where fermentation continues. Thence it is passed to the omasum where the real digestion takes place and then to the abomasum, which pellets the food for passing on to the duodenum or small intestine where digestion continues and the nutrients are absorbed. All this bacterial action produces an unwelcome by-product – gas. Methane and hydrogen are flammable gases produced by the fermentation of cellulosic matter; mixed with air it can be explosible. Methane is a very potent greenhouse gas that contributes to global warming. It is reported that 44% of New Zealand's global warming is caused by the farting and burping of its millions of cattle and sheep! Vets dealing with severe cases of bloat are at risk of setting fire to themselves or straw and burning the farm down when venting the gas in the presence of a flame. The fact that human farts are flammable has been discovered and demonstrated by many people of an investigative or humorous nature. One of the 'Hairy Bikers' did it on TV on their Lands End to Cape Town trip! Some have, however, managed to set fire to their clothing or hair while indulging in this experiment and done themselves quite an injury in a very sensitive area. As they say, don't try this at home, unless you do it in the bath, it is an experiment at which I have yet to achieve ignition. One feature of the ruminants is that they possess no upper incisors or canines and the lower incisors bite only onto a bony pad. The incisors of rabbits, however, like those of the rodents (Order: *Rodentia*), are continuously growing. Rabbits and hares used to be classed as rodents, but as their cheek teeth also are continuously growing they are now placed in a separate order, the *Lagomorpha*.

Hares

The European brown hare (*Lepus europaeus*) of central and southern Europe, the Middle East, and Asia is common in the UK. Unlike its smaller relative, the rabbit, it is an animal that lives above ground and depends on speed, it can run at up to 45 mph, and dodging to escape its predators.

Hare © Arthur Boyt

This does not work well with fast motor cars and they frequently get hit. In the space of two weeks three hares were killed on a wide road close to my home in Cornwall. The mountain hare (*L. timidus*) of Asia and **Northern Europe,** including Scotland, Ireland and parts of England changes its coat to white in winter and so can be easily seen (except in snow). It is the only hare found in Ireland where it is as common as its bigger cousin, the brown hare, is in East Anglia. I found one once in the highlands of Scotland that had had its head knocked clean off by a car. They change colour in the winter to merge with the snowy slopes on which they live. But come the spring they stand out as white dots on the hillsides. The wildlife sound recorder, Eric Simms, once found 39 mountain hares dead on 10km of road. There is no record as to whether he took any of them home to eat.

Fox

While I was cooking a lump of seal's back with spuds and leeks from the allotment, the phone rang: it was Mrs. Kimber from Redbourne for whom I had stuffed two fox heads, she had another fox and wanted me to do the head. I collected the fox from Redbourne after work and suggested I do it for them as a rug with a stuffed head. I had a quick dinner of rabbit and blackbird, corn, spuds and cabbage, but instead of starting on the fox, I tried to learn some songs from the Sound of Music. This played on my emotions as my wife had left me and I was living on my own. I had a tearful evening; better to have stuck to a bit of butchery! So it was not until three nights later, after a meal of seal breast and cabbage, that I got down to skinning the fox. As I was doing it to make it into a rug, I began with a long incision from under the jaw to the tip of the tail and then incisions under each leg to the pads. I started by skinning the tail, a fiddly job, fighting through the long hair, and trying not to make the cut spiral around the bone. Once the tail was out I skinned the back legs down to the feet; each toe had to be skinned right down to the claws and detached. I then hung up the body with a hook in the pelvis and worked my way down to the shoulders. Each front leg was then skinned out in the same way as I had done to the back legs. The body now hung, red and bare, with the beautiful pelt hanging down over the head to the floor. Then I heard the phone ring. It was Dudley, one of the 'priests' from the Brethren. I suppose I had better put my reader in the picture; it is a long and complicated story but I will cut it to the bone. Having both grown up in the Exclusive Brethren, my wife, Prudence, and I were zealous adherents of this tight-knit sect or rather cult that is marked by its practice of 'withdrawing from' (excommunicating) its members for any conceivable moral issue, doctrinal deviance, or financial failure, or any difference of opinion as to any of the

Fox © Arthur Boyt

above, or any disagreement, however trivial, with the opinions of their Man of God or any jumped-up local leader, and banning any contact between those kicked out and any relatives still in the fellowship, even husbands and wives.

The same treatment of sending to Coventry was meted out to persons not considered bad enough to be 'withdraw from', but whose words or conduct had aroused the suspicions of the leader of the meeting or some member of the 'priesthood'; this was called being 'shut up' as laid down in the law of Moses in the bible in Leviticus chapter 13 for the treatment of possible cases of leprosy. I had been excommunicated early in 1976 for being 'a bad influence on young people' an unfounded charge based on something I was alleged to have said to two boys in sympathy with them for their parents being 'shut up' and which was taken to be derogatory of a 'priest'. But now the voice grated in my ear, "*Timothy and I should like to come and see you tonight, er, at 9.30*". I acquiesced. I had been 'out' for nearly a year. They had last seen me on Christmas eve and when they left I had thought nothing was outstanding to hinder my recovery to the fellowship. The fact that three weeks had now passed meant bad news for me: they had more issues to rake over. They almost always came at night and usually were later than their stated time; it was an easy way of building up apprehension. At ten past ten, there was the dreaded knock at the door. It was they. I showed them into the sitting room and we all sat down. I began to feel as I always did on these occasions, like a man standing with his back to the wall facing a firing squad. Once they had settled and paused for effect (no common courtesies like asking how I was or how I was managing on my own), Timothy asked, "*Have you been getting help?*" As his last question to me three weeks ago had been "*Have you abandoned your natural proclivities?*" I kicked off by saying, "*I have been thinking of what you said on your last visit about abandoning my natural proclivities and I have to say that I don't think you can abandon your natural proclivities.*" "*Judge, judge your proclivities*" said Timothy. I said, "*I was going by what you said, and 'abandon' is not the same as 'judge'*". I should have known that contradicting them was not the best way to start. They must have realised they were on a slippery wicket here, so changed the subject to try to show me how I had despised the 'priestly' service to me over the previous year when similar priests had overseen my wife and me being, 'shut up' for almost a year for just asking a question about a matter of church procedure. I asked Timothy if he remembered my saying to him (on the evening before they excommunicated me from the fellowship nearly a year ago) that I had been wrong and had sinned and repented of that sin. No, he did not remember. I was not surprised, he had not wanted to hear it. It was now obvious they were getting nowhere; it was getting on for midnight and, despite the gas fire, I was shaking like a leaf. Timothy stood up saying, "*We are looking for repentance*" I volunteered, "*And you have not found it?*" He made his first encouraging sound of the evening by saying, "*Don't give up*" and then they left. It was then too late to get on with the fox, so I went to bed, but my mind was in such turmoil that I did not get to sleep till after 2 a.m.

The next day was Saturday and I spent the morning cycling around the town trying to buy some plaster of Paris with which to make a cast of the fox's head. A cast would enable me to make an accurate form to use for stuffing the head. Eventually, I got some at a DIY store. I called on my friend Vic Davies, the other taxidermist in the town, to return the book he had lent me. He showed me into his basement workshop where I was amazed to see he had already skinned, boiled and mounted a Dorset Horn ram's head I had given him only three days earlier; what a worker! The place was crowded with stuffed foxes, squirrels, various birds and a black cat curled up on the floor – stuffed. Back home again I heated some seal meat with cabbage, sweet corn and spuds for lunch, followed by raspberries and cereals. I then got back to the fox. One has to take care skinning a head for stuffing and ensure that the skin at the eyes, ears and lips is separated close to the bone and no holes cut in the skin. The nose is the last to part company with the carcass and then one can spread out the pelt and marvel at how beautiful it looks. The rich russet browns of the head and back, merging with the grey of the belly and trimmed with black eyes and feet. How lovely a fox really is! Two hours disappeared while I scraped muscle and fat from the skin. A pause for a high tea of macaroni and toast and back to the fox. I split the eyelids and lips and turned the ears inside out. Each whisker has to be carefully freed of its muscles without cutting it off beneath the skin. I made a plaster bandage cast of the head. The meat looked so tasty I cut off the whole of one leg with the shoulder and steeped it in a bowl of saltwater intending to have some of it to eat to see what it tasted like. I spread salt over the inside of the skin and folded it up to start the curing process.

I arose shortly before 9 a.m. on Sunday just in time to see my brother and his family setting off from across the road for their second meeting of the day, having already attended the Exclusive meeting breaking of bread at 6 a.m. I decided to have something new for breakfast. I cut a lump of meat, the size of an egg, from the shoulder of the fox, and, without washing or rinsing it, popped it in the pressure cooker for 20 mins. I served it up for my breakfast. The meat was firm but tender, but the flavour – Ugh! – a powerful aroma of fox musk which tasted like a mixture of petrol and onions. Swallowing did not get rid of the taste, it lingered on and then kept repeating itself (like a powerful cucumber) until about 5 p.m. when it must have got past the U-bend in my intestines. I cut the plaster cast off the head but, as it was a bit fragile, I made a new cast of wood adhesive soaked into a hemp bandage. For lunch, I cut off the lower front leg (which had been soaking in saltwater since the night before) and cooked it for 30 mins in the pressure cooker with various herbs. I served it up with mint source and it had a pleasant muttony feel to it, but the musky taste, although not nearly so bad, was still permeating the meat. I put in several hours more work on the fox skin, cleaning fat and tissue from the skin and pads. On Monday I had the upper part of the leg for dinner, cooked as before, but this time garnished with red-currant jelly. Again it was an enjoyable piece of meat, but yet again I could detect the musky flavour lurking in the back of my throat. On the following day, I ate the shoulder, which had by then been soaking in brine for three days. I cooked it as before in the pressure cooker with herbs and salt. This time I served it with lashings of mint sauce and red currant jelly. It had the feel of a shoulder of mutton, but not so greasy. As for that lingering foxy flavour, well, you could conjure it up if you shut your eyes and let your imagination run around visiting your taste buds. Which all goes to show that even that infamous old stinker, Reynard himself, can become, with due care and attention, a tasty dinner, er, well, almost.

The fox has not been high on the list of any nation's favourite dishes for a long time, if at all. I have met only one other person who has eaten this colourful and audacious denizen of both town and country. But it was not always so, examination of stone age middens (rubbish tips) has revealed Reynard's bones occurring with an element of regularity. I believe that in Eastern Europe, in communities where McDonald's burgers and Kentucky fried chicken have yet to penetrate, fox is a welcome addition to the family's protein intake. It may be that Reynard's lovely pelt was the more dangerous component of his constituent parts and eating him was but a by-product of his place in the stone-age clothing market. But two of Reynard's most dangerous assets have, over the last century or so, been his predilection for things that belong to man, like chickens, ducks, and pheasants eggs, and his propensity to run away when pursued. The first has led man to endeavour to encompass his destruction by whatever means he can: snare, shot, bullet, poison, or digging, however cruel and inhumane (although that term is itself a misnomer, the human capacity for inflicting cruelty has so dogged his dealings with both animals and his own kind, that it is more appropriate to use the term inhumane for acts of kindness and mercy) and the second to give man the opportunity to turn his propensity and love of cruelty into a national sport that the English have developed into a fine art and exported all over the world – fox hunting.

Originating as the common man's substitute for hunting the noble stag, pursuing the fox became an industry of its own. Foxes were so persecuted that they had to be imported from France and were to be found in large numbers on sale in Leadenhall market. Taking the red fox *(Vulpes vulpes)* to the eastern seaboard of N America was no great disaster as the New World red fox *(V. fulva)* was already present and is considered to be conspecific with *V. vulpes*. But taking the fox to Australia for hunting has resulted in the extinction of at least 10 of the native marsupial species and the diminution and threat of extermination of many more. In the debates leading up to the banning of hunting with dogs in Scotland (2002) and England (2005) a well-worn slogan was, 'Country affairs should be left in the hands of country people'. The story of the fox in Australia is but one example of why the activities of 'Sporting people' (not all country people get their kicks from killing things) should be controlled. Hunting with dogs was banned, not because it was anti the 'upper classes' as so many people like to think, but because it was cruel. If a hound had been the quarry for every meet of the hunt the 'upper classes' would have been as ardent to ban it as every other right-thinking person. The fox is a member of the dog family, the *Canidae*, and setting dogs onto a fox is no more appropriate in a civilised society than dog-fighting, cock-fighting, or bear-baiting. These 'sports' had neither the pageantry that fox-hunting has, nor the genuine thrill of galloping across country, nor the monied supporters to fight the law. And while the savage cruelty of these activities was concentrated for all to see, the foxhunt looked colourful, splendid, and even innocuous because the cruel business was enacted out of sight. When hounds ran riot, as sometimes happened and pets were torn apart in their own backyards, the country people who applauded the pageantry in the town square before the hunt saw for themselves and felt the sickening savagery that lay at the root of the public display. The average farmer was and is, indeed, going through hard and lean times, but the Countryside Alliance hijacked his cause to add substance to its vociferous anti-class campaign to maintain the sickening thread of cruelty in its 'sport'. Drag hunting, adopted by many as a cruelty-free way of continuing the pageantry of hunting and the fun of riding to hounds, is seen by others to be 'not the real thing'. The pageantry is there, the thrill of a cross-country gallop is there, and what is more, the drag hunting does not cross motorways or railways, nor enter private property to savage people's pets; the 'fox' pursued by such a hunt only goes to ground at a pub. I came across the North Cornwall Hunt on one occasion after the ban on hunting was in force. I saw a fox pursued by hounds on land where hunting was not permitted and where no human 'fox' could have found the footing to lay a trail. Upon asking what was going on, I was mendaciously told they were drag hunting. There were a few people on horseback but they stood about doing nothing while the master went on with his normal illegal hunt. The obsession with killing and cruelty dies hard. More recently I watched the same hunt send a man with a bit of fox scent tied to a rope around his waist to lay a trail. Good, I thought, they are actually drag hunting today. However, moments later he was back. He had laid a trail to the nearest covert where the hounds would resume hunting illegally.

So much for legal hunting. I once got caught up in one of these false trail hunts in Cornwall. The hounds, while supposedly following a hunt-laid trail were not giving tongue, (ie. no trail had been laid) picked up a fox scent, gave tongue, and in 200m had chased a fox onto the road where they killed it. The hounds were called off and passed me by with blood on their muzzles. The kennel-man picked up the fox and threw it into his pick-up and left. I went to the scene of the kill and there was blood, guts and fur littering the ground. I took a few photos and on leaving, to my surprise, came to the kennel-man's pickup truck inside which was the dead fox. Just then the men returned and I said, "*Right, I'll have a photo of you two*". As I raised my camera they set on me and while one picked me up and swung me around the other tried to wrest my camera from me. I started screaming for help as I knew there was someone else nearby. They put me down and I was able to get away. They had managed to split the camera but did not get it off me. When the matter was presented to the police the kennel-men claimed it was in self-defence as I had attacked them - as if a single old age pensioner would be able to do anything to two strong young men! The police ignored the photographic evidence I had and took no further action. I told my tale to the press and a billboard appeared in the town 'Pensioner attacked by hunt'. I went in to buy a copy and Lo and Behold the story had already been pulled from the paper!! It just goes to show the power and influence the hunt has in rural communities. I am glad to say that in December 2021 the Western Hunt master was fined over £1600 for his out-of-control hounds killing a cat in Madron near Penzance.

Research by Professor Harris has shown that fox numbers did not rise when hunting was suspended during the foot and mouth epidemic in 2001 and that fox numbers are not altered by culling. The much-trumpeted reason for the continuation of hunting is thus shown to be a fallacy. It is estimated that 20,000 to 25,000 foxes were killed by hunts per annum and 100,000 are killed on the road. This brings me back to eating foxes, there are a lot of meals in red coats out there for the adventurous gourmet.

After my initial tests of this readily available delicacy, I did not feel the urge to indulge myself again until I was introduced to a new recipe book. Patience Gray in her book, *Honey from a weed*, gives a recipe for fox along with recommendations on how to remove the acridity. The recipe was given her by someone she describes as an old anarchist in Carrara in Tuscany, that bit of North Italy, East of Corsica. *"A male fox shot in January or February. Skin it and keep the carcass in running water for three days, or otherwise, hang it up outside in the frost. Clean it and cut it up into joints like a rabbit, then put it in a lidded pot with some olive oil on a slow fire. In this way, a certain amount of liquor will be released. Continue to simmer until this liquor is reabsorbed; the process abolishes a certain acridity in the taste of the fox.*

"Now it is ready to prepare alla cacciatora – that is, pour a little more oil into the pot, add 3 unpeeled cloves of garlic, slightly crushed, raise the heat and brown the pieces, sprinkling them with mountain herbs (thyme, savory, fronds of fennel). Add a little salt.

"When the joints are thoroughly browned, say in 10 minutes, add a glass of red wine, a few peeled and crushed tomatoes and a glass of good stock. Put on the lid and cook until the liquor has practically evaporated."

She comments that the same method can be applied to badger, though it takes longer to cook. *"The preliminaries are vital since they remove the rather bitter 'foxy' taste."* Having read this I decided to have another go at making Reynard palatable. I took the advice of the old anarchist and put a hind leg into the stream that runs past our gate. I hoped that it would not get trampled on by one of the moorland ponies or some of the many sheep that use the stream for drinking. I was away for a few days, so it stayed in the stream for four days. When I came to get it out, I could not see it, it had become covered in mud! I washed off the mud and, instead of following the recipe, I dipped the pieces in seasoned flour, fried them in garlic and onions, and then casseroled them for 3 hours. It was delicious! No trace of fox whatever and so tender.

The children I picked up every morning on the Haberdashers Aske's school bus were a very nice lot. They didn't go out of their way to be a trouble and I made very good friends with some of them, even getting little gifts at Christmas time. I would occasionally pick up something like a pigeon while taking them to school and whilst it produced some questions and incredulity that I was *actually* going to eat it, no one raised any objections. However, one day I found a lovely fox and stuck that under the driver's seat. One or two children expressed surprise at seeing it, but no one was unduly put off by the new passenger that morning. The next day I got a phone call at work from Ron Hearn the proprietor of the coach company: he laughed a bit and then said, *"Arthur, I have had a complaint from a number of parents about you, they say you had a dead fox on the coach yesterday, is that true?"* *"Yes Ron, I am afraid it is"*, I replied. "*Well, I don't mind very much myself, but I am afraid I shall have to ask you not to pick up another one*" and he laughed again. "*I'm sorry about that Ron*", said I, "*people can be so unreasonable, but I will take care not to offend them again*". Ron was such a decent bloke that I would not want to do anything that got him into trouble. "*Parents often get upset over minor silly things but I cannot afford to ignore them, so, if you don't mind don't do it again,*" he added with a chuckle. I did, however, tell the children one day that I had been eating badger the night before (a regular item on my menu at that time in my life); they had refused to believe me, so I promised to bring some the next day and eat it in front of them. This, indeed, I duly did. The morsel I selected that I happened to have available the next day was a badger's testicles! The children who witnessed the event expressed unfeigned horror at what I did, but I did not have any repercussions from their parents, I am glad to say.

After moving to Cornwall I was very quickly engaged by the Webbers coach company of Bodmin and Blisland. The children I picked up here were a very different ilk from the studious scholars of Pinner, Ruislip, and Stanmore; instead of studying their books or discussing Latin verbs, as was the norm with Haberdashers kids, the subjects that seemed to occupy them most were sex, drink or drugs, or perhaps I am being a bit unfair and they were only talking about farming. Anyway, one day there was a lovely freshly killed fox in the road as we approached Camelford. I hopped out and picked it up. I noticed a bit of a smell, but nonetheless shoved the beast under my seat and got on the move. As we proceeded the most foul stench imaginable filled the coach, the children began to voice their protest and even I was overcome by the strength of the effluvia. I quickly stopped and stashed it away in the hedge. Funnily enough, there was no comeback from the parents of these children, which goes to show that different communities have different levels of sensitivity.

I have picked up many a dead fox over the years. Some I mounted the head and others I skinned, tanned, and sewed them to a felt backing to use as a wall hanging or as a rug and gave them to friends. Very recently I passed one in the dark and only stopped because I thought it was a Siamese cat. I picked it up and chucked it into the boot of the car. It had been there for a few days when I got a phone call from a lady who was doing a dinner called *Dining with Death* and needed something odd to cook for it. I told her I had a fox and she asked me to skin it and cut it into joints. This I did, but only with difficulty because I had only just moved house to Devon and had somehow lost all my scalpels. I had to skin it using a blunt kitchen knife. She rang to say she was arranging for a courier to fetch it for her as she lived in at Deal in Kent. Then she rang to say she could not get anyone to collect it for her and she would be coming herself to collect it. She arrived with her daughter after a five-hour drive and would have started to journey home had I not persuaded her to stay the night.

Pheasant

The pheasant *(Phasianus colchicus)* is a handsome bird that was introduced into much of Europe by the Romans but was probably introduced into the UK by the Normans. Nowadays, 40 million birds are released every year to be shot. It is not surprising that an estimated 2 million manage to collide with vehicles.

I have never sought while driving to run anything down, no, not even a pheasant. The sight of any bird or beast on or close to the road makes me at once take my foot off the accelerator. I do the same if a horse or a cyclist is using the road, or if children are playing near the road. It is, I believe, the only safe way to drive if you do not wish to be a hazard to wildlife and vulnerable people. I do not like even hitting a moth and within the bounds of safety, I try to avoid hitting one of these little beasties. However, there have been occasions when I have inadvertently been responsible for roadkill. The first time this occurred was in 1963 while driving to Norwich with my twin brother, Dennis, and my nephew, Stephen Whitbourn, in our 1936 Morris 8, Series 1. We were stooging along the A11 between Newmarket and Thetford at about

Pheasants © Arthur Boyt

50 mph, with half an eye open for anything dead beside the road, when I noticed a cock pheasant take off from the field beside us to our left and fly in the direction we were going. It then began to veer right so that it swung across the road and with perfect timing it hit smack in the middle of our windscreen. BAM!! The car shook and swerved as if hit by a rock. The windscreen did not

break, but the pheasant burst into 1000 feathers and sailed on to crumple onto the verge. We leaped out to ensure that it did not run off without leaving its name and address, but no need to hurry, it gave a last flutter and lay still.

Collecting pheasant © Arthur Boyt

On another occasion, again while driving to Norwich, somewhere between Royston and the A11, I hit another pheasant. I was driving my Aunt Emmie's 1956 ivory-coloured Rover 90. It was sometime in the early '60s before the overall 70 mph speed limit had been imposed, and I was, as usual, in a hurry. I was doing 90 mph. The pheasant was on the road, but not on my side of it. I, in my youthful lack of wit and experience, did not slow down, hoping it would stay where it was. It didn't. It flew up and straight into the radiator grille. BAM! By the time the car stopped the feathers had begun to settle. I ran back and collected it. It was in one piece but felt pulverised. The fine aluminium bars on the radiator grill were stove in; they cost £40 to repair, a lot of money in those days – more than a month's salary, a very expensive lesson! When we came to eat the bird, we found that almost every bone in its body was broken! Tasted good though.

Partridge

An entry in my diary in 1976 reads: 'Had a late lunch of young partridge (*Perdix perdix*). It was green, slimy, and smelled very, very high. I cooked it in the pressure cooker to make sure all the bacteria were dead and it smelled as if I were cooking a dirty nappy. When I opened the cooker the smell nearly bowled me over, but when I began to eat it – Oh Boy! It was scrumpulent! Full of flavour! I think we should eat more carrion.

Woodcock

Cycling through Bushey towards Cox's Corner one morning on my way to work I passed a bird, mottled with browns and black with a long bill and about the size of a partridge, lying in the gutter. As I whizzed by I thought it looked like a woodcock, but it couldn't be, not here in a housing estate in Watford. Having circled back and picked it up I found, indeed, it was a woodcock. I was amazed and, when I got to work I rang Chris Mead at BTO and he assured me they are known to drop out of the sky on migration into the most unlikely places. I skinned it to preserve it and had the rest for dinner. I did not cook it with the trail (a euphemism for the guts) as is recommended in one old recipe but pressure-cooked it in my usual way with plenty of onions and carrots and potatoes. It was most enjoyable if not memorable. I still have the rest of it stuffed and it makes various excursions to wildlife meetings for educative purposes and as an unusual quiz question. I cannot take it to RSPB (Royal Society for the Protection of Birds) meetings, however much it might be of interest to the members to handle and inspect a real woodcock because RSPB has a rule forbidding the use of dead or stuffed birds at their meetings. This stance would be most laudable were it not for the fact that they are quite content to allow the killing of these declining birds in their thousands every year from September to January as long as it is done by the shooting community. In fact, the killing of woodcock is such a speciality (due to their rarity) and the chance of seeing two in the air at once so infrequent that there is a club (the Bols Snippen Club, but more generally known as the Woodcock Club) whose membership is restricted to those who have achieved the immoral (not immortal) distinction of having managed to shoot two woodcock with a quick left and right (or shots from a repeater in quick succession). This band of worthless wretches, who doubtless see themselves as the vanguard of 'sporting' nature conservationists, regard their accomplishment as so acceptable to society as a whole that they flaunt their endeavours by holding an Annual Dinner to celebrate their membership of the club. What amazes me is that the antis haven't got wind of it and upset the digestion of these elders of a fellowship that celebrates the killing of this beautiful and innocuous species.

The long-term trend in the population of woodcock shows a decline of 74% from 1970 - 1999. This should have stirred RSPB to take action to stop the killing of these birds but they say that they *have no evidence that it is shooting that is causing the decline*". To listen to a woodcock roding (flying around its territory at dawn and dusk uttering its strange calls, alternately squeaking and growling), watch it patrolling its woodland beat, or starting up suddenly at your feet as you walk through the woods, its wings sounding a soft, hollow drum beat as it gets underway, fills me with wonder and a thrill of pleasure. What kind of demon is it whose only wish when experiencing the same is to blast the birds out of existence, so that it, its mate and no one else can ever again enjoy the pleasure of that bird's existence? Unfortunately, that sort of question is never asked at the annual dinner of the Woodcock Club lest it disturbs the conscience or digestion of its shameless members.

Snakes

Adder © Arthur Boyt

My first encounter with a snake on the road was in the summer of 1956. My two brothers and I, and a friend, Eric Parnell were on a cycling tour of the Cotswolds. I was riding my heavy three-speed Raleigh Tourer, Dennis was riding his single-speed Rudge and John was his bike made by a local company, the Leeming Brothers; Eric who had done a bit of cycle-racing in his time was using a much lighter machine. Eric made us do a sprint (even with all our luggage) every time we saw the name sign marking a town boundary ahead; he called it a 'preme'. Coming down into Malmesbury on our way from Stow-on-the-Wold to Bath, we had started one such preme when I saw a snake, 3 or 4 feet long snaking its way across the road ahead, at that moment a car whizzed by and its nearside wheels went straight over the snake's head….zap….zap. The snake writhed and coiled in the road as if in agony. The race was stopped and we dashed back to get it out of the road before something else came along. As I took hold of its tail, it galvanised into life and I quickly let go. But moments later, touching it ceased to provoke any reaction and we got it off the road. It was dead. It was green and yellow and grey, it had to be a grass snake. I don't think I took it on with me because I have no memory of skinning it, instead, I do remember skinning a whitethroat and a willow warbler that we had picked up that day. I skinned them over the hand-basin in the posh hotel that we stayed in that night in Bath, the only accommodation we could find and it cost us a guinea each (£1.05).

My first snake to eat was found much closer to home. I set off from work at lunchtime one day to go for a run. I had hardly left the gate from the Fire Research Station into Melrose Avenue in Borehamwood when I came across a grass snake lying in the road. It was about 75cm long and was dead. It had been squidged a bit in the middle and some of its insides were lying in the road. Upon examination, I found that the insides on the road were, in fact, eggs, snakes' eggs. Grass snakes lay eggs with leathery shells in a nest in rotting vegetation where the eggs are incubated by the natural heat of the places where they are deposited and hatch into baby snakes. I took it all back to the office with me and in the evening at home, skinned the snake and cooked it and the eggs for dinner. I am afraid I hard-boiled the eggs a bit, but the yolks tasted much the same as the yolk of any other egg. The snake itself was surprisingly pleasant; although there was not much of it and what there was required a lot of extrication from the bones. It was tender but had no strikingly noticeable flavour. However, it went very well with some well-buttered new potatoes and some nice spinach leaves.

Cattle

While writing this book I myself had a frightening experience of colliding with a large animal. I was driving on a moorland road where cattle, sheep and horses are allowed to graze and are often in the road. I was keenly on the look-out for animals on the road and had just had to slow down for some horses. It was dark and a little misty. I had seen a car's headlights coming towards me, veering around as though he were off-road. When I passed him he was going slowly and I wondered what was the matter with him. I glanced in the mirror after he had gone by and when I looked back in the direction I was going -- NO – there, not 3m away was a black bullock, standing in the road facing me. I slammed on the brakes and shut my eyes. I hit the animal with a sickening thump. It crashed against the windscreen, rode up onto the roof and fell off the car taking the roof rack with it. The windscreen was crazed but had not given way. Amazed that I was still alive I turned off the engine and got out expecting to see a dead or dying cow. There was nothing there, only a hole in the road made by the animal's horn, it had got up and walked away! I must have hit it at 40 – 50 mph! The car was a wreck. The farmer told me the next day that one of his bullocks had a broken horn but otherwise seemed to be OK. Up to then, I believed that people who collide with moose and deer ought to have been taking more care and not going to sleep. Well, now it has happened to me and I could not have been more aware of the danger.

But things don't always turn out so well. As reported in the Daily Telegraph for 11 June 2009, Amanda Russell, 25, a Tesco stock control manager of Yeovil, Somerset, hit a cow at 60mph on the A3088 while driving her Fiat Punto to work. She lost control and veered down an embankment where she was found dead, having fractured her skull. The cow, which had wandered onto the road through a gate left open by a member of the public, was also killed.

My car after hitting a bullock © Arthur Boyt

76

Roadkill Predators

We have all seen crows and magpies trying to feed off roadkill on busy highways. They have a pull and a peck and then a car comes along and they fly off for a minute or two; no sooner are they back than along comes another vehicle. It is enough to give even a magpie indigestion. They probably manage to get a crop-full in the early hours, but why is it that they have never learned to pick the thing off the road, take it somewhere quiet and consume it at their leisure? Perhaps one will get the hang of it one day and then we shall see if the idea catches on. I have never seen a buzzard carrying off roadkill either. I have seen scavenging kites in India dropping quickly into a crowded market and once into a back yard to seize a small chicken and carry it off, degutting over the shouting owner. The red kites we now have in this country are very much snatch and carry away birds than are the corvids and buzzards.

But deaths of predators at the scene of a roadkill is a problem the world over. Bears, skunk, wolverines, and opossum in N America, Tasmanian Devils in Tasmania and, as I found on a trip through Sudan, vultures in Africa. On that occasion, I had cycled up the Nile valley from Cairo to Karnak - there was very little roadkill and no wildlife - and, after taking the ferry up Lake Aswan and the train to Khartoum I was on my way cycling to Kassala, when I discerned in the shimmering haze on the flat dry savannah of Northern Sudan, some lumpy objects on the road ahead. As the picture came into focus with my approach I could see several large animals of some description. Wow! They were camels! But there were some huge birds too, six dead Griffon vultures lay scattered among the corpses! What a scene! I got off to examine the carnage and immediately entered the stink zone, the sweet sickly aroma of long-dead meat. Only the rotting barrels of gut contents remained wet the rest was stiff and dry. How could anyone mow down three camels in an empty horizon? Had they been running beside the road and veered across or had they been standing in the road and been mown down in cold blood? The vultures had come down for the feast, but heavy with camel meat they too had become victims of more drivers proceeding 'without due care and attention'. A camel's skull was too big, and too smelly, to take on with me, but the vultures were another matter. I tore the desiccated head off one and pulled several of its pinions from the wing - what specimens to add to my collection!

I have come across birds whose interest in roadkill really took me by surprise when I first encountered it; you too may be a bit credulous when I tell you about it. I was driving one day through Chorleywood in our 1936 Rover 10, the long, low-slung, rectangular saloon that I had obtained at no cost through the kind intervention of J Stanley Hutchinson, a solicitor's clerk in Station Approach, Watford, (with whose family Dennis and I had lodged in 1959) who in disposing of a client's effects had found the car hidden unused for eight years in a garage and finding it to be of no market value offered us the opportunity to remove it for him. It was a super machine! It only needed the plugs and points cleaning and some new petrol in the tank and away it went. It had a self-lubricating system (Lubrivac) for the springs which were wrapped in leather gaiters; it had a freewheel control on the dashboard to save fuel, advance and retard levers on the steering wheel and a sunroof; it could do 70mph! It purred along, a real luxury limousine. Anyway, back to Chorleywood, a cock blackbird burst out of the hedge from the left followed closely by a second and flew down low in front of the car, only one bird made it to the hedge on the other side. I looked in the mirror and saw a feathered lump in the road behind me. I braked and pulled over. I saw it move as I jumped out and went back to it. But as I approached I could see that it was two birds with the one cock sitting on the other, wings and tail spread, and bill open in a posture of defiance and victory. Mesmerized by its sudden supremacy, it hardly noticed my approach until I was almost on it when, startled, it flew away. The injured bird was still alive and probably only concussed. I decided the best thing was to put it safely off the road and let it recover in its own time. I picked it up and placed it as far as I could reach under a hedge and went on my way. I had been taking my aunt and some old brethren to a meeting at Amersham and on our return, I stopped to check on the blackbird. To my surprise, it was just where I had left it but when I picked it up and examined it I found its head was open and the brains pecked out! There is no question in my mind this had been done by its rival. I experienced another instance of this behaviour when I saw a cock chaffinch fly up from the body of another cock chaffinch that was lying by the road. Stopping to examine the bird I found that it too had had its brains pecked out! These sweet songsters we love to have in our gardens have a dark side to their nature awaiting the right circumstance for it to come to the fore. Could this be true of us all?

On the opposite side of the spectrum, I have often seen a bird calling anxiously from the phone wires overhead as its mate lies dead in the road below. We love to arrogate to ourselves alone such feelings of concern for a loved one and regard the lower animal orders as incapable of any altruistic emotions or feelings. It beggars belief that we humans can kill birds returning to succour a dead or dying mate as recounted by Farley Mowatt in *'Sea of Slaughter'* we need to face the facts of our exterminating character.

Adventures in Scotland

In the summer of 1988, I was invited by my good friends Stephen and Kathryn Reed to join them and their two young boys, Jonathon and Jamie, for some of their summer holiday on the Isle of Mull. I had never been to Mull before and, knowing it would be a great activity holiday as well as a visit to a new part of the country, I accepted with alacrity. I had at the time my cousin, Duane Henderson, from Ontario staying with me so he was included in the invitation. Duane and I drove up to Scotland in the Maxi with two sea kayaks on the roof and slept one night beside Loch Lomond. Because of the camping gear in the car there was not room for both of us in the car. Duane volunteered to sleep out. It was just at the time when the A84 was being dualled and there were large civil engineering works in progress. Duane found a huge drain or sewer pipe to sleep in and claimed in the morning that he had been warm and dry all night. We made good use of the empty roads in the early morning, but repeatedly had to stop for dead rabbits. By the time we reached Oban, where we took the ferry to Craignure, we had collected no less than seven dead rabbits, all in pristine condition. On the ferry, Duane and I fell into conversation with a pretty young lady who wanted to get to Iona. I said we were going in that direction, but not all the way and if she wanted a ride we would be delighted to take her as far as she wanted. On the drive we told her about our plans for the next few days, camping, kayaking, swimming, visiting Iona and generally having fun. She then asked if she could join us. I was a bit worried about how Kathryn would take our picking up a young lady and adding her to their holiday party, but I need not have worried as Kathryn was delighted to have her join us as another lady in a party of five males. Anna, was a young Cuban émigré who lived with an aunt in central London. I had a go at teaching her the Eskimo Roll, the skill of righting a capsized kayak. Steve caught a bucket of mackerel during the day, so we had a feast in the evening; four or five mackerel in one helping is quite an experience. They did sit rather heavily in the stomach though while trying to get to sleep! Dinner for the following evening was reserved for the rabbits and we held a mass rabbit-skinning teach-in on the beach at Uisken near Bunessan where we were camping.

I had brought my pressure cooker with me, so this very quickly turned the pile of rabbit pieces into some very tasty and tender meat. It was certainly the most magnificent and enjoyable rabbit feast I have had in the finest scenery imaginable with the mauve Paps of Jura sitting low down on the horizon 27 miles to the South and the deserted unspoiled coast and beach around us. We crossed to Iona the next day with Duane and me doing the one-mile sea crossing by kayak. There was a bit of a sea running and I was very nervous about Duane's capacity to stay the right way up. I had had some practice with him in Swanage Bay the week before and he had capsized three times. Each time I got him back in by a process known in canoeing terms as x-rescue while still in deep water, but, fit and strong as he was, he was tired after the third x-rescue. I dreaded his capsizing in the far less friendly strait between Mull and Iona, where quite a sea was running. However, much to my relief, we made the crossing without incident. Anna decided to stay on the island, so we bade her goodbye. We found ourselves caught up in a religious festival with the Iona Community doing a tour of the island with occasional stops for hymns and prayers. This was also being televised for Scottish TV, so we added our voices to the singing even though it was only heard by the seabirds and the wind, Oh, and the microphones; and so we made a crossing to Iona and gained access to many Scottish homes. The return crossing was made again without incident. A few days later we met Anna in Tobermory and she rejoined our party. Stephen purchased a bucket of scampi there and we duly had a feast of that when back at the campsite.

While returning from Mull with Duane and Anna, who joined us for the trip back to London despite the fact that we were stopping in the North York Moors for a week's camping and orienteering, I came across an animal that I had never eaten as roadkill before. It was a red deer. We had just come out of the top of Glen Coe when we spotted it. It had been there for a little while and ponged a bit. The smell was nothing that I could not have put up with for myself with the window open, but with two sea canoes on the roof and a lady inside there was not really much room for it. We took a photo and journeyed on, feeling disappointed but relieved. It remains the only roadkill red deer I have ever come across.

A rotten pick-up, or a cautionary tale

Dead animals are not all I pick up when I am driving about, anything of interest or value that catches my eye will usually get examined and if there is room and it is not smelling too much it comes on board. Hitchhikers come into this category. I used to hitch a bit when I was younger and know well the surge of joy and expectancy when a car's brakes are applied and it stops for you, and I like to give people that pleasure if it does not interfere with my journey. Besides people can be most entertaining and are very good at helping you to stay awake as well. If I see they are smoking I take my foot off the brake and drive on. It is not just people smoking in my presence I object to, but these people emanate smoke for a good half-an-hour or more from their lungs and then continue to pollute the atmosphere with the general reek of their clothes, bodies and hair which soon transfers itself to my skin and lips and clothes. The trouble is that often you do not catch the smell until you have agreed to take them and they have got in. If you stop at a garage and they fish out the fags, I say 'I am afraid I shall not be able to take you on if you smoke'. This makes them feel that their human rights are being removed and they quickly try and grab a few drags while I am not looking and pretend they are following my instructions. We get started and it is only then I realise I have been cheated and rather than put them off or have a row I drive on in stony silence. Then there are the ones who have been travelling for a while and have not bothered to wash or change their clothes, or do they always smell like that? I have suffered in silence too many times and very rarely do I stop now and give them another chance. I mean, animal parasites are one thing, but human parasites are something else, who knows what they have crawling over them?

And so it was in the spring of 1977, during my age of innocence and benefaction that I picked up one of the jewels of the younger generation at a motorway service station near Newcastle. I had set off for Scotland from my home in Watford, but diverted via Hatfield for Wheathampstead to pick up a rabbit that my friend at work, Mike Richardson, had cached for me on Nomansland Common, a regular site for roadkill spotted by Mike on his journey to work. I managed to run into some traffic jams, the rabbit had disappeared and I took an hour to finally reach the M1 at Luton. Here I picked up a couple of hitch-hikers and to oblige I diverted to drop them at their destination in Edgbaston. I made a fuel stop at Newcastle and, heading back onto the motorway, there was another young man with his thumb out: he was in his twenties, untidy, scruffily dressed and carrying a big bag. He said his name was Nick Crane (not the Nick Crane whose travels feature on British television) and he was travelling north; to my annoyance he brought into the car with him that aroma of stale tobacco and sweaty clothes that seems to be the hallmark of these pioneers of the free life; a freedom that to my way of thinking is more a freedom from the discipline of regular work and any attempt at self-discipline in their personal habits and morals.

I was going to spend the night at Leighton Moss, the RSPB nature reserve near Carnforth, and get in some late-night and early-morning birdwatching and sound recording. I turned off the motorway at Carnforth and expected him to get out and travel on his way. However, Nick asked if he could stay and join me for the night. I was a bit surprised but, in an effort not to seem unfriendly, I agreed. We found the reserve and walked out to the hides. To my amazement there was a bittern skulking in the reeds. When it stopped and stretched its neck it became invisible, then it would move and become visible again. A peregrine falcon appeared and hunted a huge flock of starlings, which balled and flowed and snaked as the peregrine dived at them, opening like a doughnut to allow the falcon to whizz through the centre of the flock. I heard two bittern calling and resolved to get up early to record them. The warden offered us sleeping space in an old farmhouse, which I accepted. I got my Primus stove going and cooked some spuds and sprout tops (from my allotment) in the pressure cooker. Having failed to find the rabbit and having been on motorways ever since, there was no roadkill to cook so I had to open a tin of pilchards. We then had soup, tea and custard. I cooked and Nick washed up. We went to bed at 10.45 p.m. and then the noises began: scratching, knocking, bumping and pattering, over our heads. Apparently two barn owls were kept in the room above! I was sleeping (or, more precisely, trying to sleep) on a safari bed, but the cold came through from below and drove sleep from me. I gained a little respite from sleeping on one arm, but that caused pins and needles, so I was quite glad to rise at 5.30 a.m. and go out to record the bittern. I was carrying with me a parabolic reflector for collecting the songs and calls of birds and animals to be taped on my cassette recorder. I took this reflector everywhere with me just in case I heard something rare or unusual. I had made it myself out of resin and glass fibre using a concrete form that I had taken from a dish that a like-minded friend at work, Stan Ames, had lent me that he too had made himself! The sound recording industry was never going to make a killing out of the likes of us. Nick came too and I got quite a good recording despite the terrific wind. Back for porridge and scrambled egg and, while Nick washed up, I went out to get some photos.

On my way back to the car I had a nasty feeling that Nick might have used this opportunity to steal the car as I had left the key in it, so it was with considerable relief that I found the car where I had left it. I paid for the night's accommodation for myself and Nick as he said he had no money with him. I never thought to ask how he would have got food and accommodation had I not been there. Once we were on our way on the M6 again, Nick did actually say that I should not have left the keys in the car as he could have stolen it. While being a little apprehensive that he should think such a thing, let alone mention it, I took confidence from this comment that I was building an element of trust with him by showing I trusted him. Nick had said he was going as far as Glasgow and would get out at Bothwell services, but after going into a phone booth at the services he returned to the car and said he had to go to Aberdeen to join his ship and could he come on with me. I said I was going camping and walking in the hills at which point he said he did not have to join his ship for two weeks as it was in dry dock and could he join me. It did not occur to me to wonder why someone should go to join a ship that was not sailing for two weeks. I thought it might be nice to have a bit of company but I was afraid he might hold me up, so I queried whether he would be able to keep up with my pace. *"OK, Nick, what about doing a long fast walk?"* I asked. *"Nothing easier,"* he replied, *"I walked from London to Brighton only last month."* *"Well, what about running?"* I enquired, *"I often do my long walks at the double."* *"No trouble,"* he said, *"I'm good at running, in fact, I did a mile in 4 minutes and 2 seconds last summer."* Having myself broken several school records for the mile and never having bettered 4 minutes 30 seconds, I guessed this was a vain boast. *"Oh, so when and where did you achieve that performance?"* I asked. *"Well, actually it was on a road and was unofficial,"* he replied. I remained inwardly sceptical, although I could not be certain it was a lie, as the year before I had run a mile in under 4 minutes, but it was done during a before-breakfast run from one end of Fair Isle to the other and was downhill most of the way! I asked, *"What about eating roadkills?"* *"No trouble, I am always eating hedgehogs. I wrap them in clay and cook them like that and I am always snaring rabbits."* My bells of incredulity rang again, but like an innocent damsel taken in by the blarney of an experienced roué, I agreed to take him on with me.

We were heading for Braemar and a campsite at Linn o' Dee, but I wanted to go via Glenisla to meet one of my father's cousins, Major Denis Boyt, whom I had discovered in the family tree and had never met. My father, William Dennis Boyt, had served in the Royal Garrison Artillery in Gibraltar in the First War and had passed his dress sword on to his cousin, Denis, when he joined the army. My trip into history ended rather abruptly when I learned upon arrival that Denis Boyt had died three weeks earlier and, no, I could not visit his grave, he had given his body to research. On the long drag up to Glenshee I picked up a mountain hare from the road, a welcome supply of meat for the next few days. Just before the Devil's Elbow, a notorious black spot on the road across the mountains, it began to snow. It was a blizzard by Braemar and was inches deep at Linn o' Dee. Nick looked scared stiff as I got out the tent and in the face of his protests got it and the awning up in a lull, taking care to face the entrance away from the prevailing NE wind. I skinned the hare and soon had the pressure cooker sizzling merrily with the hare's hindquarters inside. What a super meal! Lots of lovely grub. Nick ate well and without complaint; there was obviously no alternative. We drove round to the bar at Mar Lodge which served as a local pub at 10pm and met Bob Scott, the old stalker, and Alex Dempster, who did not recognise me from my visit of the year before as I was now adorned with a beard. After buying a drink for us both, we had a pleasant evening fraternising with the locals. We eventually left the cosy cheerfulness of the bar and the log fire and returned to our rather bleak camp in the snow.

One advantage of sleeping badly is that it makes it easy to get up early and get away from the tossing and turning. It was thus that I found myself out in the icy cold at 5.30 a.m. and walking up through the woods in the snow and the dark to try and get a tape-recording of capercaillie. These massive birds assemble at dawn at a patch of ground that is known as a lek where the males display to any females present. Unfortunately nothing was happening there that morning, so I returned to the campsite and made a pot of tea and some porridge. Nick decided he would take his in bed! We drove into Braemar to the toilets and to have a wash. Nick went to the bank, to 'get clearance' for his money. When he returned he said they had told him to call back later. I drove up to the Glenshee ski centre where there was plenty of snow. Nick said he would like to have a go but would have to borrow from me, as he still had no money. I asked what standard he was at in skiing, plough, stem or parallel turns. He said he could do parallel turns OK. He had no gloves, so I bought him a pair. I booked a lesson for two at £5 and ski hire at £2 for him and £1.80 for me. A pleasant New Zealander from Dunedin called Ross was our instructor and we set off for the draglift. Nick fell off the lift at once and had to walk up. When he got to the top of the trainer tow and put his skis on again he could not even stand up. It was evident that far from being capable of parallel turns he had probably never been on skis before in his life. Ross sent him down and then spent two hours trying to get me to stem turn less and parallel more. He kindly fell over three or four times (which I was well able to follow). I stopped at lunchtime for a sausage roll and some tea in the car. Nick had spent the morning in the bar and continued this form of exercise in the afternoon while I got a lift pass and tried to put my instruction into practice. Generally, I came down so fast I only had time to think enough for snowplough turns. The leather ski hire boots were so ill fitting, uncomfortable and painful that, when taking them off, I experienced what I have heard others describe as 'the second most pleasurable sensation in life. The fact that they presented no barrier to the ingress of icy water, slush and mud did not make them any more comfortable. When I got back to the car park I found I had no car keys. I must have lost them on the slope. What was I to do? I went to ski hire and asked if any one had found some keys. Yes, some had been found in the restaurant; they were mine, thank goodness! We returned to the camp and I cooked another meal of hare for us both. Nick had grown tired of my greens and made so bold as to complain that I thinned the custard and drowned the tea. I am afraid that my expressed apology was somewhat thin. After dinner we walked the one and a half miles to Mar Lodge and sat by the log fire enjoying the company present and a little to drink (once again at my expense). A couple from the campsite gave us a lift back and a wee dram before turning in. I went out like a light when my head hit the pillow.

I cooked the usual breakfast of porridge and we went into Braemar for a wash and then on up to Glenshee. Although the sun was shining there was a terrific wind blowing so only the trainer tow was working. I set to work putting into practice the things I had been taught yesterday. Nick decided conditions were not for him so stayed in the bar, at least I did not have to pay for ski hire for him. At lunchtime Nick said that the bank would have something for him, so we went down to Braemar. He went into the bank and came out shaking his head, *"No, nothing has come through yet."* I thought to myself, *"Banks can be such a nuisance, just when you need something in a hurry."* And so, back up to Glenshee.

I got back to serious practice, non-stop, up, down, up, down. I was determined to become a parallel skier that afternoon. I kept count of the goes I had on the lift; it gave me something tangible as evidence that I was getting value for money. The idea of stopping for a cup of tea was anathema to me, it would have robbed me of quite a few goes, and it would have spoiled the afternoon. However, after 40 runs even I began to feel that the repeated descents of the short training slope were beginning to become repetitive, and besides, I had not become the graceful parallel skier, the likes of which I could see descending the Tiger with perfect style and ease nearby, as I had so dearly hoped. (The Tiger is the steepest run at the resort and is truly frightening to all but the very competent; if conditions have been wet in the day, it freezes in the late afternoon into what seems like a wall of ice.) The other lifts began working so I went on a drag-lift that took me up higher. I always took care to keep my footing on the drag as to come off is so embarrassing, so uncomfortable and such a wicked waste of time. However, the slope was different, or I was looking somewhere else and Woops! my skis were crossed and down I came. I tried to hang on to the bar for a moment or two, but it was painful and wet and I let go. I had quite a struggle to get out of the way before the next skier being dragged up got entangled with me. My next attempt was more successful and now I could make a descent down a real hillside. I ought to say here that those machines which flatten, no, groom, that's the word, which groom the hillside and are so essential to every ski resort today, they did not exist in 1977. Well, they might have on the continent, but certainly not in Scotland. Snow fell, people skied, snow became slush, people went on skiing, slush froze and people still skied. Moguls, mounds of snow, slush, or ice formed by the action of turning skiers on them, appeared like huge goose-pimples on the steeper slopes More snow fell and so it went on, organic skiing to coin an expression.

And so it was that I started slithering cautiously down a real mountain. I gathered pace, found I could turn and slow down when needed, so let myself go and revelled in the exhilaration. After a run or two I even went off piste if you could call it that and found myself near the bottom of the Tiger in a mogul field. It was like emerging from a calm backwater in a canoe and entering a raging torrent. I was very soon on my backside and bumping helplessly to the bottom. I decided then to take the chairlift up Cairnwell. When I got to the top I found that my ski had become unscrewed so took the chair lift down again. At the bottom my pole got stuck in the chair and tripped the lift emergency cut-off switch. Having had a repair effected to my skis, I went back up Cairnwell and found it to be much steeper than anything I had encountered before. What is more as evening approached the place became very icy and I had to apply my newly learned skills to stay upright, leaning out precariously while traversing to get an edge. I came down slowly but enjoyed the extra difficulty and being able to cope with it. The lift had stopped by the time I was down so that was it for the day and I could squeeze my screaming feet out of the instruments of torture that came between my feet and the skis.

Back at the camp we found that deer had raided our site and eaten what remained of the hare, so I opened a tin and we had Spam instead. After dinner we walked up Glen Geldie beside the Dee. Nick walked so slowly we did not get far. On the way back I plucked up courage and told him his feet smelled and would he kindly wash them before going to bed. To set an example I washed mine in the freezing water of the Dee perched on one of the granite boulders of which the river bed was comprised, but sissy boy had to boil a kettle and then had a fag before coming in. I asked him not to come into the tent until he had got the stink out of his lungs. When I protested at the smell he brought in with him he told me I could smell the campfire. He had insisted on our having a campfire but when he proved incapable of getting it going I had had to show him and help him do it. I washed the potatoes and got the meal. He did offer to wash up in the morning, but, of course it was not done and the job fell to me. Dear reader, you are doubtless wondering what sort of a sucker I am. I wonder too myself as I look back and see how I went on day after day seemingly unable to remove this leech from my person. Every day increased the loans I was making in anticipation of his money arriving at the bank. I was becoming a personal servant to this smelly unpleasant, boastful and incompetent individual. Maybe it was because I had recently had an upheaval in my life that had propelled me from a close-knit upper-middle-class religious community into a wider world with which I was unfamiliar that caused me to try to embrace every member of humanity, however, low my instincts told me they were in the strata of society, with the trust and confidence that I had been used to showing to those with whom I was more thoroughly acquainted. I hoped that my trust and kindness would make this specimen respond in kind and become in character a person worthy of my trust and confidence. I had much to learn, but two more days of lessons in this difficult school had yet to be endured.

Nick said he would get breakfast on the morrow at 8 a.m. Having brought a bike with me on the roof rack, I was now able to cycle out to a blackcock lek and saw two birds there despite the bitter cold wind. I got back at 8.20 but there was no sign of Nick getting the breakfast, so I got it. He wasn't asleep so I said *"I thought you were getting the breakfast today. What happened?"* *"I didn't know what the time was"*, he replied. I drove into Braemar to get milk and then we set off to walk the 3 mile gravel road from Linn O' Dee to the isolated house at Luibeg, home of the stalker, artist and Taxidermist to the Queen, Willie Forbes, whom I had met there last year. As I suspected, Nick, when actually made to fulfil his boast of being a good walker, had to stop and rest every mile and then dawdled like a child. I got fed up with waiting for him and walked on at my own pace. Luibeg was empty; evidently Willie had moved out, so after chatting to some walkers at the hut at Derry we began to dawdle back. Luckily for Nick's muscles and my temper a Nature Conservancy Landrover came by and we got a lift. We drove into Braemar to check the bank. This time I went into the bank with him and watched him ask if there was anything for Nick Crane from his London bank. The staff looked at one another and said *"No."* By now I knew I was being taken for a ride and once outside I said, *"Would you give your bank a ring and find out why the money has not arrived?"* He was unwilling at first but agreed to give it another try. *"And I am going to listen in to your call"* I said. *"Oh no you are not"* he said angrily. *"And why not, pray. What are you trying to hide from me?"* I countered. *"My affairs are my business, not yours,"* he asserted. *"Yes but it is my money you have been borrowing"*, I retorted. Eventually he agreed to phone if I stayed outside the phonebox. Through the small rectangular windows of the red-painted telephone box I watched him dial. He dialled a number and then almost at once pressed the rest to cut the call. Then he dialled a different number and again cut it off. A third time he did the same thing and came out. *'I can't get through'*, he breezed. *"You liar!"* I said vehemently. *"I was watching you dial and you have not been ringing your bank. You dialled any old number. You are deceiving me."* *"No I wasn't, I couldn't get through, honest."* At this I finally lost my rag and stormed and raged at him. *"You have been living at my expense for the past five days, you have borrowed a lot of money from me and all the time have been lying to me about 'Money coming from London' and 'I'll repay you tomorrow' you are nothing but a cheat and a bloody liar"*, I roared. Now it takes a lot for me to swear so I must have been really upset and I began to feel ashamed of myself at once. However, it had its effect, he became quiet and subservient saying: *"I am sorry, really, I have drawn all I can this month, I do have some money due but it will not be released until the end of the month which is tomorrow. I am sorry and I have been lying to you, but the money will be through tomorrow."*

His apology and free confession somehow convinced me that, after all, things would turn out right and I had been unfair in condemning him too quickly. Funnily enough, it never occurred to me to ask myself what sort of nanny bank administered his affairs so strictly, or whether he was heir to a massive fortune whose trustees acted with extreme parsimony in the administration of his funds. Oh, why didn't I trust my inner instinct and get shot of him there and then? Instead I took him with me in search of the golden eagle. (Having tested my readers' incredulity to the limit with this saga of naiveté or stupidity, I would gladly terminate it here to limit the dreary exposition of my own folly. Things could hardly have got worse, but they did, so I guess you will want to hear about it.) We drove past Balmoral and turned off the Tomintoul road onto a track, driving deep into the wilderness of the Grampians. The track became ever more rutted and degraded. We occasionally passed derelict cottages and ruins of long-forgotten communities, but we saw no occupied habitation and no body. Birds there were aplenty: wheatear, redshank, curlew, mistle thrush and (Wow) even some ring ouzel. We were almost two miles from help when the front wheel, the driving wheel, of the Maxi dropped into a hole, the body crunched onto the ground and left the wheel spinning ineffectually in mid-air.

The car would go neither forwards nor backwards. Nick veered from panic to despair, but I had been in such a predicament before and now had every confidence I could get us out unaided. I got Nick to collect small rocks while I got out the jack and wound it right down. It was one of those that has a stub on a worm drive that slots into a jacking point under the door sill and can raise the car without anyone having to position it underneath the car. I banged the jack stub well home into the channel with a rock, getting it only halfway in would be courting disaster. I placed a flat rock under the jack and proceeded to wind the handle. Now, the channel into which the jack slots on the Maxi is prone to rust, in fact, the whole sill is prone to rust and this propensity is either discovered at the MoT or in a situation like this when everything, literally, hangs on the integrity of the jacking point. Winding carefully, I listened for the telltale crunching sound that would indicate incipient disaster. The car rose up and slowly the rusty sill began to scrunch and collapse. I wound on slowly, the scrunching ceased and, slowly the tyre cleared the ground. I filled the hole with stones. Then, digging and scraping little channels behind each wheel, I paved the track to give a good surface over which to drive out. As I wound down the jack I said to Nick, *"Get in."* I threw the jack in the boot and jumping in started the engine. I hung my left arm over the seat back, engaged power very gently and taking care to neither to spin the wheels nor stall the engine, I reversed out in one long steady manoeuvre until we were safely on terra firma and I could turn the vehicle. Only then did I allow myself a sigh of relief.

We didn't get to see any golden eagle. Once back on the main road and with civilization just around the corner, Nick began to complain that an enlarged lymph gland in his groin was giving him trouble and could I take him to the doctor? Still feeling guilty about my outburst earlier, I was only too pleased to be able to do anything to make him comfortable and off we went in search of a doctor's surgery. I had to hang about while he waited to see the doctor; he reported that the doctor said he had a lump of Hodgkinson's on his foot! I had no idea what this might be, but at any rate he had a prescription to be procured at the chemist's shop, could I pay for it? Why of course I would be delighted. I wanted him to feel we were still friends. I hoped that perhaps, despite so many signs to the contrary, he might even now be won over to the ranks of the righteous and reward my not inconsiderable investment in time and trouble, not to mention the little matter of money. Hope springs eternal...

By now I had run out of roadkill again, so we had to have a large tin of baked beans on bread for dinner and a tin of strawberries with custard for afters. The wind was getting up a bit so we tried to settle down early instead of going to Mar Lodge for a warm-up. The wind had swung round to the south and was now blowing right into the mouth of the tent. It was a three-man cotton tent by Lamont of France that I had bought 17 years earlier for a trip to the South of France in which my two brothers and I had, with four other young bloods, hired a Dormobile, hopped over the Channel from Southend in a converted Argosy operated by Silver Cities Airways, driven to Toulon via Geneva and back across the Alps having to buy snow chains to cross the snowbound Grand St Bernard pass. The tent had a sewn-in groundsheet and was yellow with a sky blue flysheet. It was bell-ended, which made it important which way you pitched it relative to the wind, and had an awning which doubled the length of it at the other and which was now catching the full force of the wind. It had two steel poles of interlocking sections and the poles were held rigid with a steel connecting pole at the top. It looked good and had given years of service. There was a hole at the bell end where a rat had torn its way in to get at some food while my brothers and I were camping in the Welsh mining village of Cilfynydd; this allowed a bit of extra ventilation. Extra ventilation, however, was the last thing we wanted that night. I tied the mouth of the awning together with string as best I could. I should have turned the tent round when the wind changed, but with a gale already driving heavy squalls I did not feel tempted to do so now. I crawled into my sleeping bag. I could hear each gust as it approached down the valley, tore its way into a copse of Scots pine 200m away, roared across the intervening ground, threw itself onto the ancient relict of the Caledonian forest under which the tent was pitched and savaged my frail habitation, threatening to tear tent and occupants from the ground to which they were so insecurely pegged and hurl us all away into the darkness. Despite all this, somehow I fell asleep.

At midnight I was awakened by an ominous and persistent flapping: something had given way, something had to be done, NOW. I struggled into my boots and anorak in the darkness and ventured out into the roaring vortex of wind, tent and trees. I found what I had feared. Half the flysheet had unpegged and the awning was flapping like a rampant elephant. Just then a violent gust roared up. I grabbed the flysheet to stop it taking off and held on for dear life. The gust seized the tent, the rear pole bowed and the front pole folded neatly into a right angle. Yelling at Nick to grab the poles, I managed in a temporary lull to repeg the flysheet in the soggy ground. Then with Nick supporting the tent I replaced the two sections of damaged pole (I happened to have two spare lengths) and we were back in business, well, back into bed, it was 12.45 a.m. Would it last the night? At 1.30 a.m. after another hard blow I got up to inspect the pegs. The rain was coming on in earnest and a small stream was developing at the back of the tent. I went back to bed. At 2.15 a.m. I found my Safari camp bed, which stands up off the ground on a sprung steel frame, was standing in water. The stream was right under the tent and had found the little holes that pepper the groundsheet. Nick had his waterproof bivvy bag and, besides, was on the dry side of the tent. I got up and betook myself to the car, a true haven in a storm. I ought to mention here, as the Austin, Morris or (as it later became) the British Leyland Maxi is almost extinct, only its fans will know that whatever faults the Maxi may have had - and it was not without them, particularly the gearbox - it was an extremely comfortable car to sleep in. The front seats moved forward, laid flat and mated with the rear seat and backrest to provide an ergonomically designed, therapeutic setting for a really good kip. In fact, if the truth be told, the Maxi was actually designed around the sleeping arrangements. It may have been the first five-door saloon, boasting a transverse engine, front-wheel drive, fifth gear, and front and rear compensating hydro-elastic suspension system, but all, that was secondary, the sleeping accommodation was the *raison d'etre* of the vehicle, it was, in fact, a bedroom that could be used for motoring about in. I proved it that night. Oh how I slept! It was so comfortable! By the time I woke up, the storm had abated and the wind gone withersoever it would. Would that Nick had gone with it, debts and all, and I could have closed this chapter here and now, but I can't for I know that you will not be satisfied till you have heard it out to the bitter end.

We had a leisurely breakfast of the usual porridge and cups of tea and made our way, as usual, to Braemar to see what the bank had to offer. Oh dear! Still no money. Surprise, surprise! But it is due today, isn't it! Maybe we are so remote from the Fort Knox where his money is guarded that it takes extra long for it to reach this uncivilized region of Her Majesty's kingdom, but, always obliging, the bank agreed to call Glenshee when the money arrived. What a good idea! I am now convinced that all will be settled by the end of the day. I suppose I so wanted it to turn out all right that I went on deluding myself that it would. Is this how battered wives go on putting up with shit husbands? Or partners of drunks hang on in the belief that they will mend their ways? You can't bear to see the investment of years disappear and so you go on ruining the rest of your life day by day, week by week and year by year. Is this where qualities like hope and patience turn their possessor into a victim? I did not believe that this chap whom I had sheltered and fed and been kind to for so long could possibly do the dirty on me. Human nature is not like that.... We drove up to Glenshee. I left Nick with the car keys as usual so that he could get anything he needed from the car without having to seek me out. I skied for four hours non-stop. It was sleeting and wet, but there was plenty of new snow except it was wet and heavy. At 3 p.m. Nick came out of the bar and asked for money with which to hire skis and get a lift pass. Without a murmur I dipped my hand into my pocket and gave it him, after all, my accumulated loan to him was about to be reimbursed, so what is the problem? Nick knew he could trust me to pay for his fun and I knew I could trust him with my car keys. No, I was pleased he was doing something active. He spent too much time lounging in the bar, the exercise and fresh air would do him good, he might even learn to ski! By the end of the day the discomfort of my cold wet hands was only exceeded by the scrunched agony of my feet. I seem to be programmed to try to get the maximum value for money out of anything I have to pay for, whatever the personal suffering I have to endure to obtain it. At 4.30p.m. the lifts stopped running. I got the instruments of torture off my feet and, bathed in the relief that ensued, went to find Nick, first to the bar and then the restaurant, but there was no sign of him. A little apprehensively I went out to the car and breathed a sigh of relief: the car was still there! But when I looked in it I saw Nick's haversack was missing. The car was locked; Nick had the keys. He was not in the, now almost empty, ski centre, so I phoned the bank in Braemar. No, he was not there.

The good fellows in the ski hire had a box full of the keys that had been dropped on the slopes and among them I found one that fitted. Thank heavens for that! But when I got into the car I found my camera and long lens were missing. He had done a runner and stolen my camera to boot. I was furious. But I was so convinced his money was coming in that I phoned the bank again and asked them to hold him and call the police should he arrive. I reckoned if he was doing a bunk the first thing he would do would be to go and get that money. I then jumped in the car and tore down the 9 miles into Braemar at horrendous speed, sometimes taking off on the hillcrests of the old military road down Glen Clunie, thinking all the time that I would catch him on his way to the bank. I screeched to a halt and dashed into the bank. He wasn't there, and, blow me down, he hadn't been in either. Then it was that I found myself in the police station relating my sad and sorry tale. The police came out to the campsite and took away Nick's bivvy, that being the only item of his possessions that he had left behind; I certainly did not want the stinking item. Although I had picked up in the previous few days a barn owl, a peewit, a black-headed gull and a stoat, I did not regard these as edible and cut myself some slices of Spam and cooked spuds and greens in the pressure cooker. I entertained a caravan party with my sorry tale and then went to prepare for bed. My sleeping bag had been in the car the night before; it was not there now. The bastard had nicked my sleeping bag to replace his own when he had scarpered! I drove along to Mar Lodge and Eileen, Bob Scott's daughter, lent me two double blankets for the night. Some of the human race are wonderful, some are not. I lay awake and cogitated about the events of the day. Why had he not taken the car? Perhaps my efforts had been rewarded. He had become a little bit of an honest man after those few days with me, or was it that he couldn't drive or had no money for petrol? I shall never know. I should have made sure he had my address to which to send Christmas greetings and thank me for the exciting break we had together. Silly me, I don't think ahead.

This chapter should end here, but as the rest of the journey became something of what the Americans would call a 'roadkill fest', I shall take you on with me. I had planned to visit Skye and travel on to the Outer Hebrides, going first to Harris and Lewis and then taking the ferry south to North Uist and visiting Benbecula and South Uist. I had never intended to spend so much time at Braemar, but, well... you know the story.

The Hebrides

The next morning after an excellent night, I had a more relaxed breakfast of porridge, scrambled egg and marmalade. I returned the blankets with thanks to Mar Lodge and called at the police station. Apparently Nick was on the run, as he was wanted for some offences south of the border! I went back to Glenshee and collected the boots and waterproofs that I had left behind in the panic of yesterday. The ski-hire blokes reported that Nick had hired skis and had left an address. So was this a last minute, spur-of-the-moment act or had he arranged to get a lift away earlier in the day? Who knows? I was glad to be shot of him, but I was furious that not only had he deceived me when I was befriending him, but he had stolen all the pictures I had in the camera as well! He didn't even do the decent thing and send me the film that was in the camera. Well, come on, how could he, did he have your address? No I suppose he didn't, but he could have found out what it was. Oh really! Look this happened nearly 40 years ago and you are still smarting over it! I know I am, but...

Before leaving Glenshee I cached the owl and other beasts in a deep bank of snow and headed for Skye. I picked up a new sleeping bag in Pitlochry for the sum of £7.75, nothing very special, just something to see me through. Then I saw two boys standing by the road ahead and as I approached their thumbs went out, oo-oh, hitchhikers, should I leave them where they are, or should I pick them up? They looked innocent enough. My good nature got the better of me and I stopped. They were students from the University of Strathclyde. I did tell them they were lucky to be getting a lift. I dropped them off for the ferry at Onich on Loch Lynne and stopped myself for a walk on the shore a little further on. Here I found a dead (long dead) Great Northern Diver. Wow!! One of Britain's rarest birds. This I could not leave where it was, I had to take it on with me. You see, I have been collecting skulls, used birds' nests (but not eggs), rocks, pine cones and things since I was old enough to do such things. There was no point in picking this bird up to eat or even to skin and stuff; it stank to high heaven. No, it was really the head I was after, but I wanted to examine it more closely when I had time to look at it at home. I stuffed it into a sack that I found nearby and it went into the car; the atmosphere in the car became somewhat unpleasant. A little further on I came across a still-warm Mallard beside the road, ah! that is more what I want. That bird stood me in good stead for no less than four substantial meals. I stopped for the night between Fort William and Spean Bridge. Here, in the shelter of a dilapidated hut by the roadside, I cooked a leg from the duck, the pressure cooker sizzling away merrily. As always, when the meat is nearly done I open the pressure cooker (after the pressure has been released, of course) pop in some spuds, after another six or seven minutes I depressurise again and pop in some greens and give them two or three minutes. Then all is ready. The liquid is poured into a mug and the solids tipped out onto a plate. No nutriments wasted or washed away and no unnecessary heating of water that is thrown away; a truly economical system. The duck tasted extra special.

The next day I set off up the Great Glen beside Loch Lochy crossing the Caledonian Canal near Lagan little thinking that in a few years I would be kayaking this way in a triathlon from Spean Bridge to Inverness, 10 miles run,

17 miles canoe and 35 miles cycle. Lochs Garry, Loyne and Cluane, artificial though they are, were sparklingly beautiful with the browns and greens of the hills set off against the snow-clad hills. To someone from the London Basin this was scenery beyond the imagination. But this was to be surpassed by what lay ahead as the road dropped down to Loch Duich, Eilean Donan Castle and the grand beauty of Skye from across Loch Alsh. Why had I never been to a place in my own country so wonderful as this before? I was wrapped in a great vista of snow-clad rocky peaks; a panorama of glorious mountains. I took the ferry over to the island at Kyle of Lochalsh for £1.10. Skye seemed to be asleep. The presence of the diver was making life in the car a bit unbearable, so I cached it somewhere safe to pick up on my way back to the mainland in a few days. I needed a walk in this incredible scenery, so headed towards Elgol to the south of the majestic bulk of Blaven. Leaving the car near Kilmarie, I walked over to Camasunary, one of the biggest and most isolated beaches in Skye, a south-facing beach on Loch Scavaig and sheltered in part by the mass of the island of Soay. I find the tide line on any beach, but most especially an isolated beach like this, irresistible. Dragging myself from its diverse attractions, I followed the coast path to Loch Coruisk and crossed a river on a scary, swinging suspension bridge. The coast path became a steep rock traverse with a three-inch ledge only five or six feet above the sea. Was I in the right place or is this the bit that is known as 'the Bad Step'? Not a route that anyone should try to take with a zimmer frame! But the reward - four or more peaks of over 3000 feet rising black and threatening out of the sea, their jagged outline broken up by patches of snow and the tops hidden in ominous clouds that leaked rain and sleet and snow. A lonely spot indeed. Even the very rock under my feet was smoothed and scratched, direct evidence of the massive grinding machine that worked here when all the land about lay under the slowly moving grinder of a huge glacier. Awe inspiring. I climbed up and over Druimhain with Sgurr Alasdair behind me and Blaven before me and descended again to Camasunary beside Loch an Athain and Loch na Creitheach. Wet through and weary, I got back to the car six hours after setting out. I was too tired to get a cooker going and stuffed myself instead with bread and marmalade and honey.

The wind rose again in the night and buffeted the car. Warm and cosy though I was, it seemed to my groggy mind that the wind had become embodied and was trying to roll the car over, using the bicycle on the roof rack as a lever; it did not succeed. I slept long into the morning and then moved to a more sheltered spot to feast on porridge and omelette, after which I cleaned and cut up the rest of the duck. I drove to Elgol and phoned a neighbour at home to keep a watch out for Nick in case, knowing I was away, he might choose to help himself to more of my possessions. Elgol is off the beaten track but the views from there are absolutely fantastic: the cluster of menacing peaks that form the Cuillins across Loch Scavaig, the great mass of Rhum with Eigg and the diminutive islands of Canna and Soay. This Soay, by the way, is not the Soay from which the breed of primitive sheep that bear that name originated, that is an island in the St Kilda group. I drove to Sligachan picking up a pair of hitchhikers on the way and stopping to examine a sheep lying by the road; I decided not to take it on with me, I might as well collect it on my way back. I then got the bike off the roof and cycled the 11 miles over towards Glen Brittle. I hid the bike and in two hours walked back over the snow-covered ridge with the great panorama of the Cuillins to the south. The rocks underfoot were volcanic, mauve, blue, green, brown and purple. I could not resist filling my pockets with such treasures as these. I spent the night at Glen Brittle and met a party of boys from Rugby School, one of whom had fallen, bouncing and rolling 900 feet down the mountain before saving himself with his ice axe 30 feet before a precipice. I collected two interesting sheep skulls on the beach before realising I had only 30 minutes to cover the 40 miles to Uig to catch a ferry. I subjected myself to two scary moments while overtaking a lorry on one humpbacked bridge and passing an oncoming car on another, but I made it in time. The round trip from Skye to Harris to N Uist to Skye cost £33! I had wonderful views of a black-throated diver on the way over and sightings of black guillemot and red-throated diver when we docked at Tarbert on Harris. As I drove north to Lewis there was a huge bird in the mountains being mobbed by ravens that looked in comparison like starlings to a buzzard. My first Golden Eagle, what a majestic bird! I ate my dinner as I nestled by my Primus on the harbour at Stornoway, starting with soup then more of the duck with spuds and cabbage, then peaches and custard, finishing off with a pot of tea.

If you examine a map of the Island of Lewis you will notice that the north end of the island is circled by a road save for a stretch of eight miles on the east coast between the Butt of Lewis and Tolsta Head. Well, I had noticed this and decided to complete the circuit on my bicycle, if need be pushing the bike on the coast path. I set off in some truly foul weather battling into sleet and rain in bottom gear for 12 miles from Stornoway to Borvas. Here the road turned NE and I rode the 15 miles to Lionel downwind in top gear and with no hands much of the way. Dead sheep lined the sides of the roads (at one place there were seven in as many yards), I could not tell if they were roadkill or whether they had just chosen to die beside the road. There were raven and hooded crows everywhere and I am not surprised with so much food available. Each habitation I passed consisted of a new brick-built, white-painted croft with an old black house behind it now used as a shed, though at Europie, a tiny hamlet, a few of them were still inhabited. No tree was to be seen and every dwelling had a huge mountain of peat beside it and most had a tractor; pervading all was the tang of burning peat. It was like a foreign country. The frontage of each house was policed by a border collie who shepherded me by in a rude and noisy fashion. I visited the Butt of Lewis where I saw five corn bunting, their brief unmusical rattle alerting me both as to their presence and their identity. I then set out from Skigersta to ride and walk the eight miles along the coast to New Tolsta. I reckoned it might take me three hours. The path soon disappeared and I found myself slithering across open peat moors bisected every so often with rivulets, gorges, bogs, marshes, open water, ravines and rivers.

It poured with rain and sleet and I was soon wet through; not even Gore-Tex could cope with this. Far from riding the bike I had to carry it over rivers on stepping-stones and jump ditches with it. A line of cairns and posts was intended to show the way; they were often hidden in mist. On and on it went from one mound to another, round one lochan to the next, over one headland only to see more ahead. Darkness began to fall. I couldn't understand why I didn't arrive somewhere and wondered whether I had got into some sort of time warp and this would now go on forever. But at last I came to a track, which led to a road; lights and habitations came into view. I had made it. It had taken me eight hours! Enquiring of some chapel-goers as to how far it was to Stornoway, I was disconcerted to know I still had 12 miles to go. I had no lights, but I couldn't care, I was nearly done in, but the bike carried me on. When eventually I reached Stornoway, I tried to get a B&B, it was full; so, propping up my bike and staggering into a fish and chip shop, I ordered two meals and went back to the car to change out of my wet gear. Chicken pie and fish with a double large portion of chips were waiting for me when I got back to the shop, such a meal never tasted so good! Replete, I went to bed in the Maxi at midnight and slept for eight and a half hours.

Not long after my father's death in 1947, my mother was asked by the meeting of Brethren which we attended in Watford if she would have the visiting 'ministering brother' to dinner on the Saturday. This was something that would have been my father's duty and pleasure had he still been with us. The visitor, who had been invited to lead a special bible reading, was Mr A.P.Cecil Lawrence of Stornoway. In Stornoway, he was the owner of one of the biggest woollen mills producing the world-famous Harris Tweed. To us, he was a beloved servant of the Lord. He drove a Bentley and, while taking us to the first meeting, got stuck in a traffic jam. Anxious not to be late, he asked if there was a way round, however far, that he could take to avoid the hold-up as he could go very fast on an empty road. I was forever disappointed that he was not able to put this into effect and have treasured this memory of the man to this day. It was therefore with some astonishment to find that the first person I asked in Stornoway about him told me he had actually worked for him! This was a man operating a weighbridge at the harbour. He said that APCL had died only three years ago while on a cruise in the Mediterranean and that he had been buried at sea. As we parted, the man gave me three fresh herring; a very welcome present!

I then returned to Tarbert whence the N Uist ferry departed. Caledonian MacBrayne's ferry service between the north and south islands of the Outer Hebrides operated only via Uig on Skye. This gave me extra time at sea and an hour and a half at Uig, and allowed me to wander the shoreline at Uig where I found among the jetsam a woolly hat, a long sock and an oil-soaked woollen waistcoat. I cached these in a fish box to collect upon my return. There was a force eight gale and showers of sleet and hail. I felt distinctly queasy as the big ferry pitched and rolled its way across The Minch. The ferry had to circle before attempting the narrow entry to Lochmaddy in the gale. N Uist is bleak and rugged like Harris, but is pockmarked with lochs and lochans everywhere. I found a spot in the lee of a shop where I could cook my dinner or, where I could try to cook my dinner. The fact was that the freezing wind was carrying away the heat from the Primus and preventing the pressure cooker coming up to pressure, that is until I wrapped it in socks which I had to take care not to set on fire. I had the last portion of duck, which had been with me for five days and was still very savoury.

Next morning I again had trouble with the Primus in the freezing wind and had to boil my kettle inside the car. I visited the RSPB reserve at Balranald where I met Charlie Pickup, the warden, and had a long chat about birds. A flock of about 100 twite flew over and, with red-throated diver on the water and corn bunting rattling by the crofts, the visit quickly made my day. I drove on to the crossing to Benbecula, a causeway that links the two islands that takes you onto the rather large sand dune that is Benbecula. As I drove, I sang over and over a lovely song I had learned from a tape of Scottish folk songs:

To Benbecula I'll hie me,
Where the spray is flying high,
Where the winds are wild and stormy
Where the lonely seabirds cry.

It seemed so appropriate. But no sooner are you on Benbecula than you are driving off again, it being no more than five miles across. I drove down to the RSPB reserve at Loch Druidibeg and there met the warden, Colin Brown. He was packing up for a trip to St Kilda, but readily marked up my map with the best places to see what the island has to offer in the way of interesting birds. I went off to see what I could find and came across a rubbish dump. I am afraid that I am rather partial to rubbish dumps and this was no exception. It was full of such useful and exciting things. There were the remains of an old solid fuel stove, which of course I could not leave there. I loaded the bits into the car. There was also a car battery. It seemed such a waste to leave it, after all I could get 10/- (50p) for it at home. I put it on the roof between the bars of the roofrack; by the time I got home it had worn the paint below it right down to the metal! There were some cars there too, but generally speaking cars are left where they die in those remote islands. There is no scrap metal business there and cars litter the fields, gardens, moors and even the beach. I did see a beautifully decorated coach in someone's garden; it was covered all over in seashells, what a sight! The sandy soil is manured here with seaweed and even with the bodies of dead seagulls partly buried in the sand. I should like to tell you more about the wild beauty of these islands, the rugged, rocky eastern coastline compared to the gentle sandy machair of the west, the 2000 foot peak of Beinn Mhor on South Uist and the flat soft outline of Benbecula, the wild geese, long-tailed ducks and whooper swans, and the easy-going slower life peculiar to islands. But space does not allow it, you will have to go and find these treasures for yourself. If you are constrained from travel by circumstances or ability, Lillian Beckwith's novels capture the unique life of the Hebridean crofters and the atmosphere of the islands free from the turmoil of city influences. I have cycled and driven across the Alps in Europe and the Rockies in North America, they are on a grander scale, but the Hebrides have an unrivalled beauty that is all their own.

The patter of rain on the car next morning told me all I wanted to know about the weather, it was Good Friday. I lay in and listened to what sounded like a barking fox flying over, then it changed to the familiar "*Kok-kok-kok*" of a red-throated diver and moments later changed again to the amorous wailing it employs to woo its mate. I drove as far south as it is possible to get on South Uist to Polachar; it was my furthest point from home. I got out and drank in the view across the Sound of Barra. As I stood there, I thought I heard a hissing noise. It seemed to be coming from the car. I looked underneath and something was dripping onto the ground. Was it my imagination or was the car creaking spasmodically and sinking slowly on one side? I thought it must be the radiator boiling and went off for a little exploration. Wild and deserted though this little corner of the globe is, it is steeped in history. The island of Eriskay, which lies on the east side of the archipelago and between South Uist and the Island of Barra, is the point at which Bonnie Prince Charlie in 1745 made landfall on his first arrival from France in the land to which he claimed title to the throne.

Incidentally, the words *"Over the sea to Skye"* of the well known Skye Boat Song recounting the Bonnie Prince's escape to Skye after the battle of Culloden in 1746, do not refer to his crossing the narrow strip of water, barely half a mile across, that separates Skye from the mainland at the Kyle of Lochalsh, as so many people think, but to the 40 miles of stormy sea that, while disguised as a woman named Betty Burke, he braved with Flora MacDonald in a boat rowed by six men from Benbecula to Skye. Also the Sound of Eriskay between Eriskay and Uist was the scene, in 1941, of the wreck of the SS Politician while bound from Liverpool to Jamaica with a cargo of more than 250,000 bottles of whisky and £3 million of Jamaican currency. The whisky was 'rescued' by the islanders; an event which has been immortalised by the book and later the film, *Whisky Galore* by Compton MacKenzie. My upbringing in the Exclusive Brethren barred me from going to the cinema, but when *Whiskey Galore* was shown by the school film club in the mid 1950s, I was somehow allowed to go. Not being familiar with the film world, I found it incredibly exciting as I believed I was watching a record of the real events!

When I returned to the car, it had an odd list to it; it was down on the off side. There was a pool of liquid where I had seen the drip and my nostrils engaged with an aroma to which they were not accustomed (but which they would over the next 20 years become very familiar indeed): the alcoholic mixture of the hydro-elastic suspension system. The car body was now resting on the rubbers on one side. This was a right old how d'you do. I drove tentatively to a garage in Loch Boisdale but everyone was at church. I came back later and found they needed a part from Inverness to effect a repair. It looked as though I was going to have to drive home in this rather lopsided attitude! Fortunately the failure had occurred on the off-side so the camber of the road offset the list and evened things up a bit and, after driving about a bit, I found it did not affect the handling or driving qualities of the car. Maybe I could possibly drive it home as it was. Snipe were drumming overhead as I cooked one of my fishes and I rounded this off with a tin of rice pudding. The mainstay of the camper's equipment in that day and age was the Primus stove. It was powered by paraffin and required a preheating of the vaporising pipework with methylated spirits before it could be cajoled to operate. This was an art in itself, a valve had to be closed to allow pressure to build up. Close it too early and you got a long tongue of yellow flame and had to begin again, close it too late and the meths burnt out without lighting the gas, which billowed around while you struggled to get a match lit. The stove then had to be pressurised by means of a pump; this pressurisation had to be repeated during the cooking process, operate the pump too vigorously with the pan of food balanced on the ring as I did that day, and disaster, the pan and contents fly off!

My last day in the Hebrides began before dawn with an expedition to record whatever sounds there might be as dawn unfolded. There were the wails and honks of unseen greylag geese, a plaintive buzzard and a flock of twittering twite. After breakfast I motored up to the rocket-tracking station on Rueval a 286ft (87m) high hill crowned with strange globes and antennae, and from which the distant silhouette of St Kilda could be clearly seen nearly 60 miles away. I puzzled over the sight of the huge statue of the Lady of the Isles set on the side of Rueval. That it should have been paid for by the impoverished islanders staggered me; it looked more suited to the ruins of Karnak but with the toddler Jesus being held up as if to get a better view of St Kilda. I boarded the ferry back to Uig and watched as Benbecula quickly slipped below the waves as we steamed eastward. Skye, Rhum and the whole of the Hebrides stood out sharp and clear. I made good use of the first washing facilities I had seen for some time and stripping down to the waist made myself feel fresh and smell less. When we had docked, I collected my cache of oily clothing from the beach and set off round Troternish, the northernmost lump of Skye. What a panorama unfolds as you drive round in a great loop, first heading north then eastwards and finally heading south. North Uist, Harris and Lewis to the west and north, the great mountains of what used to be known, until three years ago, as Wester Ross and then Applecross behind the islands of Rona and Raasay. I stopped near Kilmuir on the northwest side of Troternish and visited Flora MacDonald's monument at her grave. It is a high Celtic cross of granite that has become a 'must see' for tourists. I must have rubbed my eyes to see better and dislodged a contact lens into the long grass. Confound it! Luckily no one was there to witness my apparent frenzy of devotion as I crawled systematically to and fro over her grave hunting for the damned thing for half an hour. I did not find it. If an excavation of her grave at some time in the future purports to reveal that she wore contact lenses, let me put it on record here that she didn't; the lens is mine. This meant that the rest of my holiday and all the driving back had to be done with clear vision in only one eye. I stopped on the moor south of Portree and cooked the last of the fish from Stornoway. It was a calm evening so I took the recorder and taped golden plover calling and snipe drumming, what magic!

Next morning it was raining again. I found a pile of dead ravens by the road which had not been killed on the road, but which all had their upper beaks missing. I surmised that a farmer or gamekeeper had shot them and sent their bills somewhere to claim a bounty as had been done for some years in England with a 1 shilling and later 2 shilling (5p and 10p) bounty for grey squirrel tails. I removed four of them and some wings to take on with me. They smelled a bit. Then I found a sheep in the ditch. It had been dead for two or three weeks and was just a little bit smelly. I managed to heave it up onto the roof rack. On my way I retrieved the great northern diver I had cached earlier and which, when tied up securely in a plastic sack, did not add to the aromas in the car. I then had a little walk beside Loch Ainort and found a red-throated diver this time. Wow, it did smell, Pooohh! I stowed it with the great northern and reduced its effluvia to an acceptable level. The only trouble was that to touch either of them contaminated ones fingers with a rich, warm, nose-watering smell that proved extremely difficult to get off! I also picked up the ewe that I had examined a week before. It was very heavy and the only space left for it was on the rear passenger seat! After crossing to the mainland, I picked up a hitch-hiker, a student of English and economics at Berkeley, California. He did not seem unduly perturbed by sharing the car with a dead sheep. I stopped a bit further on to pick up a stillborn lamb and a herring gull. When I dropped off my passenger he wished me well with my carload of carrion. I drove to Braemar and parked again at the scene where my adventures had begun two weeks earlier.

I had a day and a half skiing at Glenshee. At last, I felt I had actually mastered the skills enough to cope with whatever the slopes presented even if it was not done very gracefully. On the way back to the camp at Linn 'O Dee, I picked up three fresh blue hares, though one of them was a bit squashed. I was able to gorge myself on fresh meat again with spuds and cabbage followed by gooseberries and custard. Before settling for the night, I had to get the second ewe onto the roof, as it was a little disconcerting to have it next to me in bed. This proved to be harder than I thought it would be. It was heavy, but I managed by first pushing it up the tailgate and then climbing up onto the roof and pulling from above to get it safely up with the other one. The first ewe had a hole in its side from which gurgles emanated every time I moved it and which leaked a strange brown fluid that ran down the back of the car in a long trickle, I was afraid it might fetch the paint off. In the morning,

I again made my way up through the woods in the dark and snow and managed to get a recording of a capercaillie lek. I was quite surprised to find how quiet the lek was, not nearly as noisy as a blackcock lek. It comprised strange grating and bubbling noises finishing with a distinct pop like a cork being drawn from a bottle. I recovered my cache of owl etc hidden in the snowdrift and set off before 3 p.m. for Perth, Glasgow and Carnforth. I had been happy to drive about the wilds of Scotland with a dead ewe on the roof of the car, but I felt it might be a little disconcerting or even distasteful to parade such specimens of rural life (or death) to the squeamish gaze of civilization in the towns and cities of the South. To this end I wrapped the offending items in an old blanket and weighted it down with the car battery I had collected in South Uist, all jammed up against my upside-down bicycle. On the lovely drive down

Glenshee beside the Blackwater River, I came across a dead blue hare that had actually had its head knocked off by a car. I had never seen that before, nor have I seen it since. I had one stroke of luck as I ran down out of the mountains, I stopped to pick up a pheasant and found another one hard by and a grey partridge as well! When I came into Perth with its great stone bridge over the Tay and ornate granite spires, I noticed that heads were turning to watch me go by. I thought at first it was my Flying Enterprise[1] simulation that was catching their attention, but when I stopped to refuel I discovered that the blanket had blown away and my cargo of ewes were on full public display!

I was a bit amazed that, throughout the 500-mile journey, no police considered my lop-sided attitude to be of sufficient interest to stop me and at least talk about it. Some years later I blew the suspension system on the Maxi by hitting a ramp at speed and this time I had hardly travelled a mile before police stopped me and allowed me to continue only on condition that I was going straight to where I could get it repaired. I ought to comment that although the Maxi handbook says that the vehicle may be driven on a deflated suspension system and speed should be limited to 30 mph, I found that the vehicle handled perfectly at any speed albeit giving a less comfortable ride. I drove on and spent the night at Leighton Moss regaling the warden with all my adventures since my last visit where it had all begun 18 days before. It was too windy to record in the morning but I did see a sparrowhawk discomforting the colony of black-headed gulls and I heard the bittern again. I made it back to work for the afternoon and so ended this rather long and exciting saga.

Some weeks later I rang Sgt Murray of the Braemar constabulary and he told me that Nick Crane had been tried for his original offence in England and had been sent to prison for three months. I asked if any compensation order had been made regarding my camera and lens. He told me that compensation is not an automatic part of a penalty in English law, although it is in Scottish law. Compensation has to be obtained by a civil action in England. This struck me as being a bit daft. The law may be satisfied by a prison sentence, but the victim gets no satisfaction and is no better off. The criminal has benefited from his crime and is not required to restore that which he stole from his victim. Those detained at Her Majesty's pleasure do not have to pay for accommodation or meals, in fact, for someone like NC, if he has no home and no job, then a prison sentence is actually a gift of three months accommodation with warmth and

---

[1] The Flying Enterprise was a cargo vessel whose cargo shifted in a storm 600 miles out in the Atlantic in 1953 and, listing heavily, was gallantly towed for many miles by the little tug Turmoil until the tow parted and the listing freighter went down. It captured the imagination of the public, just as I was doing now.

light, the electricity all being paid for, a clean bed (the washing all taken care of) and nutritious free hot meals, cooked and served without any of the bother of shopping, preparing and cooking to worry about. I am prepared to admit that for NC the meals might even have been more inviting and palatable (certainly to a conservative palate) if not as varied and nutritious as those he was served on his trip with me. I know there is the little matter of a certain curtailment of liberty, but with books to read, TV to watch, games to play, interesting conversations with persons who may well be the leading exponents of their profession (with all the financial advantages that has to offer when once more set at large to implement this education). No, all in all, I think the English system of justice actually promotes a criminal way of life for the down-and-out specimens of life's failures and encourages them to indulge in their nefarious practices during those periods when they are having to provide for their own well-being. It enables them to fall back on a more predictable period of stability and build up their bodily reserves at no expense to themselves when their criminal incompetence has led to their apprehension.

I later learned that NC was convicted in court of the theft of my camera and was fined. Did he ever pay the fine, or are they still waiting for his bank to give clearance for the release of the money?

I do not know if such a judicial system is practised anywhere today, but the penalties for stealing as given in the book of Exodus in the Old Testament are simpler, more appropriate and fairer to the victim, and would make larceny a very unprofitable business. It reads: *'If a man steal an ox, or a sheep, and kill it, or sell it; he shall restore five oxen for the ox, and four sheep for the sheep. If the thief be encountered breaking in, and be smitten so that he die, there shall be no blood-guiltiness for him (*tell that to farmer Martin[2]*). If the sun be risen on him, there shall be blood-guiltiness for him; he should have made full restitution: if he had nothing, he would have been sold for his theft. If the stolen thing be actually found alive in his hand, whether it be ox, or ass, or sheep, he shall restore double.'* Exodus 22 v 1 - 4. *'If anyone...hath robbed or wronged his neighbour...he shall restore it in the principal, and shall add the fifth part more thereto; to him to whom it belongeth shall he give it, and his trespass offering,...a ram without blemish...shall he bring to... the priest'.* Leviticus 6 v 2 - 6. [Quotes from translation by J.N.Darby] It is a pity something along these lines is not employed today.

---

[2] Tony Martin (55) a Norfolk farmer was jailed for life after being found guilty of murdering Fred Barras (16) a gypsy who had broken into his lonely farmhouse, Bleak House, at night in 2000. Martins conviction for the shooting was later reduced to manslaughter and he was released after 2 ½ years in prison.

Roadkill Abroad

North American experiences

New Orleans to Winnipeg by bike

In the summer of 1982, I planned to cycle across the US. The three and a half weeks holiday available to me did not give me time to cross America east to west, so I had to opt for a south to north transit. I had just completed assembling my new bicycle with its Wester Ross frame and had only enough time to give it a short road test the night before I left. I flew to New York with the bike and then to New Orleans in Louisiana at the mouth of the Mississippi on the Gulf of Mexico. My route on the bike took me north through the states of Mississippi, Arkansas, Missouri, Kansas, South Dakota, and North Dakota. I entered Canada to end my ride at Winnipeg. This is not the place to recount all my adventures, but I shall mention some of the more interesting roadkill encountered on the way. I did not expect to be able to eat roadkill on the journey, but I had brought a minimal taxidermy kit with me in case I found anything I could not leave behind. Down in the south I encountered strange beasts indeed: opossums, armadillos and even turtles; but I had neither space nor time to carry them on with me and deal with them, I had to be satisfied with only their photos. I did pick up a lot of birds, some of which I skinned in motels and others which became unpleasant and requested to be put down. Approaching Baton Rouge in Louisiana, I saw the sign for a taxidermist's establishment and called to have a chat and see what he was doing. He was delighted I had called and invited me to see his workshops and a number of completed specimens. I asked if he would like some birds I had picked up that day and had in my bag. He at once became agitated and told me not to get them out of the bags. If he was found with protected birds, even roadkill, on his premises he would be fined and possibly even closed down. I asked if he had any spare skulls and he responded by raking about on the roof of his building and producing a few, which he gave to me. They were the skulls of a brown bear, a peccary, a bobcat and a coyote. No matter about the extra weight, I strapped the box of skulls onto the carrier and rode off, a very happy person.

A week or so later after spending a few days in Missouri with cousins I had never met before, I was riding during the evening rush hour, somewhere near Kansas City, in very heavy traffic, when I saw something small and bright red lying in the road ahead. As I approached I saw it was a bird. I stopped on the road and picked it up. What an incredible bird! It was all scarlet but for a black face and throat, with a scarlet crest and bill. I knew at once what it was, a cardinal *(Richmondena cardinalis)*. As I stood astride my bike admiring this gorgeous creature, a police patrol car drew up alongside me, the window wound down and an officer of the law drawled, *"Do you mind stepping off the highway before you get killed?"* That night in the motel, I skinned the wonderful cardinal and a yellow-shafted flicker that I had also picked up. The skins would keep once they were dried. Somewhere else I came across a freshly killed raccoon. What a beautiful beast! And such a lovely tail! I dug out my taxidermy kit: a scalpel and some borax powder and sitting down right there beside the road proceeded to skin the lovely striped tail to take on with me. I would have loved to have skinned the whole animal, but I had so many miles to cover, I could not afford the time. After 1700 miles in less than 15 days, I crossed the Pembina river and arrived at the Canadian customs. The officer asked me what I was carrying and I said, *"As little as possible."* *"Any weapons?"* *"Only a penknife and a scalpel."* I got him to take a photograph for me and then rode hard down wind into Winnipeg to meet my cousin, Paul Cavenagh, whom I had last seen 36 years before when he was in Britain with the Canadian forces after the war. It marked the start of a long friendship with him and his delightful family.

Skunk

No, I have never eaten skunk *(Mephitis mephitica)* and I am not sure that I want to, but I have met a lot of dead ones by the roadside and smelled many more. If a skunk gets flattened on the highway, the unique perfume that they carry about with them is born on tyres for a very long way from the scene. Lying in the verge, they emanate this perfume for months so that as you pass by you know when you are passing through a skunk-kill zone. I had encountered one on my ride from New Orleans, but it was on another ride to Winnipeg, this time from near Kitchener in Ontario, that I decided to collect a skull and bring it home with me. I was cycling along without a care in the world, as they say, well, actually I had quite a sore bum, when my nose hinted to me, '*Skunk;*' then it said boldly, '*Dead skunk;*' then it shouted to me loud and clear, *"There's a dead SKUNK right here!"* I circled back to where the effluvia was strongest and dismounted. A short excursion into the long grass and there was some black and white fur. Yes, skunk it was. That there was only a ruptured skin clinging to a disjointed skeleton told me it had been dead for months. But this gave me an idea, could I extract the skull and take it on home with me. This raised an important question. Would I be able to contain the powerful niff that was coming off it? I thought it was worth a try. I put each hand into a polythene bag and, holding the body down with my foot, I tried to peel the head out from the skin. It would not come away until I had severed the connection with my penknife. I then pulled one bag over the skull and then the other. That should keep the smell in, I thought. I shut it into the back pocket of the pannier and cycled on my way. The next time I stopped I thought I could smell skunk, so I sniff-checked the pannier: it reeked. The smell was escaping! I put it in more bags, and still it smelled. It was not until I found a foil crisps bag that the smell was contained, but the pannier and its contents retained a gentle reminder of skunk for the rest of the journey. I put it in a screw-top honey jar for the flight home and that succeeded in protecting my, and everyone else's bags, from this penetrating natural perfume.

On another visit to the States in 2005, I was driving into Sioux Falls to stay with my cousin, Bob Boyt and his wife Jeanne, when I saw a dead body that I thought was a mink beside the highway. I was on a three-lane dual carriageway and could not stop at once. I noted the position of the body with a view to coming back to get it, which I did the next day before going for a run in a nearby park. I had to go back on the other carriageway to beyond the point where I had seen it and then come back again. It was a diversion of more than 10 miles! When I drew up beside the beast, I saw at once it was a skunk. I had but seconds to make up my mind as I was not supposed to stop. I elected to take it on board as it did not seem to smell terribly. It very soon began to register its presence, even with the window open. I knew I could not expect to deal with it at my cousin's place. So I sought out an empty parking lot and as discreetly as possible cut the thing's head off with a blunt scalpel blade which I carried with me on the trip, using the old polythene bag technique I had used on the previous occasion. This reduced the specimen to a manageable size. I managed to break the blade, which made the job fairly difficult. I was able to hide the head outside the house during my stay and procure a honey jar in which to put it. As I pulled out of Sioux Falls the next day, my eye was caught by a swollen headless carcass under a tree in a corner of an empty parking lot....Ah! That's where my skunk skull came from. The skunk must be one of the first animals recorded as becoming roadkill. The Royal Natural History[3], published in 1894, states *that in many parts of the United States these creatures are not unfrequently (*sic*) run over in the evenings on the roads by passing vehicles.* This same authority also states that *"the flesh of these animals is said to be white, delicate and highly palatable."* Well, perhaps I should try one when I next get the opportunity.

Red-tailed hawk

"No Arthur, I am sorry, you cannot skin it anywhere here." *"What, not even outside in the garden?"* *"No, not even in the garden."* So went the

---

[3] Published periodically and collected by my grandfather, kept by my father and bound by me.

conversation with my cousin, Mavis Legg, when I suggested I was going to skin a red-tailed hawk *(Buteo jamaicensis)* that I had picked up on the way to her home in Edmonton, Alberta. It was that which led me to be skinning the thing beside the road the next day on my way to an orienteering event near Edmonton. It was just too beautiful to be left to rot. Everything was a bit messy and the flies began to gather but I managed to get it out of its skin in 20 mins and spent another 20 mins cleaning the muscles off the legs and wings. A little later when I was back on the road, a common crossbill flew across and disappeared in front of the car: a glance in the mirror told me it did not come out the back. I stopped and went back to look, it had managed to fly right under the wheel. What was left could not be skinned or eaten; it had been absolutely flattened onto the tarmac! It had become what the uneducated first think of when they hear of me eating roadkill - a meat and feather pizza.

There was no time to do any more to the hawk after the orienteering, as my friend, Jim Prowting, and I were to be travelling through the Rockies for a few days. Our next port of call was Calgary at the home of another of my cousins, Gordon Taylor. I wanted the skin to dry out as it would keep better dry if I didn't have time to give it more attention, so I hung it in a tree in Gordon's garden. I did get to clean it up a little, but in the few days before my return home it became as stiff as a board. It had become a bit oily and certainly did pong a bit, so when the time came to pack for the flight home I put it in a polythene bag and wrapped it in my pyjamas in the bottom of the case. On arrival at home everything in the suitcase ponged a bit, but it was difficult to tell what was smelly socks, what sweaty O-kit and what red-tailed hawk; the pyjamas never did lose all trace of that memorable tang. Eventually I got round to finishing it off at home, scraping and peeling fat and muscle off the skin and scraping the bones left in the skin. It had to be soaked in borax solution to mothproof it and then dried. It was during the washing and drying process that an awful lot of the feathers fell out and I was in two minds as to whether to continue or dump it. After spending so much time on it, I couldn't bring myself to dump it and went ahead and stuffed and mounted it. It didn't look too bad from a distance and I still have it to this day.

I have since learned that picking up a roadkill hawk in America is a criminal offence, as is picking up almost any roadkill! It so happens that First People (Red Indians) use bones and feathers in their ceremonies but the authorities have made picking up such things illegal. There was the case of Velasquez, a well-known artist and singer of American Indian songs. As Dana M Nichols wrote in an article in 2007: *when Velasquez, saw a dead red-tail hawk next to Highway 12, he stopped, picked up the bird and began a prayer,*

promising it would once again feel wind pass through its feathers during
ceremonies. A California Department of Fish and Game warden was watching
Velasquez through binoculars. She gave him a ticket and took the bird. The
ticket said he could be jailed for a year or fined $1,000. Velasquez does have
plenty of dog bane, a plant he uses to make twine used for a variety of purposes,
including decorating musical instruments. Even the dog bane requires him to
jump bureaucratic hurdles, getting a state highway permit to collect the plant
from a shoulder and filing other papers so that highway crews won't kill the dog
bane with herbicides. David Irey, the supervising district attorney decided not to
prosecute the case. "I don't think there's any jury in California that would have
convicted him for what he was doin." Can you believe it? A game warden
watching a carcass by the road with binoculars and booking a native for picking
it up! A year in jail or a $1000 fine! The warden could have planted the hawk. I
suppose the reasoning is that someone could shoot a hawk and say it was
roadkill when challenged. OK, examine the bird, has it been shot (or poisoned)?
Even then a year in jail is very severe. And you have to file papers to stop the
highway crews spraying the verges and then get a permit to pick a wild flower!
What a morass of legislation to restrain the activities of people from doing
something that is causing no harm to anyone or anything! 'The land of the free' –
you must be joking!

Short-eared owl

I had the opportunity after I had been made redundant (not that I was
actually redundant, mind you, that is just the mendacious term given by my
employer to a management process that involved doubling the number of staff
while keeping the salary budget the same, and don't ask about it or this book will
double in length to provide the answer), anyway, as I was saying, after I had
been made redundant I had the opportunity to travel round Canada and America
to meet some of my many relatives. I spent 7 weeks in N America and travelled
some 9000 miles from Winnipeg westwards to Vancouver, south to Los
Angeles, east to Texas, north to Minneapolis for some orienteering, and so back
to Winnipeg. A second cousin of mine, Ken Boyt from London, joined me for
the trip from Calgary round to Des Moines. For those who don't know what a
second cousin is let me elucidate: first cousins are the children of siblings,
second cousins are the children of first cousins and third cousins are the children
of second cousins and so on. So Ken's dad and mine were cousins, our
grandfathers had been brothers and we had a common great grandfather. The
relationship between cousins of different generations from their common
ancestor are known as cousin-once-removed, twice-removed or more, depending
on the number of generations between them in their line of descent from their

common ancestor. So Ken's children are my second cousins once-removed. Do you get it? It is not quite so simple, I am afraid, as people sometimes refer to first cousins once-removed as second cousins and to make it worse, first cousins are sometimes called cousins-german.

Anyway, Ken had put onto the computer all the family-tree data that I had researched and collected for over 20 years and from it produced a roll of paper 27ft (8m) long containing a tree with 741 names. We travelled together from Calgary and except for two nights in the Rocky Mountains, he and I stayed every night with relatives where the family tree would be unrolled and crawled over by our hosts with great interest. In Tucson, Arizona, Quent and Ana Quiner's basset hound jumped right through the paper! In the course of our travels we came across some good roadkills. Get yourself comfortable and I shall tell you about a few. Starting from Winnipeg on my own, I first picked up a short-eared owl (*Asio flammeus*). It had been dead a day a two and had begun to smell, nevertheless I stowed it into the boot (I suppose I should say trunk to be idiomatically correct) to do something with later. That night I stayed with Glen and Julie Hope and their family in Gravelbourg. He is the son of my cousin, Joan Stowell who married George Hope of Maple Creek, and he is therefore my first cousin once-removed. I did not have time to do anything with the owl that night as it would have been a bit invidious to spend an hour skinning some smelly bird when you are staying as a guest with someone you have never met before, you obviously have a lot of talking to do. The next day was no better as I was invited to see Glen's workplace where he is in charge of a municipal recycling plant! What a job! Picking over the chucked out stuff for the whole town and being paid to do it! He and I are obviously kindred spirits as he had filled his basement with stuff saved from the incinerator. He made me a gift of some books he had salvaged, he must have considered me a scholar for they were all in French!

When I was able to tear myself away from Glen, I set off for Calgary. I believed I was to meet my cousin, Gordon Taylor, at his daughter, Wendi's house in De Winton in the suburbs that evening, but when I arrived after following a very faded memory of the way to get there and the shape of the house, I found that I was not expected at De Winton until the next day. I then set off for Gordon's place in the city, but got stuck in so much traffic that I had to divert to get to the airport in time to meet my cousin, Ken, who was flying in from London and with whom I was scheduled to continue the trip round America. I waited patiently at arrivals eagerly scanning the faces of the American Airlines flight from London as they came through from customs. He was not among them. Enquiry at the airline information desk revealed that he was not on the list of passengers, but further investigation revealed that he was due on the same flight tomorrow! It was now nearly 10 pm, I had not eaten and Gordon had been expecting me for some hours. My faded memory of how to get to Gordon's place was too sketchy and, after driving in what I thought might be the right direction I realised I was lost. I had to phone. I stopped at a call box but found I had no change. I stopped at a store to get change and then found another call box; then I realised I did not have the phone number. I rang directory enquiries: Name? Taylor, G for Gordon. Address? Ah! That I had forgotten too! In much of N America you need a house number, the number of the street and the sector, all I knew was it was on the west side of the city. Luckily there was only one G Taylor, who, when I eventually got through to him, was very relieved to hear from me, but when he asked me where I was, I had no idea! I then had to make an excursion to find some street names and call back, no, I had not run out of change. You can understand why I am not usually allowed out on my own! At last after much manoeuvring of the big Buick I got to the house. Gordon and his wife, Delorna, were nearly as relieved as I was! To my surprise another of my cousins, Bob Stowell, had been waiting there for me since late afternoon. It is always a pleasure to meet Bob, he is not only very interesting, but is also a highly successful artist. Some of his work has become well known attractions in Calgary: the dinosaur park in the zoo, the relief ironwork sculpture depicting the history of the CPR on the subway walls beneath the CPR building and the a column decorated with Indian tribal designs in the hall of the a building in Calgary. But what became of the owl? You may well ask. Getting into the car on the following day to go to the airport, my nostrils told me something was amiss: decaying meat. Then I remembered the owl. I should have liked to take the wings, but even they were too far gone to be acceptable travelling companions for a few weeks, so I had to be content to pull out a few wing feathers and some from the tail. But I could see that the carcass had leaked somewhat and the carpet in the boot was stained with dissolved owl that was continuing to fill the car with its gentle aroma. Purchase and application of an air freshener alleviated the crisis somewhat and by the end of the journey, well, you couldn't really smell anything untoward at all.

Coyote

It was surprising how few roadkills there were on the highways of N America compared to Britain. Perhaps there is less traffic on roads through the countryside. However, in Missouri, near to my second cousin Dick Boyt's property in Neosho, I found a freshly killed, fully grown coyote *(Canis latrans)*! I jumped out and rescued it from under the nose of a street-cleaning gang about to collect it. It was heavy and required quite an effort to lift it into the boot; I was careful to spread a newspaper down for it to leak onto if it felt so inclined. It was just like a big lean dog, longer than an Alsatian and of a light-brown sandy colour. When I got off the main road and had a chance to inspect it I realised the coyote was pretty heavily infested with fleas that were now beginning to look elsewhere for their next meal as the ground under their feet began to cool. We were due to leave that day for Dyersburg, Tennessee, and no way was Ken, or even I for that matter, going to be prepared to travel with so many hopping and hungry companions. The coyote had to go. It was the most exciting roadkill I think I have ever picked up, and here I was chucking it out as I might have done to an over-ripe rabbit. In thoughtful consideration for my cousins, however, I did not take it and its little companions to infest my cousin's yard and dogs, but I buried it by the farm track in the hope of coming back one day and retrieving the skeleton all clean and ready for my museum.

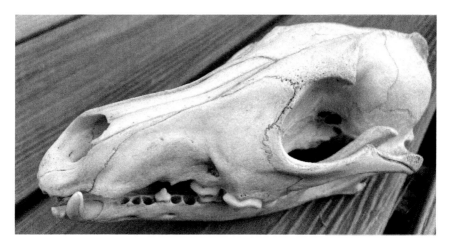

Coyote skull (minus a few teeth) © *Arthur Boyt*

Eight years later I again did a 9000-mile tour of Canada and the US. I revisited Neosho and arriving there, my first concern was: is the coyote still here? However, before I give you the answer, some events occurred on the way that I know you would like to hear about and there were some interesting roadkill finds on the way, including another coyote, that I will tell you about first to get the story in chronological order. I had flown to Calgary to stay with Delorna, my cousin Gordon's widow, for a few days. Gordon had died of cancer a month before and it was strange visiting his home without his cheery presence. My next stop was Gravelbourg in Saskatchewan, to stay again with Glen and Julie Hope. On the way I ran into a pretty big storm. The rain was so heavy I could not see out of the windscreen, so I had to stop. Then it turned to hail. The hailstones went from the size of grapes to walnuts. I turned the car round so that the back window was facing the wind, as I was afraid the windscreen would get shattered. I was parked near a creek, which rapidly became a roaring torrent with a river running down the road threatening to sweep me away. Just then an emergency warning broke into the car radio: *"This is a tornado warning for the Cadillac area."* Where was I? Cadillac. *"People in the Cadillac area should take cover in a basement. People in mobile homes should go into a building. People in automobiles should get out and lie down in the ditch."* I looked at the ditch beside me; it seemed a much quicker way of dying than staying where I was. I stayed belted in and tried to enjoy the fury of nature around me, the constant crash of hail on the roof, the lashing of heavy rain on the windows, the spouts of water thrown up by the balls of ice falling into the growing lake beside me and the tumult of the rising torrent in the ditch (in which I was supposed to be taking refuge). Lightning flashed and thunder crashed. At last, it began to diminish and I was able to see the road and where to go next. I had not been whirled up into the heavens and dropped to my death. There were hailstones as big as golf balls on the road. I stopped, picked one up, wiped it on my sleeve and popped it in my mouth, some gobstopper! What kind of updraught had been operating in the cloud to grow a raindrop into this huge ball of ice. I was amazed to discover that the car was not covered all over in dents from the icy rocks.

The next day I paid a visit to Glen's workplace, where I was invited to have a look in the salvaged clothing bin. There I found a pair of cord trousers, not the latest fashion it must be said, but nonetheless, very smart and a perfect fit. Proudly wearing my new trousers, I was taken to see two of Glen and Julie's married daughters, Tracey and Roseanne, at Assinaboia. Roseanne and her husband, Dwayne McDonald, had a daughter, Megan who was engaged to a young man named Brock. He told me he knew where there was a coyote's skull as he had killed it two months ago. It had crossed the road safely ahead of him but had turned back and run in front of the vehicle. I asked him for directions to the site to see if I could find it. It was then that I learned it was 200 miles away, as he came from a farm close to the Manitoba border. I was due to pass that way in two days time. He said he would see if it was still there and, if he could arrange something, he would. The next day, Brock rang to say he had found the coyote and would hide the skull for me to pick up from the SE corner of a crossroads on Highway 13 north of Antler. I duly stopped at the prescribed crossing on my way to Winnipeg next day and started searching in the long grass. Sure enough, there was a bulging polythene bag. I picked it up. It contained one lovely big coyote's skull!

On the way to Winnipeg that day I also picked up a robin and a Swainson's thrush. I stayed with Joyce, my cousin, Paul's, widow in her neat and clean flat in the city. I knew better than to suggest skinning anything in the flat, so I slipped out and skinned the two birds in the boot of the car. Two days later, I left Winnipeg and drove south to the customs post into the US at Pembina. As I drew up, four officials, pulling on rubber gloves, advanced on the car. "*Oh, oh!*" I thought, "*Will I have my treasures confiscated because of some obscure bylaw?*" I had to leave the vehicle to this search party and have my documents scrutinized in the nearby office. When I was informed that I could proceed, I went out to the car. One of the officers was deferentially holding the car door open for me and as I slipped into the driver's seat he asked, "*May we ask what the birds are for?*" I said, "*They are roadkill, and I am writing a book on roadkill.*" "*OK, Sir,*" he replied, and I was free to travel on. I started the engine, pushed the lever into drive and pulled away. I breathed a big sigh of relief.

I spent a few days in Des Moines with my second cousin, Jack Boyt. He is a most interesting person to be with as he is so full of novel ideas. He worked on the Manhattan project in his early years and later pioneered the use of air-supported structures that are sprayed with concrete to create novel and bizarre building shapes with high thermal efficiency. Before setting off for a drive with him on my last morning, I eased myself into the front seat of his car and slipped my money and document pouch under the seat for safety. We went to see a big dam on the Des Moines river, the outflow from which was what Americans would describe as awesome.

On the way back I noticed a dead muskrat by the road. It did not look particularly fresh so I did not request him to stop and pick it up. We called at his son Doug's sewing factory for a last farewell and then I hit the road for Neosho in Missouri over 300 miles away to the south. However, I decided to head north again to pick up that muskrat, 20 miles or so in the wrong direction. I managed to find my way there and just before arriving at the spot the thought crossed my mind, "*Have you got your bum bag with you?*" So when I stopped at the creek where the muskrat was, the first thing I did was look for that little buff and brown bum bag which held my credit cards and passport. I couldn't find it. I hunted systematically through everything and it was not there. What a good job I had taken this little diversion. Had I not done so I could have been 200 miles away before discovering my mistake when I had to stop for gas. I then approached the muskrat. It seethed with maggots and stank to high heaven; not the best choice for a travel companion. I thought I would remove the skull and make do with that, so I attacked it with the broken scalpel recently used on the skunk. The neck was pretty tough, the blade was blunt and the skull began to break up under my attempts to free it. Worried about the lost wallet, I abandoned the smelly corpse and headed back for Des Moines. Jack was not in. I managed to remember where his friend, Mable, lived and called on her. First, she tried to get Jack on his mobile, no reply. Then she rang our second cousin, Brian Thompson, with whom we had been the day before, no bum bag. Then she tried Jack's daughter, Maggie, where we had been in the evening, no bum bag. Then Doug's works, no Jack. Jack had left to take his car to the Toyota garage, so she rang there, Jack had not arrived. We chatted awhile until the phone rang, it was Jack at the garage. Yes, he had the bag! Maggie collected him and brought him home and I was reunited with my money, cards and passport. So, useless as the muskrat was as far as its skull was concerned, it had possibly saved me from a lot of bother had I arrived in Missouri without my bag.

The drive to Neosho took 5hrs, with no time to stop and inspect fur or feather beside the road. As I arrived on the farm track where the coyote had been concealed eight years earlier, I realised the road configuration had altered. Where the track had crossed a ditch there was now a bridge. The ground in which the animal was buried had been removed!

Porcupine

Porcupine © Arthur Boyt

In 1997, my last port of call in the USA was Minneapolis, where the

114

World Veteran's Orienteering Championships were being held that year and in which I was competing. Before going on to Minneapolis, I stayed with my second cousin and his wife, Bob and Jeanne Boyt, in Sioux Falls. On the morning of my departure I went with Bob to a meeting he had arranged with some First Nations to whom he was giving some land for a hospital. During the meeting, the natives, Gene Thin Elk and Nikki Pipe-on-Head, were asked to sing one of their own traditional songs, which they did. It was a very moving performance, certainly one of the most memorable moments of my whole trip. I had arranged to stay for the last two nights in Minneapolis with my twin's brother in law, Rutherford Aris, a professor in chemical engineering at Minnesota University, and his wife, Mercedes. But I had not arranged other accommodation for the preceding week. Only during the trip did I discover that I had two second-cousins-once-removed in the vicinity and, far from being without somewhere to stay, I now had to balance the invitations lest I disappoint any. Thus it was that I spent a few days with Greg and Mary Madsen (Bob's daughter) at Plymouth and a few days with Tom and Carla Price at Anoka while doing the Championships, both in the environs of Minneapolis.

Next day, on my way to an orienteering event, I saw something big lying on the road ahead but could not make out what it was. It was black with some white, shaped rather like a small bear, unlike anything I had seen before. When I got out to inspect it, I could see it was covered in quills; it was a porcupine *(Erethizon dorsatum)*. What an animal! This really was something! I carefully picked it up by its feet and put it into the boot of the car. I took it back to Anoka and tentatively enquired whether Carla might like to have a go at cooking some of it to see what it tasted like. She bravely agreed to give it a try, so I skinned some of it and prepared a few joints. The whole animal, save for its face, feet and belly, was covered in short thin white quills, 1.5 – 4in long, with black tips, each with an invisible hook on the end. Despite taking great care I kept getting the short spines hooked into my flesh. The quills did me no harm, they are not tipped with poison and did not break off and work their way to my heart and cause me to suddenly drop dead: not yet anyway. The quills cannot be easy to pull out if you only have paws with which to do it. If attacked, the porcupine turns its back on its assailant and reverses into it swishing its tail. Any wolf, coyote or dog not smart enough to get out of the way will collect a face full of quills which are not readily removed and work their way in to fester and maim their recipient. They can cause blindness and can sometimes be fatal. Many a dog in areas where the porcupine is at home has returned whining to its master to have its painful trophies of the chase removed. I should think that for a predator even eating a dead porcupine would be quite a hazardous operation, the quills detaching so readily. I cut off its head to procure its skull for my museum, knowing it would not begin to smell too badly before I got it home. Two days later after staying at the Aris's Bloomington flat, I called on the Prices, and Carla and I had the porcupine for lunch. We both agreed that it was deliciously tender but did not really possess a distinct flavour.

Funnily enough, while visiting Alberta for the World Master's Orienteering Championships nine years later in 2006, I found another fresh porcupine. I was unable to partake of this one, but I did skin the head and boil the skull to bring both mask and skull home with me. I could have eaten the meat from the skull and would have done so had I not boiled a very rotten skunk's head with it in the pot at the same time. I was staying on the farm of my first cousin and her husband, Win and Wilf Waters. I did my bit of cooking in a hidden corner of the farm watched by a couple of my cousin's grandchildren (my first cousins twice-removed). They were fascinated by this strange old relative boiling heads in a tin. I put the remains of the porcupine out in a field well away from any farm dogs, in the hope that some hungry coyotes might find it. In the morning there was not a sign of the porcupine's remains, the whole thing had disappeared.

Mountain Lion

In 2011 a mountain lion (*Puma concolor*) was killed on the road in Michigan. There has been no mountain lion in Connecticut for 100 years. Where had it come from? Examination of its DNA revealed that it originated in South Dakota – 1500 miles from Connecticut. It had taken two and a half years to travel via Minnesota, Wisconsin and Michigan, then into Canada, Ontario, back into the US, New York and Connecticut. Was it searching for a mate?

Cycling in Austria

In the summer of 2006 I took a holiday in Europe, orienteering, cycling and visiting relatives. Germany and Austria are well supplied with cycle routes, either beside ordinary roads or using minor roads, or very extensively on dedicated tracks from which traffic is largely excluded. Even on these roads, little used by vehicles, there was roadkill. The mole (*Talpa europaea*) is a species rarely seen dead on the road, but I encountered four on those cycleways. Had they been run over by cyclists? There were also places where the large edible

Edible snales eating a recent companion, now roadkill © Arthur Boyt

snail, the Roman snail (*Helix pomatia*), had come out onto the tracks, some had been squashed and others had moved in to partake of the flesh of their kin where it had been made available. I felt it was my duty to stop and throw these animals off the road and out of the danger; their very size (big as a golf ball) giving them importance beyond their place on the tree of evolutionary development. These big snails do occur in the South of England, but, tasty though they may be, you are prohibited by the Wildlife and Countryside Act from collecting them. Our native snail *(H. aspersa)* is equally edible and is not protected but next to nobody bothers to eat them. Another phenomenon that delayed my travels was peacock caterpillars (*Inachis io*) migrating across the track and facing certain suicide by attempting to cross the road. In one place I threw 25 of the black spikey wrigglers back whence they came. I hope that some survived to grace the world with their magic and beauty. There were also plenty of slugs and worms but they failed to interest me either as a rescue endeavour or as edible roadkill. I have eaten both, but I see no great future in stopping for slugs and worms.

Between Munich and Salzburg I came across a freshly killed pine marten (*Martes martes*) on the main road, what a beautiful animal. Dark chocolate-brown fur with a cream-coloured throat, a sharp foxy face and such large padded feet. I had no space to take it on with me and was able only to secure a photo before regretfully leaving it behind.

Pine marten © Arthur Boyt

I found another pine marten (well rolled out) on the outskirts of Vienna. I was able with this one to put my foot on the disrupted flesh and peel off a lower mandible that was exposed to view. Later on the trip, I saw what I took to be a pine marten in Wiener Neustadt, when a something in the dusk, not as big as a cat, slipped under a parked car and when I peered under the vehicle, was not to be seen, but which reappeared and ran up the road as soon as I had passed.

I came across a slow worm (*Anguis fragilis*) dead but undamaged, possibly having died by getting trapped by a high kerb and roasted in the midday sun. Also known as a blind worm, it looks like a shiny snake, but is, in fact, a legless lizard. It gets its Latin name from the fact that if it is molested it can go so rigid that it becomes brittle and can break into pieces.

Slow worm © Arthur Boyt

At one point my nose told me I had passed downwind of roadkill. I circled back to where the effluvium was strongest, and, sure enough, there was brown fur marking the outline of a twisted and maggot-infested corpse of a roe deer. Nothing for me there. I came across two dead hares on my ride, one fresh and the other well past its regular eat-by date. The hare is such a big animal that at first, from a distance, I thought one was a small deer. The road was stained with splashes of blood which suggested that the hare had taken time to die. It remained only for me to move the carcass from the road and let nature's undertakers clear up the tragedy. The fresh specimen I was unable to make use of as I was cycling and camping, and had no tools to skin with and no cooker with which to cook. I waved the good hare at a local but he did not take up the opportunity – at least not while I was present. What a waste of good dinners for a hungry family!

Bloody record of hare's dying moments © Arthur Boyt

My one overpowering memory of that ride was the number of painted lady butterflies (*Cynthia cardui*) slaughtered on the road. They were there in thousands! They overwinter in North Africa and spread northwards every year. Cycling enables you to see and appreciate the numbers that would be missed in a car. I have only once seen more butterflies and that was in Canada near the US border in 2005. I drove through a continuous cloud of this same lovely insect blowing in their millions across the road. I must have killed thousands. Had I been on a bike then I should have been choked by breathing them in! In N America they overwinter in Mexico and migrate northwards every year.

South Africa

Barn owl © Arthur Boyt

I visited South Africa in 2009 on the first leg of an orienteering world tour. I spent two nights in Kruger National Park and during my stay, I picked up a roadkill barn owl, an African wood owl and a common fiscal and cut off their wings and tails, cleaned and dried them to take on home with me. On my way to the airport, I found a freshly killed hyena. That was amazing. Almost as good as finding a dead lion. However, its head had been crushed so I was not able to salvage its skull and had to be content with mere photographs. I did manage to buy a small crocodile's skull from the National Park shop.

Striped hyena © Arthur Boyt

Australia

I flew to Australia from South Africa and was rather perturbed to find a card handed out before we landed asking if I had any plants, animals or parts thereof to declare. I owned up to what I had and was siphoned off in customs for questioning. Their eyes grew big when they saw my wings. I asked what I would have to do to make them acceptable. They said they would need the attention of a taxidermist. I said I was a taxidermist and the specimens had been treated. But that was not enough and they were confiscated after I had taken a farewell photo. The croc skull was returned after fumigation or something and I was allowed on my way. I hired a car and drove from Perth to Albany where my cousin lived and on the way came across several dead wallabies, which I stopped to photograph. One was very fresh and beautiful, so I cut off its head right there and took it on with me. Six days later I had an opportunity to cook and eat it while camping. Unfortunately, I only had an empty baked beans can in which to do the cooking. It occasionally boiled over and messed the stove up, but a regular topping-up with water and I reckoned it was done after one and a half hours. However, it was still a bit tough and the flavour was nothing to write home about but it was well worth the exercise.

Pretty-faced wallaby © Arthur Boyt

Australia was a goldmine for roadkill as every time I stopped to examine a specimen I came across several more in various stages of decay. Thus I collected several kangaroo and wallaby skulls and even a red fox. It was on a gravel road near Lithgow that I found a long-dead fox that made a super photograph for this book.

I saw a wombat (*Vombatus ursinus*) ambling across the road on more than one occasion and also found several dead wombats in various states of decomposition. Some were oozing with maggots, while others were dried skin bags full of bones. The wombat's skull is quite remarkable. It is nearly four times the size of a badger's skull and is very powerfully built as though it had evolved in a climate of savage beasts. But it has no predator in Australia other than the recently introduced dingo (*Canis lupus dingo*). So you have to look back in history to find the Tasmanian devil (*Sarcophilus harrisii*), the Tasmanian tiger (*Thylacinus cynocephalus*) and the marsupial lion (*Thylacoleo carnifex*) which could have influenced the robust nature of the skull.

Wombat © Arthur Boyt

Approaching Canberra I noticed a kangaroo sitting by the road and watching the traffic roll by. It was quite obvious to me that it had been hit and disabled so I stopped at the next garage and asked them to call the phone number (given on billboards along the highway to contact someone if an animal should be injured) and tell them where the animal was to be found. The garage agreed to make the call for me.

New Zealand

Going on to New Zealand I found this land to be equally good for roadkill. The flightless weka *(Gallirallus australlis)*, a bird rather like the British water rail, sometimes ran across in front of me and one or two would have a scrap in the road so that I had to brake hard to avoid them. Consequently, I found one or two as roadkill and I have their wings as mementoes. The animal most often dead on the road was the common brushtail possum *(Trichosurus vulpecula)* This is a marsupial imported from Australia by Europeans in 1850s both for its flesh and fur. It has no predator in New Zealand and so became widespread and now has occupied the whole of the two islands. It is a herbivore that enjoys birds' eggs and young and results in considerable damage to the forests and to the bird populations. It is also a vector of bovine tuberculosis. Attempts to control it involve dropping doses of poison from the air into the forests where it lives. Several dead possums that I found had babies, known as joeys, in their pouches. Marsupials by the road being new to me I had to stop and investigate whether they had a joey in the pouch. In one, the joey was not 50mm long, was naked and undeveloped, a bit like pictures I have seen of foetuses in placental mammals but with a big mouth attached to a teat in the pouch. On one occasion while in an orienteering race in NZ, I came across the

Brushtail possum © Arthur Boyt

skeleton of a possum. I could not stop long but I snatched up the skull and scapulas (they are interesting too) and, having no pockets, shoved them down the front of my running trousers. This was all right for a while but the skull began to slither down inside one leg and was soon right behind my knee which made bending it for climbing over gates and fences a bit uncomfortable.

Galapagos

Having the opportunity in the winter of 2009 to visit the Islands of Paradise, my wife and I spent a week in Galapagos during which we did some kayaking, snorkelling and camping in addition to the usual things that tourists to the islands do. Despite the enormous slaughter of wildlife perpetrated by man since his arrival and discovery of the islands, many of the birds and animals on the islands still treat humans with indifference enabling us to move among them and watch them without their taking fright. Coupled with this, many of the animals are unique to the islands and some are unique to just one or two of the individual islands in the archipelago. It was this that sparked Charles Darwin's interest when he visited on board the Beagle in 1836 which led to his conception of the theory of survival of the fittest and his promulgation of the theory of evolution. The unique nature of the islands is that they arose from the sea as volcanos upon which plants, animals and birds were cast and where their isolation, 600 miles from the mainland of Ecuador, enabled species to develop to occupy every ecological niche that occurred without the influence of the breeding stock from which they originated. The archipelago is either a 15 million-year-old field laboratory for the study of evolution or it is a postscript to Genesis chapter 1. Like an adopted child who discovers in later life that his real parents are not the ones he has grown up to accept as such, humanity has discovered that its real parents derive from a much older stock than the Adam and Eve of the Bible that it grew up to believe; and the Galapagos phenomenon was the key to that doorway of intelligence.

But to the question "*Is there roadkill on Galapagos?*" the answer I found is a definite "*Yes*". Not only did I see with my own eyes a dead cat, a rat and a finch, but I learned that there was so much concern over the amount of roadkill when the 45 km road from Puerto Ayora in the south of Santa Cruz was constructed to serve the airport on Baltra to the north that a speed limit was imposed and police timed the passage of vehicles crossing the island, fining those who broke the limit. I am not sure what the limit was, but the vehicle I travelled in touched 80 kph (50 mph) quite enough to kill anything it hit.

Although the Galapagos is probably the last place to observe the phenomenon, the speeding vehicle predator must be having an effect on animal survival and hence on evolution itself. Animals that have a predilection for lying on or lingering on roads must be selected against compared with those who cross quickly or avoid them altogether. I have heard the theory proposed that hedgehogs no longer curl up when approached by a vehicle as those that had this tendency have been eliminated and only those that keep running have survived to breed. Whether this is true or not I have no idea. Maybe someone could work on it for a PhD thesis. But the very characteristics of road avoidance that could benefit an animal can also be to its detriment. Animals that are loth to cross roads may suffer a loss of territory or range or be restricted or delayed on migration. Where animals are endangered and their numbers reduced, the vehicle predator could easily tip the scales towards the extinction of certain threatened species such as the Florida panther (*Puma concolor coryi*), the American crocodile (*Crocodylus acutus*), the Florida Key deer *(Odocoileus virginianus clavium)* and the Marsican brown bear *(Ursus arctos arctos)* in Italy.

Roadkill while orienteering

Let me ask a question. What is the most popular sport in Britain in which people of either sex, from an age range of very young to very old compete (not spectate) throughout the year? It may come as a surprise to most were I to say that I believe that sport is orienteering. Argue what you will, the popular national sports are seasonal, are played by fit and mostly young men and are popular because they are spectator sports. No one goes to watch an orienteering competition; it is a participation sport, not a spectator sport. But hundreds and sometimes thousands (and often three generations from the same families) can compete, each at their own level, at orienteering events every week up and down the country throughout the year. It may be esoteric and is not yet to be seen at the Olympics or any of the big games but is run by thousands of volunteers at club level under the auspices of the British Orienteering Federation. I have indulged in other esoteric pursuits such as rock climbing, horse riding, hang gliding, windsurfing, rowing and canoeing, and less esoteric sports such as skiing and snowboarding, and have competed in athletics, cycling, cross-country, marathons and triathlons; but I have found my home in orienteering. I am an orienteer and I am proud to say that I have competed for my country, in my age class, quite a few times. Not as a member of the elite GB team in the World Championships, but selected as best or second best in my age class in a Home International match or in a five-cornered match for England against Belgium (separate teams for Walloons and Flemish), Netherlands, part of Germany (Nordrhein-Westfalen) for the Interland Trophy. To put you in the picture, age classes in orienteering are every two years for juniors and every five years for veterans over 35 years; the senior class is from 21 to 34. Juniors are selected to represent their country from three age classes: under 14, under 16 and under 18 for boys and girls separately for the Junior Home International and Interland events. So it was that I found myself travelling overnight by coach to Cologne in March 1996 to compete for England in the 50/55 class. I tried to get some sleep but was too cold. I asked the driver to turn up the heat and managed to doze off for about an hour before we arrived at an army barracks at Bruggen at 6.30 a.m. Here we were awakened with breakfast. It was one of those 'Eat as much as you like and come back for more' style canteens, of which I duly took full advantage. They actually had kippers on the menu, so after porridge and cereals, I had a few kippers. I haven't had such a good breakfast since I stayed with a fish market auctioneer, George Thom in Lowestoft many years ago, who never started the day without five or six delicious kippers for breakfast.

However, a surfeit of kippers is perhaps not the best thing to have before going for a run! My training run seemed a bit heavy going, and I did find it a bit hard to climb all the stairs in one of the towers in Cologne Cathedral when we visited that great city later in the day, but by the time we stripped off for a short park race my belt was feeling a little less tight. The thing I liked best about the Interland competition was the meal, or should I say Banquet that the host nation laid on for the visiting teams. I have generally found it possible, despite the language barrier, to ask for second helpings at these events, which always adds to the sense of satisfaction and value for money. After the event and on my way back to get changed in the coach I found a dead red squirrel lying beside the road. It was quite fresh and was apparently undamaged. Having been a taxidermist since my teens, I could not leave such a desirable specimen there beside the road to rot so I picked it up, tucked it into a polythene bag and stowed it in one of my bags in the luggage compartment. I showed it to one or two before we set off for England and word got around among the juniors that I had a dead animal on board. A note was passed to me intimating that I should not smuggle it into the country, so I returned the note with an invitation to a meal of said animal. I think some felt it was against the rabies regulations, but dead animals or meat is not prohibited from entering the country across the Channel and I saw no reason to give an officious customs officer the opportunity to rob me of this lovely beast. However, when I got out at Watford, I completely forgot about the squirrel and it stayed on the coach to its terminus at Birmingham. When I discovered the next day that I had no squirrel, I thought at first someone had pinched it. I got in touch with Andy Hemsted who was last off the coach and found he had taken custody of my bag. I then asked him, if he did not mind and if his wife did not object, to stick the squirrel into his freezer until such times as I could arrange to collect it. Many months later my wife and I had a very enjoyable cup of tea with Andy and his wife, Penny, when we stopped off on a journey south from some event in the North to collect the little red animal. There has been a special bond between us ever since.

I had had a visit from a journalist a few days before the Interland competition in March 2003 and this had left me with quite a bit of badger, which needed eating up before I went away, so I made up some badger rolls and sandwiches to take with me on the journey to the Netherlands. This worked out quite well because, when everyone bought a meal on the ferry, I was able to have my badger rolls and then help tidy up some people's leftovers. We spent the first night on the premises of a rowing club in Belgium and travelled on to Arnhem for lunch where I had some more badger rolls by the bridge fought for so bravely by the British in WWII (A Bridge too Far). I felt rather old and slow in the training run that afternoon and then did a bit of birdwatching in the woods until dinnertime. Gavin Clegg, the team manager, appointed mentors from the seniors for each of the juniors. I was allocated to a super lad from the Midlands, Adam Bushnell, and because there was a bit of noise developing at his table joined him for dinner. The trouble mostly stemmed from a lad named Iain Embrey from Birmingham who loudly expressed his opinions (of which he was well possessed) to all who wanted to listen (and many who didn't). As to the food, Iain had many likes and dislikes, but mostly dislikes (he even wiped extra cream off his ice cream), so to try and concentrate his mind on the food, I challenged him to an eating competition – I would eat twice as much as he could. This had the desired effect, quietened him down and turned his attention to the food. We started with soup, I had four, but Iain did not like soup, so I won that round. I had three and a half legs of chicken and Iain had two and a half. One problem was getting the extra food and we had to go around the room scavenging for uneaten vegetables and leftovers. Iain got his hands on more beans than I did and so did better than me on that score. We engaged others on the table to scout the hall for extra puddings on our behalf, and Iain and I remained, when all the others had finished and had left the room, to plough our way through the queue of plates waiting to be emptied. We lost count of the extra puddings each consumed and agreed in the end that the result was a draw.

I did not do very well at the event next day, but I don't think it was due to the meal the night before, but more to problems with my brain. I took 55 mins, but my teammate, Ivor Noot, beat me by 10 mins. Two Belgians beat me too, but one of them was non-competitive, perhaps he had drawn the map. Anyway, England won and we were soon on our way home. On the road, I had everyone at the front of the coach looking out for birds. Someone spotted a moorhen off to the left which began to run across the road ahead of us, sensing its danger, it jumped into the air, and disappeared below the windscreen - I gave a yell - there was a dull thud and black feathers swirled in our slipstream. The driver took no notice of my cry to stop and so I lost another bag of tasty meals. I ate the last of my badger sandwiches on the boat and did quite well out of others' leftovers again.

I ran again for England in the Interland competition in the spring of 2006. I travelled to Poole to get a lift with Gavin Clegg in his nifty little Porsche to the rendezvous at Uxbridge. I passed at least six good badgers beside the road, but could pick up none as the car would be standing in the sun for a few days and could get a bit smelly; I noted where they were for the return journey. I got out my badger sandwiches on the ferry to have while the rest of the team bought themselves meals; when Jane Morgan (one-time lady fell runner of the year) learned what it was that I was eating she moved to another table! Beth Clayton, however, was made of sterner stuff and swapped some of her chicken for a badger's heart. The competition was staged in Germany near Warendorf and we travelled by coach as usual and stayed the night at a sort of youth/sports hostel in Oost-Dunkerque. Breakfast was served only between certain hours and unfortunately some of the younger members of the team, without a parent to chivvy them to breakfast, put in their appearance only after breakfast had stopped being served. It was a lovely frosty morning with the sun breaking through the mist and glistening on every twig. We had passed Eindhoven and were heading for Munster when a wood pigeon appeared flying along ahead of us on our left. At first I was a little surprised to see here what at home is such a common species, until I remembered this was Germany not France. In France, the wood pigeon is pursued by the shooting fraternity with a fanaticism that borders on madness, and it hardly dares show its face in that country without getting it full of lead pellets. It, like any wildlife in France that wants to survive, has learned to be wary. To overcome this wariness, the shooters there have devised a system so intricate that it defies the imagination. A number of little platforms are fixed high in the branches of trees. Each platform has a sprung trap door to which a captive pigeon is tied. Each trap door is connected by a string to an operator hidden in a hut on the ground. When a flock of wild pigeons is seen flying over, the operator pulls the strings, which causes the trapped birds to flap their wings, this attracts the passing birds who circle around to come into what they think is a safe place to roost. Bang! Bang! Bang! Hidden gunmen blast away at the unfortunate birds. Do you believe me? No, I thought you wouldn't, but it is true. But to come back to the pigeon on the road to Munster, it began to veer in our direction. It was going to pass over the coach, no, it was dropping lazily into our path. Seeing the inevitable intersection of our two trajectories, I began to shout "*Oh!*" and increased the volume as the distance diminished, "*oh, oh oooOOOOH!*" There was a hard thump as the bird caught the edge of the windscreen and I jumped up to see grey feathers billowing in our slipstream. Everyone on board, their attention gained by my shout, was witness to the horror. They all thought I must have been responsible for it! That I had somehow mysteriously drawn the bird down out of the sky to collide with our coach! It was roadkill; it must have been me!

I have never actually picked up roadkill while engaged in an orienteering competition, but I did once find a red grouse that had been shot on the Yorkshire moors. It was at an event, staged every year on the North York moors in August.

While bounding over the heather, I spotted the grouse lying among the purple blooms. The area had been shot over in the previous day or so and this bird had been missed both by the gun who shot it and the dogs which accompanied the pickers-up. The gun was obviously not interested in the least in what became of the things he hit, too occupied trying to hit another.

It is the act of killing that makes these people cough up good money to pursue their blood-letting pastime. If it weren't for that, think how much simpler it would be if live birds were dispensed with and the whole business of raising them and getting them over the guns could be a thing of the past. Instead, there could be an array of clay pigeon machines carefully hidden in the heather in front of the butts giving a wide assortment of shots simulating grouse coveys, high pheasants, ground-level hares and jinking snipe. Each gun would get a guaranteed number of shots; no one would feel left out or on an unlucky peg, and what is more there would be no bad seasons with few or no grouse to shoot. This would ensure a steady income for the estate, without the anxiety of bad weather, disease epidemics and plagues of foxes. They could go round the hills just as they do now with a fresh range of targets and challenges with each change in the view. The guns would hardly notice the difference. Another drawback to shooting real grouse is that the estate can raise only so many birds to go over the guns and so the number of days shooting is limited. Whereas with my grouse-friendly targets, any number of shoots can be held and, what is more, they can be held in the close season too. Without the overheads of a gamekeeper and the expense of game rearing, the price could come down. The man in the street could afford to have a go. Vegetarians, vegans and anti-bloodsports campaigners could participate with a clear conscience, and even animal-rights activists could vent their energies to the benefit rather than the detriment of the shooting estates. But as to the grouse I had found, I could not leave it behind; I had to carry it on with me. So with map in one hand and compass and grouse in the other, I continued on my way around the course. Every time I came to a control I would lay down the bird, punch my card, pick up the bird again and continue to the next control. The finish team were no little surprised to see a grouse come over the finish line with me. It did not slow me down much but provided some very good eating afterwards.

Railroad kill

Railways are elongated wildlife reserves, often acting as largely undisturbed corridors linking habitats together. Foxes used them where I lived in Hertfordshire and in several places had dens over which commuters had a grandstand view of cubs taking little notice of the train rumbling by. Railroadkill must occur more frequently than we imagine as there is no access to find it. In the early '70s I was given a kestrel and a barn owl to stuff by a lady who picked them up from beside a railway line where a footpath crossed the rails. They must always be a hazard to wildlife, but when deep snow forces animals onto the tracks a disaster is inevitable. The winter of 2007 was exceptional in Colorado with heavy snow and prolonged cold weather. Rich Tosches writing for the Denver Post website recorded how 50 elk and 1200 pronghorn antelope were killed when seeking refuge from the deep snow on railway tracks cleared for the passage of trains. The huge lumbering trains that use the tracks may only be going at 45 mph, but they cannot slow down quickly and it is enough to result in carnage. To combat this carnage the Colorado Division of Wildlife flattens the snow with snowmobiles and other snow vehicles away from the tracks at known blackspots and puts out feed to attract deer, elk and pronghorn away from danger. They report that the strategy is working. The trains run slower too in an attempt to prevent the slaughter. But railway lines run for 1000s of miles and animals may travel 100s of miles in their search for food.

Moose are also attracted to the rails as it provides an easy pass through the woods in the snow/ However, if an accident occurs, the railmen know where it is and a vehicle is sent down the track to collect it. Moose killed in this way, and on the road, are always collected and shared out in the nearest community.

Shared roadkill

On a country cycle ride one day in the early '70s, my eye was caught by a pheasant's head lying quietly on the road; I jumped off my bike to examine this strange phenomenon. Normally such an item has a body attached. I looked about to see whether there was one in the vicinity and, sure enough, there it was in the ditch nearby. The head could have been knocked off by a speeding motorcar, or there was a possibility that the pheasant had been caught by a fox, which had bitten its head off. I wasn't sure which. I hung it for a few days but when I came to pluck it I found puncture wounds caused by teeth under its wings, where a fox had carried it. I cooked it in the usual way in the pressure cooker and carved off a drumstick and a few slices from the breast. To my surprise, I bit on some lead shot (nearly cracking my teeth in the process), which indicated that perhaps the fox had collected it after a shoot. But moments later when I started gnawing on the drumstick I discovered that the tibia, the leg bone, was bent, but no, it was not bent, it had been broken and had mended bent. Two days later when I carved all the meat off the breast I found some holes in the keel of the breastbone. So the strange and gruesome history of the unfortunate bird was now revealed. It had been shot, its leg broken and its breast riddled, but it had survived and its wounds healed. Then a fox had caught it, possibly because it could not run so well due to its lame leg. The fox had dropped it for some reason - frightened by a car? Then serendipity had ruled that I should cycle by on cue and be the final beneficiary of the hunting of others. It tasted extra-special when I finally deduced the events that led up to my being the consumer. I kept this unique leg bone and had occasion, a year or so later, to use it to demonstrate to a bunch of orthopaedic students how nature heals without man's assistance. I was on an outpatient visit at the Royal National Orthopaedic Hospital at Stanmore while recovering from a fractured shoulder blade. The surgeon was showing a bunch of students how a fractured scapula disenables the affected arm to be raised sideways by more than about 50 degrees. Try as I might I could not move that arm any higher. I had sustained this unfortunate injury while cycling to work one morning down the Watford by-pass. I was struck in the back by a lorry carrying bricks into London; the driver claimed he could not see because of the fog, which evidently had not been a sufficient reason for him to slow down and drive within his limits. Anyway, the bone very quickly distracted the attention of both the surgeon and his students from my disability.

Another meal that I shared with one of nature's hunters was a grouse. Er, well, I hardly shared that pheasant with the fox, did I, it got little more than a taste. But the grouse was a different kettle of fish. On one of my winter visits to Scotland, I was skiing on the slopes at Glenshee, when feathers and blood on the snow caught my attention, and there in the heather was a grouse, well, part of a grouse. As there was no footprint on the ground around, I assumed that some of it had been eaten by an aerial predator, most likely a peregrine falcon. I pondered whether to leave it for the bird to come back, but the prospect of sharing a meal with a peregrine was too tempting to leave it behind. I don't suppose many people have eaten a meal caught for them and shared with a wild peregrine. There was no great flavour of the wild hills (whatever that may taste like), in fact, it tasted like nothing more exotic than a partridge.

I once shared a pheasant with a rat. I picked up this pheasant on the A11 near Newmarket on my way to Cley on the East coast on Boxing Day 1976 (more on that trip later). It had evidently lain beside the road for some days. A rat had stripped the feathers off its back and one leg, and eaten the flesh down to the bone. The road had been wet and it had got quite gritty too. I don't know why I bothered really. It wasn't as though I was that desperately short of good food. But the breast looked quite wholesome so I took it home and ate it. It tasted OK, but I couldn't help thinking about the little rat teeth marks as I ate. I suppose it added a certain frisson of adventure or absurdity, but quite frankly, I think I was carrying parsimony to quite unnecessary lengths, especially as I had picked up another, perfectly good, pheasant on the same day.

Eating pets?

While not everybody joins in the clamour of horror at learning that I eat roadkill, there is no exception to the condemnation when the subject of eating cats and dogs comes up. Somehow, the status of being a human being's pet confers on these animals a sanctity that puts them on a plane almost equal to man himself. I readily agree that our pets and, indeed, all the animals we domesticate and farm for our own pleasure and as food should be treated without cruelty or discomfort. And I am not advocating the slaughter of pets, or for that matter the slaughter of pet species that are bred for food, such as dogs in the Far East. But for people who happily eat cattle and sheep to express disgust at the eating, not the killing, of other mammals simply because they are pets is being a little unreasonable. As a race, we have encompassed the annihilation and extinction of many species of bird and beast, and in many cases with unspeakable cruelty. To give one example, the Great Auk, a huge and majestic, flightless seabird that took 300 years of man's exterminating activities to remove millions upon millions of these inoffensive creatures until not one was left. The Great Auk had the misfortune, as do so many seabirds, of being clad with warm feathers, well endowed with oily fat reserves and made of tasty meat, but being unable to fly was at the mercy of plundering nations, led by Britain, who in the process of their shameful work stripped the skins off the breasts of living birds and left them to wander off and die, and used *living* birds as fuel for the very fires that rendered the oil from their fellows.

A full account of man's horrifying history of his dealings with pretty well all wildlife for profit or sport is to be found in Farley Mowat's book, 'Sea of slaughter', a book which makes very uncomfortable reading, but which I feel should be on the curriculum of every school in every land throughout the globe. Sport and greed for money have robbed society of much of its wealth and variety of wildlife the world over. Man's treatment of his own species is a history shameful enough, but his treatment of the animal kingdom beggars belief. If we remain unaware of our history of cruelty and extermination, we shall continue on the same course, as indeed we are, as far as fish and whales are concerned. No amount of self-flagellation will bring back the Great Auk, but we are still killing whales and that by the most cruel means imaginable, the harpoon. OK, there is a tremendous movement afoot for the cessation of the killing of all whales, but Iceland and Japan are going ahead with whaling under the disguise of science, and Norway, in defiance of international agreements, with commercial whaling. If farmers killed their cattle, sheep and pigs with harpoons as the whalers kill their victims, they would be sent to prison for years. Every man-jack on board a whaler is as guilty as the members of the government that support it. In the same way that the command structure for the Japanese army in World War II from the emperor downwards was responsible for the atrocities carried out by their foot soldiers that gave them such a reputation for infamy throughout the whole sphere of their operations. Maybe that nation needs to examine whether the streak of sadism that was manifest in its wartime actions is not perpetuated in its treatment of the whale, and all because some of their people like the taste of whale meat! Every meal of whale meat eaten should be accompanied by the forced viewing of a DVD of the hunting and killing of whales. That might render the meal a little less palatable! Also, our partiality for fish is not only driving the tuna, toothfish and swordfish to extinction, but in the process, the long-line techniques used for catching them are killing 300,000 seabirds, including 100,000 albatrosses, a year and ensuring their rapid extinction unless something drastic is done at once. I suggest the navy gets out there and sends all pirate fishermen to Davy Jones locker along with all fishing boats not employing albatross protection procedures.

Meanwhile, we all sit on our hands and do nothing, Oh yes we do, we buy Japanese cars, cameras, computers and a lot else besides, we eat Icelandic fish and we visit Norway. The talk about having to cull whales because they eat fish is sheer balderdash; they are killed because they are big business. Proper commercial sanctions against these cruel, greedy, senseless nations would soon put a stop to it pretty quickly. When Norway resumed commercial whaling in 1993, President Clinton had it in his power to exact sanctions and he would not do it. Why? Politics. Big business and politics. Man's blood-stained history of cruelty goes on. We don't want to know about it, we are not interested in it and so we do nothing about it; just the climate for the fin and minke whales to go the way of their greater cousins.

Dog

You may well wonder how it was that I came to eat man's best friend, the dog. DNA testing has suggested that man's association with dogs goes back over 100,000 years to when he began to domesticate the progeny of wolves. In western civilizations the dog is taken into the bosom of the family; it is a member of the family. A dog's death is a family tragedy. For many a lonely person, a dog or a cat is the only family they have. Many dogs are pampered, nothing is spared for their comfort and well-being and some people's lives revolve around them. And let's be fair they do fill a gap in many people's lives. They provide a devoted, intelligent companion who will untiringly listen to all their woes. They keep many people healthy too in that their owner has to take them for a walk every day and that is good for people in this sedentary, drive-everywhere society. Along with cats, they are considered to be of psychological benefit to their owners. But to eat a dog! It is beyond the pale. In our Western civilised society eating a dog is regarded with almost as much horror as cannibalism. In the Orient, they have no such compunction. Dogs are raised for the table; the family pet is happily put down by its owner to be enjoyed inwardly as a series of excellent dinners for the whole family. And while I subscribe to the principles of the Humane Society International and support PETA (People for the Ethical Treatment of Animals), I have no desire to preach against people eating dogs, or any other domestic animal for that matter, provided the animal is not treated with cruelty in its life or in the manner of its dying. Unfortunately, this is often not the case in the Far East where dogs and cats are reared in small cages or stolen and often transported with cruelty to a cruel death. The rearing of stock in cramped and cruel cages is also true to some extent with intensive farming in the 'civilised' West. Until meat is marketed with a label indicating its manner of existence, only vegetarians can be sure they are not involved in the cruel procurement of meat; other than a roadkill eater, of course.

It is fair to say that this self-imposed prohibition on the eating of dogs was a contributory factor to the tragic failure of Scott's last expedition. He would not take dogs as a means of drawing supplies and equipment and, as their work diminished, killing and eating them. Roald Amundsen, the Norwegian explorer who raced Scott to the South Pole, had no such compunction. He used dogs to pull sledges and as stores were used up their work diminished so he killed and ate them and got out and back quicker and so survived. Perhaps it was not so much the eating of dog that stopped Scott taking them on his expedition, but the killing of a faithful servant and friend; a treacherous act if ever there was one. But Scott's party died, Amundsen's didn't. Members of the Jewish faith are prohibited from partaking of dog, but that is because it is a rule of their religion, not because they are repulsed at the idea, they have no option in the matter. But, like us, dogs too are made of meat and any barrier to their consumption is surely only in the mind.

The first time that the opportunity, and with it the temptation, to partake of a dog arose on Thursday the 19th of January 1978. I set off for work on my bike at 7.10 into a headwind with snow falling. I had to wear a cape so it was like sailing into wind with a spinnaker up. The gear lever had broken and I had not had time to mend it, so I had only one gear working, which meant I had to be off the saddle for much of the time. I was riding up the A41 on my way to pick up and drive a school bus from Brockley Hill for Ron Hearn and as I passed the huge Aldenham bus works I saw the body of a big grey animal lying on the wide grass verge, it was a dead dog. I did not have time to stop then as I had to drive a coach to Stanmore to pick up kids for Haberdashers' Aske's school. Having dropped the children off at school at Aldenham and the coach at the depot, I diverted from the direct route to Borehamwood, where I worked, to inspect the dog. It was near a permanent gypsy site, (or should that be travelling people's site?) and I suspected that that is where it belonged. It was a lurcher, a cross between a greyhound and either a collie or a sheepdog. It was a rough-coated, huge, rangy animal, looking very much like a small wolfhound. I left it so that its owner would have opportunity to see it and do with it whatsoever they wanted.

After work, I went another way home to inspect a fox I had been told about. It proved to be a small, mangy, tailless beast and not worth further attention. I had badger heart and kidney with corned beef and the usual exciting array of vegetables for dinner that evening, very nice. I passed the dog by on Friday, but on Saturday, after a lunch of rabbit and having had to push the car 100 yards to get it going, I drove to London. I collected a pair of 170 mm Roy compact skis with Salomon 444 bindings that I had ordered from Lillywhites in Piccadilly a week earlier. I stopped at Elstree on my way home having been invited for a meal with my ex-boss, Peggy Shakeshaft, who had been Librarian at Fire Research Station when I started work there in 1965. She gave me first a cup of tea with a whole sponge cake full of fresh cream and jam. Knowing she did not partake of such a delicacy I indulged myself and ate it all. Then came dinner: a huge slab of pork pie with salad, followed by treacle tart, peaches and yogurt. She knew how to spoil me rotten! On my way home the dog was still there, so I picked it up.

The next day was Sunday and I found myself still having breakfast at 10.30 a.m. I had two exciting things to demand my attention, the skis and the dog. The skis won and I spent an hour putting them on and off and practising manoeuvres as much as one is able on the sitting-room carpet. I had lunch of rabbit at 3 p.m. At 6p.m. I began work on the dog. It was 5ft (1.5m) long and weighed 48lb (22kg). It was quite clean and did not smell. I cut it open on the garage floor, pulled out the guts and then hung it up by one back leg. It was easy to skin as it had little fat on and the skin came away very cleanly. I stopped for tea, sweet corn, toast and cereals at 8.30 p.m. and then on with the job. I found it had died of broken ribs, which caused internal bleeding. I was told by one of my fellow coach drivers a few days later that it had wrecked the front of the Ford Grenada that killed it. I carved the joints off as it hung, but this allowed blood to get sploshed and splattered everywhere. I had almost finished the job when I went for a bath at 11.45 p.m. I finished jointing it on Monday evening and, with great expectation and no little apprehension, cooked my first sample of this good-looking meat. It did not smell bad while cooking, as badger often does, but when I started to eat it, it was DELICIOUS. It was tender as veal with the consistency of lamb. The flavour was sweet and pleasant, a sort of combination of veal and lamb and beef! No wonder it is hard to keep dogs as pets in Hong Kong! I once asked for dog in a restaurant in China but was told it was the wrong time of year; they eat it mostly in the winter because it warms you up! Well, that dog gave me a lot of pleasure and nutritious benefits over the next weeks. I found dog made very nice sandwiches too, but nobody believed me when, on being asked, I told them it was dog in between the slices of brown bread.

My second dog turned up almost exactly two years later (30th January) in exactly the same spot, outside the entrance to the gypsy permanent site. It was another lurcher and could have been the brother of the one I had already eaten. It was a real case of *deja vue*. Again I was on my way to Brockley Hill to drive a Hearn's coach to Edgware to take Habs children to school in Aldenham and again went back to inspect it on my way to work. This time though there were some of the travelling people about. They asked me what I was going to do with it, but I don't think they believed my reply. It was not until four days later that I was able to start skinning the beast. It weighed about half a hundredweight (56lb, 25kg) and was too heavy for me to hang up on my own. My neighbour's son, Clive Jackson, walked in as I was struggling with it and he helped me to hang it in the garage to skin. He then watched as I set to work stripping the thin almost hairless skin from the lean powerful body underneath. Once the skin was off, I took the carcass into the kitchen to cut up on the sink unit. It had a chip of bone broken on the skull, so it may have been knocked out, but the real damage was, like the previous animal, a row of broken ribs penetrating the heart, lungs and liver that resulted in a massive internal haemorrhage. When I began to cut it open and joint it, Oh the blood! There was blood everywhere. It oozed out in great clots that slurped off onto the washing machine and slithered down the side of the gas stove. Clive had never seen anything cut open or blood running out. He was quite chuffed with himself that he did not flake out at the sight. Eventually, I got it all cut up and into polythene bags and into the freezer; the gory bags of meat weighed no less than 46lb (21kg)! The next day I cooked the head in the pressure cooker but dusted it with mixed spices instead of the usual mixed herbs and it smelled more like fruit cake than meat. It was a bit tough and tasted more like beef than lamb, but it was good. Two days later I had the brains with a hind leg. The leg was delicious, reminiscent of a knuckle of lamb. That animal supplied me with about 14 more meals as well as lots of sandwiches.

Cycling through the countryside one day between Luton and Harpenden, I came across a black Labrador in the ditch. I could tell it had been there for a day or so as the vegetation beneath it was slightly paler and *rigor mortis* had come and gone. If you don't know what *rigor mortis* is, it is explained in Chapter 24. I had no means of taking this huge and heavy animal on my bike, so I had to come back later with the car to collect it; it was still in the ditch upon my return. The animal was wearing a collar, but it was not much use as it had nothing engraved on it. It happens to be the law in the UK (Control or Dog Order1992) that dogs must wear a collar that carries the names and address of the owner. Failure to comply with this law can incur a fine of up to £5000 though I have never heard of it being applied. There was no obvious place whence this might have strayed whither I could have gone to enquire of its ownership. I do recall once finding a chihuahua beside the road that exhaled a breath of steamy air that proved to be its last just as I arrived at the scene. It had no collar, but I guessed it might belong to a nearby mansion. I passed through the large wrought-iron gates and knocked on the door. Did they own a chihuahua? Yes they did. In great consternation, the man followed me to the scene of the tragedy. Yes, it was his wife's. I offered to take it home and bury it for him, to which he gave his immediate assent. I resisted the temptation to give it a more active after-life by incorporating it into my own personal operations and buried it beneath an apple tree in my garden. A day or so later I called at the mansion and let the man know that his wife's pet was safely laid to rest. He offered to pay me for my service and I am ashamed to say that I found myself putting out my hand to receive it even while I was protesting that I could not possibly accept anything from him. I suppose we all have things in our lives that make us cringe as we reflect upon them. This is one of mine. But there again, undertakers, or funeral directors as they call themselves, do this every day without seemingly the least twinge of shame at making a living out of another's tragedy.

The labrador proved to be as tasty as the lurchers. There certainly does seem to be something very pleasant about a roast leg of dog or even a joint just cooked quickly in a pressure cooker without any special preparation or seasoning. It is every bit as good as beef or lamb and I have been heard to comment that it is my favourite roadkill. However, I have not had any to eat for a quarter of a century, I suppose they get picked up by the police when a report is received. I did pick up a dog recently, it was in Sussex, a spaniel and such a lovely dog. It had only just been killed and was in the middle of the road about to be rolled flat before I retrieved it. It did have a name and phone number on the collar. I was about to ring the owner when a police car appeared and I passed the responsibility over to them.

I once had four sandwiches for lunch, three of which were dog and one was hare. I ate the hare first to give it time to get away before I sent the dog down after it.

Cats

My first cat was a small ginger moggie I picked up while driving back from my second hang-gliding lesson at the end of October 1976. The first lesson had been two weeks earlier in Winslow, Bucks, where 12 hopeful air cadets assembled to have a go at the craze that was catching on about that time. We had some instruction in a classroom and, after sitting in a harness hanging from the door arch, which served as a flight simulator, we drove the five miles to Conduit Hill near Quainton to taste the real thing – hang gliding that is, not cat. It was a little perturbing, as we walked towards the hill, to find that we were carrying three hang gliders and a stretcher with us! Our first attempts to get airborne were somewhat mixed: quite a few managed to crash their first attempt, my friend, Paul Samme, with whom I had travelled to the event, had a superb first flight, one chap hurt his leg and another could not bring himself to even get into the harness. When my turn came, I managed to have three perfect flights! The flights were so short you did not have time to do very much, a bit like flying a swing. Only half the students managed to get the hang of it. The second lesson was again at Quainton and Dave Robinson another fellow from work, Paul and I rigged a Chargus 18/50 Rogallo, a first-generation kite. We practised on this all morning and made sufficient progress to go on to a Chargus Aquila Vega with a higher aspect ratio. This gave us longer flights but was harder to control and both Paul and I managed to have a tumble. I touched a wing and flipped over so that I was left hanging in the air! It was altogether a successful venture and we resolved to continue with our training as opportunity allowed. On the way home that night I spotted this little cat in the gutter and stopped to examine it. It was quite fresh and had not been squashed at all, so I took it on with me to decide what to do with it later. Had I left it there it would quickly have become squashed and, had its owners then found it, they would have been more traumatised than having it just disappear, at least that is how I looked at it. I could not go knocking on doors at midnight to see if they had lost a cat either. But should I eat it? After all, it was or had been someone's pet. Something was going to eat it, even if it got rolled out and washed down a drain, so what is the problem with me eating it rather than a thousand wriggly maggots? I thus convinced myself that there was nothing unnatural about my eating it, the body was saved from going through the smelly stage of natural decomposition and the owners, had they known, could have taken comfort from the fact that at least some of their pet was sitting in front of a warm fire of a cold evening.

I got round to skinning it the following evening. It was easy to skin and the pelt was so attractive that I decided to keep it and put it into the freezer for future attention. I cut the little beast up into joints and found it came to 3lb (1.3kg) of very good meat. Examination of its intestines revealed three big nematode worms! I did not examine the worms to identify them, perhaps I should. I am sure that my twin brother could have told me at once what they were as he worked for some years in the helminthology section of Cooper, McDougal and Robertson Ltd at Berkhamstead Hill. He lived just over the road from me at that time, but was not associating with me as he was a member of the Exclusive Brethren, a fundamentalist Christian sect from which I had been excommunicated; but that is another story! The worms might well have been *Toxocara cati* or *Toxascaris leonine*. These parasites do present a risk to humans giving rise to human toxocariasis (see Chapter 19).

I cooked a foreleg and the liver the next day. I had it with two corn cobs gleaned from a local farm where they were grown for pig food and so were solid, tough and required much mastication. The meat was very tender but was not exactly bursting with flavour, in fact, it was rather bland and needed spicing up a bit. It was perhaps more like veal than anything else. I ate my way through the cat during the next week until I reached the head and neck, which I ate with one of the front legs. It was delicious. The tongue was very rough and felt very funny, just like a cat licking around inside my mouth – quite a novel experience! It all tasted very good accompanied by some red currant jelly.

I had several cats thereafter. One yielded 9lbs of meat. Another had got diesel all over it and required great care when skinning it. I don't know whether it got the diesel on it before, during or after its fatal encounter. Most of it was OK, but I found when I ate the head, that the diesel must have got into its eyes and mouth for it came through as an unexpected and unpleasant flavour! One thing I found about cooking cats was that they were well fed and yielded quite a bit of grease on being cooked. I used to save this in a bowl and used it for dripping whenever I did a bit of frying. My sister came to stay once while I was away and availed herself of the things she found in the fridge, the dripping included! She complained upon my return of the 'awful dripping' I kept in the fridge. I did not enlighten her then, but some months later, when her son Stephen got married, I was invited to say a few words at the reception in praise of the wonderful selection of delicious things set before us to eat and used the occasion to let the cat out of the bag about the dripping. My sister's horror turned to rage when she discovered what she had eaten and she proceeded to pummel me until I sat down.

Roadkill cat © Arthur Boyt

I have found dead cats with an owner's name and phone number on the collar. It has been my unhappy duty on such occasions to break the sad news to them. They usually come to verify the identity and take the remains with them. I have never offered to butcher and cook their treasure for them or invite them, unsuspecting, to a meal and only reveal afterwards what it is we have just eaten. There is a limit to my sense of humour.

And don't forget that Chinese restaurants prosecuted for serving cat in place of chicken are not usually rumbled because someone noticed it tasted funny, but because the dustman found a pile of cat skins in the bins.

Nearly roadkill

Dog

Sometimes animals get run over that are not killed on the spot. My first experience of this burned itself so deeply into my memory that I can relive it now with just as much horror as when it happened nearly 60 years ago. My Auntie Mary, having been recently widowed, was visiting her two sisters in Britain from her home in Winnipeg. An acquaintance of hers, a Mr Louis E.

Samuels (LES), a minister of the Lord, from Winnipeg, had just arrived in the country and offered to take her, my mother and my Auntie Emmie, along with my two brothers and me to the home of a mutual friend who lived at Nash Mills. We pottered along in this big black saloon car while the conversation hopped from people who had died to people who were about to die and back again to those who had sadly passed on. I was jammed in the back and, being only seven years old, was clutching a cuddly dog which I had named Grapes that had a white body and a black nose and black ears. LES was not used to driving on the left in a right-hand-drive car and was pursuing a course somewhere near the middle of the road. Two dogs suddenly raced barking from a house on the right. The smaller of the two, a wire-haired Jack Russell, ran into the road behind the car, raced past us on the left and I could 'see' its barks coming up from in front of the car. I was terrified. The dog was in mortal danger. Mr Samuels carried on driving relentlessly. My twin, who was sitting in the front, stood up to see better. The front nearside wheel of the car bumped over something, the aggressive barking changed to a yelping scream and a moment later the back wheel right under me bumped over what I knew for certain was the body of the dog. LES drove on seemingly unperturbed. I twisted around and stared out of the small rear window to see the little dog dragging its crushed hindquarters out of the road still yelping. "*We ran it over,*" exclaimed my brother. "*Oooh!*" wailed Auntie Emmie who was always very sensitive about the feelings of animals. LES did not stop. The image I had from that encounter has remained with me as clear as ever today

Cat

A less traumatic but equally memorable event occurred around that time. Between the pavement and our front garden was a brick wall with a wooden post and rail fence on top of it and a privet hedge behind it. I was sitting on the fence. We had a tabby cat called Tibbles. A deep maroon, 1930s Humber came down the road and I recognised it and the driver, Mr Ernie Sims, who went to our Meeting. He must have been on his way back from visiting Mr Leslie Pratt who lived in No 64 and was also in the Meeting. As he passed he caught sight of me and waved, at that moment Tibbles dashed across the road and passed right under the car, I saw her rolled over and over under the vehicle, Ernie Sims drove on oblivious to what was taking place underneath him and Tibbles came out the back and shot under the hedge on the far side. When I managed to extricate the frightened animal from her hiding place I found she had escaped unscathed. I reckoned I had seen her lose one of her nine lives.

My wife was driving along a Cornish lane one morning recently when she saw a cat lying in the gutter looking at her. She stopped and went back to hear the cat wailing pitifully. She phoned the friend she had been going to meet who told her to pick it up and take it to the vet. Afraid that it was a feral cat and would scratch her, she managed to push a coat under the cat and then lifted it into the car. She decided to stop at a nearby bungalow to see if they knew the cat. They did. It belonged to the judge who lived nearby. The judge was away but a cat-sitter was in residence but she could not drive. So the two of them took it to the vet. Did the cat have insurance? The cat-sitter assured him that the judge would pay if it was not insured. Later that day the vet rang to say it had a broken pelvis and had to go to Exeter for an operation. The cat-sitter's husband stepped in and took the cat the 50 miles to Exeter. I am happy to relate that the cat recovered, but was not so keen on staying out all night.

I was witness to a similar event while visiting my cousin in Gravelbourg, Saskatchewan, in Canada. We were passing through Lafleche after visiting his daughters in Assiniboia, when I saw a cat proceed to cross the busy highway. There was a lorry approaching. It was evident that the paths of both cat and lorry were going to cross. Lorries, or trucks, as they are called in that part of the world, are big and they have a lot of wheels. The cat was heading straight for that train of rolling wheels. Neither cat nor truck was going fast, it was all happening in slow motion. I prepared myself for a gruesome spectacle and began to gasp "*Oh, oh, oh, oh!*" as the climax of the incident approached, partly to warn the cat by telepathy and partly to prepare my cousins for the outcry that would accompany the dénouement or finale of the affair. Instead of veering off from its destination the cat began to run and dived between the front wheels and back wheels of the cab. It had escaped the first two of the cab's 10 wheels. My 'Ohs' changed to a continuous scream as the moggie disappeared from view until I saw it miraculously appear on the far side when I was able to let out a great sigh of relief. What a cat! No roadkill that day.

Tawny Owl

I used to drive around Bodmin Moor every week for choir practice with the Loveny Male Voice Choir. This involved some miles on narrow lanes which were usually crawling with rabbits, pigeons and so on. One night there was a ball of feathers on the road. I leapt out blocking the road and rescued a young tawny owl. It seemed OK, so I went to put it through the hedge thinking it had perhaps only been concussed, but it capsized every time it tried to fly; it was obvious it had a broken wing. I took it home and called a friend, Richard Arnold, who worked at a small zoo and kept a rescued barn owl. He collected it to see what could be done about its broken wing. Unfortunately, he called me back after a few days to let me know it had died. Oh well, we did our best. Two days later I was going home on the same road and saw a rabbit lounging beside the road. I knew at once what was wrong. I jumped out, extracted the wheel brace from the boot and checked the rabbit. It was as I suspected, the front end of the rabbit was unharmed and alert, but the back legs were lying idle. It tried to scrabble away, but only its front legs worked. I could see the slight kink in its back marking the place where the back was broken. I spoke to it softly to calm it and apologised for what I was about to do. As I steeled myself for the task before me, my mind jumped back to a scene seared on my memory from over 50 years ago: in a Surrey wheat field during harvest, the reaper was closing in on the last square of wheat when the driver stopped, picked up a stick and advanced into the corn. "*It 'im 'ard, Bill*" said one of the men. Bill did just that and stooped to pick up a rabbit kicking its last. One hard whack and my rabbit lay still. I did not like doing it but it had to be done.

I used to share the driving to choir practice with one of the baritones, Dave, an ex-policeman. He didn't approve of my efforts to preserve the local wildlife. One day I skidded a bit to avoid a wood pigeon. "*Stop it. You'll have us both killed,*" he cried. And whenever I swerved to avoid a mouse, he would say "*What are you doing now?*" "*Didn't you see that mouse in the middle of the road?*" is my retort. Once, while in his car, I could not restrain myself from shouting, "*Look out!*" when a rabbit hopped into the road. "*Shut up. I'm not going to kill myself avoiding one of your animals!*"

Travelling home on the A303 some miles east of Honiton where it is single carriageway, I spotted an owl (not a spotted owl) sitting up and propped against its tail. It was in the road just right for being run over. I swerved and stopped. I picked it up gently. It was a tawny owl *(Strix aluco)* and was pretty dopey. I placed it on my wife's lap and covered its head with a cloth, it gripped her leg with its talons. It occasionally fluttered on the way home. Next day it was still alive so we took it to a friend, Richard Arnold, who has a menagerie and also keeps a barn owl. He kindly looked after it and fed it for a week or so until he reported it ready for release. Sue was visiting her mother in Exeter and decided to kill two birds with one stone (not the owl) and visit her mum and repatriate the owl. Her mum went along for the ride and they opened the box off the A303 and close to where we had found the owl. As soon as it saw the open sky above it, the owl took off and powered up to the top of the tree above them; a very satisfactory end to the story.

Barn owl

Driving back home from Launceston one day I saw a dead barn owl *(Tyto alba)* lying on the road. I jammed on the brakes and ran back to retrieve it. I picked it up by its feet and as I did so its talons just tightened a fraction on my hand – it was alive. Its eyes were closed and it appeared to be at death's door. I put it in a box overnight and in the morning it had recovered enough to scrabble its feet but its eyes were still closed. I kept it a day or so until it showed signs of recovery and then took it round to Richard Arnold to feed and care for it. It made progress so after a week or so we took it out to near where we found it and let it go. It flew away low down and crashed into a fence, we tried again but another crash landing. So Richard took it home and kept it for another week or two until he felt it was ready to go. This time when we released it, it took off and flew up into a tree, we followed and it flew off. Our job was done.

Pheasant

On another occasion, in the lanes near Lanhydrock with Sue in the car, there was a pheasant lying in the road as if there was no better place for a little rest. I picked it up and it flapped its wings vigorously, so I let it go, but it crashed down into the ditch beside the road. I was on my way to a training run from Lerryn with some friends and was already late so I left it. Returning after the run and a meal, I stopped where the bird had dived into the ditch, hoping it had recovered and gone elsewhere. To my sorrow, it was still there and its legs seemed to be paralysed. I took it home and left it quietly overnight in the hope that it might have recovered by morning. It hadn't. I now had another unpleasant job to do. Again my mind raced back to another event of 51 years ago, this time at a bird observatory on Skokholm Island off the coast of Pembrokeshire. Den and I and our friend, Ian Cheshire, were there for a week recording and ringing birds under the auspices of the West Wales Field Society. We had hardly been able to believe it when mum had agreed to our going because it meant we would be away from home for a week and would not be able to get to any 'meetings' on the Sunday. We couldn't thank her enough for letting us go to paradise. On our second day there, I saw an oystercatcher walking about in a strange way. I called it to the attention of Peter, the warden, who realising it was sick, picked it up and holding it carefully swung it through between his legs so its head thwacked on a rock between his feet. It was as swift and merciful as it could have been. I picked up the pheasant and, as with the rabbit, apologised for what I was about to do; I then quickly swung it over and thwacked its head on the top of the dustbin. But my thoughts lingered over that vision of the island in the west for on the day after the oystercatcher incident the boat from Dale Fort was seen approaching. This had to be something special as it only crossed the seven miles of sea once a week on a Saturday. We went down to the harbour and watched the boatman having a conversation with Peter who then came over from the boat to us and said, *"Are you the Boyt twins?"* *"Yes"* we replied, wondering what this was about. *"I am afraid I have some bad news for you"*. He drew us aside. *"Your brother has rung to say that your mother died of a stroke this morning"*. The words penetrated my brain and the world caved in around me. The waves still lapped noisily against the rocks, the gulls still called plaintively overhead, but I had entered another world that would never be the same as the one I had just left. *"You had better pack your bags,"* Peter's words were wafting over me, *"and the boatman will take you back with him as soon as you are ready"*.

Galah

We had a pleasant Australian couple stay in our self-catering cottage. Ray and Betty Cleveland from Cootamundra, NSW, (where Sir Donald Bradman was born) told me that they had two galahs *(Eolophus roseicapilla)* that they had picked up injured from beside the road. My amazement increased when I learned they had kept these big cockatoos for 19 years!

Negative ecological effect of roads

Amphibians

Frogs, toads and salamanders are all amphibians, a class of four-legged animals having moist skin without scales. Most species begin life as gilled, water-dwelling creatures, like the tadpoles we are all so familiar with, before undergoing a dramatic metamorphosis to become four-legged, air-breathing adults, walking or hopping about on land. Present-day species are the descendants of amphibia that first appeared 360 million years ago (145 million years before the first dinosaurs) they were the first vertebrates to walk on land and now they are in trouble.

For some time people have been aware both of the fearful carnage among amphibians in certain places and at certain times of the year, and of the need to take mitigating action. Toads for instance migrate every year to the pond where they were born. Roads in the vicinity of such ponds become killing grounds as slow-moving toads run the gauntlet, well, they don't run they crawl across the strip of tarmac reserved for the unseeing, unthinking vehicles whose operators are as insensible to the presence of the natural inhabitants of the place as the inanimate vehicles they control. A British amphibian welfare organisation Froglife[4] has been running a campaign, Toads on Roads, since 1989. The campaign works to ensure measures are put in place that save toads as they migrate across roads to breeding ponds in spring. It has registered 670 crossing places in the UK, some of which have dedicated volunteer Toad Patrollers who assist in helping toads cross the road on mild nights from February to April after prolonged bouts of rain. Is this something you fancy doing? Get in touch with Froglife at the above e-mail address. Toad migration takes place just after dusk which often coincides with the rush hour. While patrols can alleviate the mortality, a system whereby a low fence is erected along the roadside has been proved to be very useful. Pits are dug at intervals along the line of the fence and buckets sunk to ground level which traps toads moving along the fence whence they can be carried across by a patrol. By the way, I don't recommend eating toads. They are known to have toxins in the skin which can cause nasty reactions. Whether skinning and cooking them renders them innocuous I don't know.

In the USA, Andrew DeWoody and Dave Glista of Purdue University, Indiana, conducted a 17-month study of the problem of amphibian mortality on roads. They found 10,500 dead animals along 11 miles of roads. Of those, 7,600 were frogs of unidentifiable species and another 1,700 were bullfrogs. More than 75 per cent of the carcasses originated alongside a one-mile stretch of road that traversed a wildlife-friendly wetland, and where, along a one-kilometre (0.6-mile) section, an average of eight amphibians were killed each day. Quoted in ScienceDaily[5], Dave Glista said, *"Several steps can be taken to help reduce road-kill. For one, development planning should take into account an area's wildlife value. Second, structures to mitigate, limit and prevent road-kill should be explored whenever possible. Options include underpasses, viaducts and overpasses to allow wildlife safe passage, and special fences to keep animals off roads. We need to avoid, minimize and mitigate. As a biologist, I do think we should avoid building roads in wetlands and other wildlife-rich areas. Mitigation structures are worth the cost, as is any measure we can take to minimize our impact on the overall environment."*

The study, published in the journal, Herpetological Conservation and Biology, significantly under reported the actual numbers of animals killed because many specimens had been scavenged, degraded beyond recognition or moved; about five times more animals died than could be recorded, DeWoody

---

[4] www.froglife.org
[5] http://www.sciencedaily.com

estimated. The dead included 142 eastern tiger salamanders, a finding DeWoody said was troubling as "*most of these individuals were mature, many of them were gravid, bearing eggs on an annual trip to breeding grounds where they lay 500 to 1,000 eggs. This could make a potentially big difference for the population.*" Researchers also found 74 dead northern leopard frogs, a species of special conservation concern in Indiana. Scientists estimate that one-third of amphibian species are threatened, and hundreds of species have gone extinct in the past two decades alone. Roadkill is believed to play a significant part in this decline.

Other species of wildlife documented in the study were 79 opossums, the most common mammal; 36 chimney swifts, most common bird; 35 common garter snakes, most common reptile; 43 raccoons; and four white-tailed deer.

Marsupials - Tasmania

Come to Tasmania and see the wildlife - squashed flat and flyblown in the middle of the road.... so began a report by Libby Sutherland in the Launceston Examiner in the Spring of 2003 declaring Tasmania to be the 'Roadkill State' and a tourist turn-off. A follow-up report by Fran Voss in 2005 reported tourists expressing their horror and disgust at the high number of mutilated animal corpses they see. State Parks and Wildlife staff suggested that about one million mammals perish on Tasmanian roads each year. Remember, this is Tasmania, a living museum, a Noah's ark of marsupial (pouched) mammals, created when Australasia, as part of Gondwana, drifted away from the rest of Pangea (Laurasia) before placental mammals had evolved allowing the marsupials to become the dominant mammal infraclass. Many of the Australian mainland marsupial species were doomed when the red fox was introduced to Australia from the 1850s by wealthy settlers from Britain who wanted to carry on foxhunting in their adopted homeland. It is estimated there are now 30 million foxes on the mainland. There are a thousand hunt members in Victoria alone who, while no doubt claiming to be helping to get rid of a pest, are following in the footsteps and benefitting from their unthinking, criminal predecessors. The government of Victoria introduced a $10 bounty in 2002 and 90,000 were shot in 9 months, but that is having little effect on the 2 million foxes in the state. Unbelievably, someone introduced foxes to Tasmania in 2001. The Tasmanian Fox Free Taskforce was set up in 2001 in response to this emergency. Its scientific advisor, Nick Mooney, said, "*It's more or less eco-terrorism.*" Could it be the hunting community again? But we are getting away from roadkill. One of the key instruments in the killing of animals on the road at night in Tasmania is believed to be the number of logging lorries driving throughout the night to conceal the vastness of the vandalism going on in

Tasmanian forests and the illegal overloading of lorries. There is a website which sets out to expose the shocking cruelty to Tasmania's native wildlife. There are morning-after pictures on this website taken on just one short stretch of road that is subject to considerable nightly logging movements.

Roadkill possum with joey © Arthur Boyt

Dr Hobday is a roadkill researcher from the University of Tasmania's School of Zoology; he clocked up more than 15,000 kilometres criss-crossing Tasmania for his study. He estimates 113,000 animals are killed on Tasmanian roads each year, and that's a conservative estimate, considering the number of animals that crawl off the road to die. From similar studies in the US and Western Australia and Victoria, the density in Tasmania is higher. In Tasmania it is about one animal every three kilometres, elsewhere in Australia it's about one animal every five or six, so they're almost double in Tasmania.

He has identified 51 species killed on Tasmania's roads. Brushtail possums and red-necked pademelons are the most vulnerable. He says: *"where it does shock me, I guess, is for things like, say, a Tasmanian devil, where it may be up to one-and-a-half or two per cent of the adults are being killed each year on the roads. And I think with the situation of Tasmanian devils are under at the moment, that is a source of concern"*. Normally, roadkill is a good sign that there are healthy populations, but at Cradle Mountain in the early '90s when the road in as far as the park was made up, it caused the local extinction of eastern quolls and halved the Tasmanian devil population in 18 months.

Jays

Researchers in Florida have found that scrub jays *(Aphelocoma coerulescens)* that nest along a highway die in greater numbers than they reproduce. From 1986 to 1995, the survival and reproductive success of jays nesting along a two-lane highway were monitored. The researchers found that 15% more breeding adult jays died on roadside territories than on non-road territories (38% versus 23% per year). Moreover, on roadsides, the number of adults that died was much larger than the number of young that survived, which means that the roadside population would have decreased by nearly a third each year if new jays had not immigrated there. In contrast, in non-road territories, the number of yearlings that survived was 19% higher than the number of breeding adults that died.

The roadside death rate was particularly high for two groups. The first was breeders that had not lived along the road previously: up to half of them died during their first two years on roadside territories. Interestingly, after three years, the death rate dropped to 29%, close to that of breeders on non-road territories. The researchers speculate that the jays that survived this long either were inherently unlikely to be killed by vehicles or had learned to avoid them.

The second roadside group with a particularly high death rate was 30-90-day-old fledglings: three times as many died on road territories than on non-road territories. During this age range, young jays reaching independence fly well and are very mobile.

Florida scrub jays do not avoid roadside habitat and may even be attracted to it, they like to forage in open areas. The researchers recommend buffering Florida scrub-jay habitat from roads. "*I think the best of the politically acceptable alternatives would be, oddly enough, clearing all vegetation of the right-of-way and keeping it mowed,*" says Mumme. "*Then the jays will be able to see well and will find less food on the road.*"

According to an article written by R. Mumme, S. Schoech, G. Wolfenden and J. Fitzpatrick for the April issue of Conservation Biology which was referred to in ScienceDaily (April 19, 2000) "*Jays and cars don't mix*",

Wolverines

A 1998 report by Beuckling on research into causes of death in rare forest carnivores in British Columbia revealed that of six radio-collared wolverines *(Gulo gulo)* that died during the B.C. study (Krebs et al 1997), two were trapped, one was killed on a highway, one was killed on a railway, one died of natural causes and one remained as unknown cause of death. While the presence of roads leads to increased human access and disturbance, trapping and poaching have a greater negative impact. Nevertheless, it is recommended that, as wolverines are carrion eaters, roadkill be removed from the highway, that highway twinning at locations where wolverines may require crossing from one wilderness area to another be restricted, and crossing structures which provide adequate cover and are established at narrow points of right-of-way must be provided.

Roadkill prevention

Twin carriageway road with a barrier between them constitute a seriously hazardous crossing to wildlife. One answer is to provide an overpass crossing. In the USA, these passes have been in operation for some time and are regularly used by wildlife. They can also be used to protect rail lines. In Sweden, one overpass, aligned to roadside fences led to a 70% reduction in accidents with roe deer. In the UK a green bridge was built over the A21 at Scotney Castle in Kent. Deer, foxes, badgers, bats and even door mice have been recorded using the bridge

The best way to stop animals getting killed on the road is to stop them from getting onto the road in the first place. This involves fences to keep animals from gaining access to the road and tunnels, underpasses and bridges to enable them to cross safely. Back in the early '80s when the M25 around London was in the planning stage, I tendered evidence of the use by badgers of a path between setts on either side of the proposed line of the motorway in Hertfordshire that would benefit from a tunnel being installed to allow them to pass freely as they had done probably for centuries without the danger of their getting flattened in the process. This was adopted, the motorway fenced and a tunnel installed under the M25 between the A41 junction (J20) and the bridge leading to Berrybushes Farm. If you are not given to attacks of claustrophobia, crawling through it (as I have done) makes an interesting transit of the M25! There are other such tunnels elsewhere on the M25 and they can be identified by the fences funnelling down to the passage under the road. Look out for them next time you are driving around that great highway, but keep your distance, you don't want to end up underground yourself, do you.

The Post Office is working with The People's Trust for Endangered Species (PTES) and the Deer Initiative to raise awareness of how to avoid accidents with wild animals, and what to do in the event of a collision. Richard Pennant-Jones, Post Office Head of Motor Insurance said: "*We want to encourage UK drivers to watch out for wildlife and help reduce the number of collisions with animals and birds by being extra vigilant at key times of the year when animals are migrating and most likely to venture onto the nation's roads.*" In researching this book I came across some very worthwhile tips on driver behaviour that would, if followed, help reduce the carnage on the roads. The following article is by Merrit Clifton, editor of *Animal People* and appeared on the website Earthcaretaker.com which is created and maintained by Walter Muma who gave me permission to reproduce it here. While much of it applies only to North America it is nevertheless of great interest; I particularly like the advice on not getting shot!

Mitigation

UK

In the UK the National Deer Collision Project[6] was launched in 2003 to define the scale of the problem and its distribution, identify key factors affecting it, assess measures to reduce DVCs, find black spots, raise public awareness and how to avoid them.

The use of reflectors and mirrors has been tried, but no conclusive benefits have been recorded so far. The Deer Commission for Scotland is examining the cutting back of vegetation near black spots and the use of fences. Suffolk County Council is testing rumble strips.

In the UK there had been, until recently, no central system for recording road traffic collisions with deer and other wildlife. The National Deer Collisions Project was launched to assess the real picture. Its aims are to investigate the key factors that affect deer accident risks, undertake research into the effectiveness of various roadside defensive measures used to reduce animal roadkill and identify black spots where future preventative efforts should be targeted - as well as increasing public awareness. It has collated, via its website[7], information

---

[6] Deer vehicle collisions in Britain – a nationwide issue. J. Langbein and R. Putnam. Ecology and Environment Management In Practice. 2005, 47.

[7] www.deercollisions.co.uk

from all over the country on collisions involving deer, building a database of where and when these accidents are happening. This research is now building up an extensive database of reported incidents to provide a basis for analysing the true scale and key factors associated with the occurrence of deer-vehicle accidents.

For the large species like red and fallow deer, October is the peak of the mating season when bucks and stags tend to run blindly across the road with other things on their mind. The greatest concentration of collisions reported so far comes from around Greater London and the Home Counties in England – where heavy traffic flows coincide with large numbers of deer and a high percentage of woodland cover, followed by areas of South Central England, Thetford Chase, the Forest of Dean and Cumbria. In Scotland, numbers peak in the Highlands and Northeast. The Foundation is urging drivers involved in or witnessing, collisions with deer or those who just spot deer carcasses at the roadside to report them on the project's website[7]. Records do not have to be perfect in every detail, as long as the details of date, road number and approximate location can be given.

The RAC Foundation and the Deer Collisions Project have compiled the following safety tips to avoid accidents:

- Take note of deer warning signs, by driving with extreme caution at or below the posted speed limit. Such signs really are positioned only where deer crossing is likely.
- Peaks in deer-related traffic collisions occur October through December, followed by May. The Highest-risk periods are from sunset to midnight followed by the hours shortly before and after sunrise.
- Be aware that further deer may well cross after the ones you have noticed.
- After dark, use full beams when there is no opposing traffic. The headlight beam will illuminate the eyes of deer on or near a roadway and provide greater driver reaction time. But, when a deer or other animal is noted on the road, dim your headlights as animals startled by the beam may 'freeze' rather than leaving the road.
- Don't over-swerve - a slight swerve might be safe but overreacting with traffic coming in the other direction or a ditch to the left could be fatal.
- Only brake sharply and stop if there is no danger of being hit by following traffic. Try to come to a stop as far in front of the animals as possible to enable them to leave the roadside without panic.
- Report any deer-vehicle collisions to the police (who should be able to

contact the local person best placed to assist with an injured deer at the roadside)

- Slow down for wildlife.

I should add to that: The moment you see any animal on or near the road, take your foot off the accelerator and prepare to brake.

Inside Out, the TV programme that examines newsworthy stories in the South West did a report on the deer problem in 2004 in which the issue of Britain's growing deer population was discussed and the steps being taken to combat it. The work of the Deer Collision Project is reviewed and how Dorset Police have put together a Deer Dispatch Unit, with 50 trained volunteers who can respond quickly and be at the roadside to assist motorists and injured deer after a collision.

Animal crossing warning sign © Arthur Boyt

North America

In North America, a great deal of research has been carried out and measures put into effect to mitigate roadkill. A comprehensive report issued in 2002[8] reviews, examines and assesses the work done on the mitigation of roadkill on a global scale.

---

[8] "Interaction between roadways and wildlife ecology, a synthesis of highway practice". Transportation Research Board – The National Academies, (www.trb.org)

This report (parts of which are quoted below) studies the effect of roads on the environment and the measures taken to mitigate the effect on wildlife. The Endangered Species Act of 1973 is one law that must be considered by states. Any species that is in danger of becoming extinct throughout all or a significant portion of its range is considered endangered and qualifies for a listing. Roads can become the final nail in the coffin of some species. It is the Federal Highway Administration's policy that states must provide evidence of compliance with the 1969 National Environmental Policy Act's environmental protection requirements.

Currently, some of the best information on deer collisions in the US is being assembled by the Deer Vehicle Collision Reduction Working Group[9], which is soliciting data on vehicle-related deer kill from the states. The site is primarily recording information on the midwestern states, but it has the potential to become a national clearinghouse for mortality information.

Databases such as WARS 2000 - Wildlife Accident Reporting System and the Washington State Department of Transport deer kill database are being developed by transportation agencies to:

(1) identify accident hotspots and trends,
(2) direct mitigation efforts,
(3) evaluate the effectiveness of mitigation techniques,
(4) provide data for highway planning purposes,
(5) model and forecast wildlife accidents, and
(6) establish policies and strategies for wildlife accident issues.

The following is a review of structural and engineering features that prevent and reduce roadkill.[10]

Fencing

Fencing is a common practice used throughout the world to keep animals off highways. Twenty-eight of the states responding use fencing to protect wildlife. California reported an interesting fencing application in areas with kit fox and coyotes. They provide a gap under the fence just large enough for the kit fox to negotiate at full run so that they can escape predators such as the coyote. One-way doors are installed to allow deer trapped between the fences to escape. Fencing is commonly used in Europe to keep smaller animals off highways.

[9] http://www.deercrash.com
[10] Transportation Research Board – The National Academies, Synthesis 305, National Cooperative Highway Research Program, Washington, 2002 (www.trb.org)

Drainage and stream culverts,

The Netherlands is a leader in modifying extant drainage culverts to accommodate wildlife. Several US states are using culverts for reptiles, amphibians and turtles. The use of the natural stream bottom rather than a concrete or metal bottom is best. By providing shallow water or dry edges alongside the stream, the greatest number of species can move through these structures. Given sufficient height, these culverts can even allow larger mammals, such as deer, bears, and other species that ordinarily follow riparian corridors for movement, to pass safely under roads. It was recommended that drainage culverts of varying sizes should be placed every 150–300m close to shrub or tree cover.

Underpasses, bridges and dry culverts

Many states are also using culverts of varying sizes in uplands areas where they have proven successful in accommodating a wide variety of species

Extended bridges

One of the most successful and cost-effective means of providing for wildlife movement down riparian corridors is a bridge longer than is needed to just cross a river.

Viaducts

Viaducts over wetlands, rivers, and variable topography and geology are a potential solution for the entire spectrum of species moving through an area.

Wildlife overpasses

Wildlife overpasses are used extensively in Europe and vary in width from 3.4 m to 870 m. Florida, Hawaii, New Jersey, and Utah reported overpasses being used by wildlife. The New Jersey overpasses were completed in 1985 at a cost of $12 million. Research on overpasses in Germany, the Netherlands, France, and Switzerland found that the overpasses were effective for a wide variety of animals including invertebrates. Overpasses at least 60 m wide were found to be more effective than those narrower than 50 m, especially for larger mammals.

Other measures for wildlife

Signage is a common approach to informing motorists when they are entering an area where the danger of wildlife collision is high. The Swiss have very successfully reduced deer mortality using a series of solar-powered, battery-operated, motion sensors to determine animal presence that triggers low-voltage, LED-illuminated warning signs that reduce the posted speed limit to 40 km/h and alert motorists to the presence of wildlife. One system developed by Sensor Technologies and Systems (STS) in Scottsdale, Arizona, uses transmitters and microwave radio signals along a one-mile stretch of highway 191 in Yellowstone National Park. It works by causing flashing beacons to illuminate when a large animal breaks a beam and so warn motorists that they could encounter wildlife. It costs $31,000 per year. On highway 260 in Arizona fences will funnel deer to a crossing area protected by sensors.

Florida

As reported by David Havlick[11] a computer-based model, that identified ecological hotspots (sections of road where high-quality habitat, vehicles, and vulnerable species intersect) and integrated its use into statewide transportation planning, has been developed at the University of Florida where Daniel Smith and his colleagues in the Department of Wildlife Ecology and Conservation have been working in collaboration with the Florida Department of Transportation (DOT). It could bring species such as the Florida panther (*Puma concolor coryi*), the American crocodile (*Crocodylus acutus*) and the Florida Key deer (*Odocoileus virginianus clavium*) back from the brink of extinction. Smith's team found that:

"Some stretches of road are simply more important—and more deadly—than others. From 1976-1999, four of every five black bears killed on Florida highways died on just five roads. The question is why? Higher vehicle speeds, heavier traffic, and wider roads definitely make crossings more treacherous. But another critical factor is where human highways cross wildlife highways. More often than not, roadkill peaks where wildlife corridors such as riparian zones or strips of forest intersect with roads.

"And that's where Smith's model comes in. He gathered data on chronic roadkill sites, wildlife movement corridors, and eight other key factors and plugged them into a computer to reveal ecological hotspots. Smith then took his

---

[11] Conservation in Practice, 2004, 5 (1) and available online at http://www.conservationmagazine.org/articles/v5n1/road-kill/

results into the field to look at 1,400 sites first-hand to make sure that the streams or forests or roads matched the descriptions that came out of his model. They did. Not only that, but when Smith checked out 290 of these hotspots in-depth, monitoring wildlife movements, tracks, and other signs of activity for a period of two years, he found that animals were actually using the areas much like his model had predicted.

"In response, Florida transportation officials are now installing underpasses at dozens of these locations so that everything from black bears and panthers to tree frogs and turtles can make safer crossings. In Wekiva State Park, on either side of a new underpass, a barrier fence extends to block highway crossings and channel wildlife to a safer tunnel. Hidden cameras at the site show that bears not only use the new structure, they seem to remember it. When the fence first went up, bears snuffled along its edge looking for a gap. Now, they tend to make a beeline for the underpass.

"On Big Pine Key, highway traffic was the number one killer of the endangered Florida Key deer. Two Winnebago-sized culverts (i.e. big as a motor home) and an eight-foot-high barrier fence now usher deer beneath the highway without their needing to dodge cars en route. Scientists had also identified vehicle collisions as the leading cause of death for the rare Florida panther throughout the 1980s whose population had dwindled to 30–50 animals. Twenty-three wildlife crossings, 36.6 m (120 ft) wide and 2.4 m (8 ft) high and 13 bridge extensions, 12.2 m (40 ft) extension over dry land were constructed on interstate highway I-75, known as Alligator Alley. 64.4 km (40 mi) in the area of the crossings was fenced with 3 m (10-ft) chain-link fence with an outrigger with three strands of barbed wire. No Florida panthers or black bears have been killed on Alligator Alley in the project area since completion of the Interstate."

With the purchase of land at hotspots where crossings have been constructed, corridors of safety are being provided to allow the safe movement of animals throughout the region and reduce the hazard created by the roads. Smith shows how animals use or avoid road sections, newly installed culverts, fences, and corridors beneath bridges. In 2001, The Los Angeles Times reported that more than 300 wildlife corridors had been identified as vital to California's wildlife populations.

Canada

Roads through national parks are particularly hazardous for big mammal/motor vehicle encounters. Moose and elk are big and heavy; they can wreck vehicles as well as kill the occupants. When I cycled the 200 miles through Jasper and Banff National Parks on the Icefields Parkway and Trans Canada Highway on a ride from Prince Rupert in British Columbia to Calgary, I saw no roadkill, only the occasional tell-tale bloodstains where something big had been killed and then cleared up by park staff. I have also driven through the parks and whenever moose or bear were about many drivers stopped to take photos. But accidents do happen and Lawrence Herzog, in an article "*Road kill: cars and animals don't mix*" published on the web, records that in Jasper National Park alone, an average of 125 ungulates, hoofed animals such as deer and moose, and five carnivores such as black bears are killed annually in motor vehicle collisions. In fact, in Alberta's four contiguous mountain national parks, Jasper, Banff, Yoho and Kootenay, this is the leading cause of mortality for large animals, culminating in an annual average roadkill count of 270 with perhaps another 70 animals later dying of their injuries. Of course, collisions with wildlife are also dangerous for the motorists and passengers involved. On Alberta roads in 2002, nine people died and 442 were injured in 11,449 collisions involving animals, with resulting insurance claims exceeding $11.1 million. But the Canadian authorities are not prepared to just sit back and do nothing about it, Herzog takes up the story:

"To help battle the sobering reality that wildlife and automobiles just don't mix, the Alberta government and Parks Canada have implemented various strategies over the last several years, including roadside reflectors, reduction of roadside shrubbery, wildlife habitat manipulation, reduced speed limits, and extensive fencing and wildlife crossing structures. For various reasons, most of these measures have failed to make a difference. Take speeding. Surveys show that 75 per cent of the vehicles passing through Jasper National Park are exceeding posted speed limits, particularly in 70 km/hr zones where wildlife is prevalent.

"One collision-prevention strategy, however, has been a success along the twinned [dual carriageway] *parts of the Trans-Canada Highway through Banff National Park, where peak summer traffic reaches 24,000 vehicles per day. Since 1982, 22 wildlife underpasses and two overpasses have been built along this stretch of highway, along with kilometres of 2.4-metre-high fencing. . Parks Canada constructed a combination of pipe culverts, box culverts, and open-span bridges of varying size and design. The two overpasses built for this section are approximately 50 m (164 ft) wide.*

"Since monitoring began in 1996, more than 50,000 large mammals have used the two dozen crossing structures in the Trans-Canada Highway Twinning

Mitigation Project. These include moose, elk, deer, sheep, grizzly and black bears, wolves, coyotes, cougars and wolverine. Overpasses were used in preference to underpasses and use of the crossings has increased with time. Between 1997 and 2002, a total of 237 animals were reported killed on the Trans-Canada Highway in Banff, Yoho, and Kootenay national parks; 143 were ungulates and 94 were carnivores. Carnivore mortalities consisted of coyotes, black bears, wolves and cougars. A review of road mortality data of large carnivores in Banff National Park from 1981 to 2002 showed that 48 large carnivores (black bear, wolf, cougar, and wolverine) were killed; mortality was highest on unmitigated, unfenced Trans-Canada Highway." And even though vehicle traffic continues to increase along the highway, animal-related collisions and fatalities have dropped by about 80 per cent.

Overpasses have proven to be very effective for the entire ecological community from plants to insects to wildlife. Research done in Europe indicates that overpasses are warranted on ecologically sensitive corridors on public lands as the most complete answer for connectivity.

Herzog goes on to say *"It is hoped that the most recent wildlife collision preventative initiative in Alberta's national parks will be equally successful. The Parks Canada-led 'Drivers for Wildlife' program is designed to boost motorist awareness of animal hazards, using direct-marketing techniques. These include larger-than-life photographic decals of different wildlife species now being posted at high-risk sites on Alberta's park roads.*

"Some of the newest technology also looks promising in terms of reducing on-the-road wildlife carnage. Recently, the Insurance Bureau of B.C. (ICBC) began testing an infrared camera and computer system that warns motorists when an animal is on the road ahead, the same way existing flashing signs warn of ice or snow. The system, designed by Edmonton's InTransTech, Inc., uses a heat-seeking camera similar to those developed by NASA to detect incoming missiles. The 'camera' detects animals up to two kilometres away, and then relays that information to a computer which interprets what kind of animal it is and flashes an appropriate driving speed limit on the highway's warning signs.

"Meanwhile, Saskatoon-based International Road Dynamics has developed a wildlife warning system that scares animals away from highways with lights and horns. The alarms, which are triggered by approaching vehicles, use alternating sounds to prevent animals from becoming too easily accustomed to them. The system is now being tested as part of a pilot project financed by the

Saskatchewan government.

"The Alberta Motor Association believes wildlife crossings have proven their worth and should be used wherever possible in areas of high wildlife traffic, such as the national parks. 'We're watching the infrared camera projects closely, since results so far are very promising,' says Scott Wilson, AMA's policy development and promotion manager.

"The effort to make roads less deadly goes beyond underpasses, road fencing, or similar attempts to modify wildlife behavior. On a scenic and road kill-prone stretch of highway in the northwest corner of Yellowstone National Park, Marcel Huijser from the Western Transportation Institute is experimenting with active detection systems that shoot a beam of high-frequency radio waves along roadsides. When a large animal such as an elk, bear, or bison breaks the beam, the system activates flashing lights and audio signals to alert motorists that an animal may be crossing the road in front of them. This approach allows animals to move across roads freely, rather than limiting them to isolated crossing points such as underpasses. But it also means that wildlife and motorists must share the road, which is what causes roadkill in the first place."

Another not so high-tech wildlife warning system is the so-called wildlife whistle. Mounted on a vehicle's hood, the whistle emits a high-pitched sound when air passes through it that is inaudible to the human ear. The whistles were mounted on ten warden patrol vehicles in Jasper National Park a decade ago, but Bradford *says "they have been found to be effective only on coyotes, due to that animal's exceptionally acute hearing. Other species in the park seem to ignore them, but he ventures that could be because they are used to people and aren't hunted".*

Deer Whistle

In an article by Janice Palmer on the website[12]; she records that: *"On the highways and byways across North America, nearly 750,000 collisions occur each year between deer and vehicles. Efforts to reduce that number have spun off a multi-million-dollar industry: deer whistles."* The testing of air-fed whistles was carried out by Peter Scheifele, director of bioacoustics research at the National Undersea Research Center, *"All in all, the air-fed whistles do not make sense to me acoustically,"* states Scheifele. Since completing the study, a new electronic whistle has been put on the market. Although Scheifele has not

---

[12] http://advance.uconn.edu/2002/021118/02111812.htm

had an opportunity to test it, he has examined its advertising claims. He says, *"the specs for the electronic whistle are considerably different from those of the air-fed devices, so there is a possibility that the electronic whistle is more effective than the air-fed devices."*

A chap reported in a blog that he had obtained wind-powered plastic deer whistles to scare deer from crossing. At first they seemed to work, then he found that deer seemed to head his way as he drove by and even run alongside him. He went to the shop where he bought it to complain. The shop keeper went to his car and knelt down to examine the whistle. He fell about laughing and took him into the store and showed him a new one, which had a label 'American Elk Mating Whistle'

Italy

In the forests of Italy's Abruzzo National Park live one of the rarest creatures on Earth: the Marsican brown bear *(Ursus arctos arctos,* formerly *Ursus arctos marsicanus)* a subspecies of the European brown bear. For the last several decades the species has been on the brink of extinction, with current estimates putting their population at less than 50 individuals, down from over 100 in the early 1980s. Efforts are underway to preserve them from poison intended for other animals and illegal hunting, to human development and vehicle strikes. Most, if not all, are thought to be living under protection in Abruzzo National Park, but that fact alone hasn't managed to curb their decline. Park administrator Giuseppe Rossi told *The Christian Science Monitor*[13] that she believes the animal's numbers are 'below the threshold of survival.' To add weight to this hypothesis one was found dead in May, presumably having been struck by a car.

Netherlands

In the article published in <u>Conservation in Practice, Winter 2004 (Vol 5 no.1)</u>, David Havlick reported that Smith and his colleagues in Florida were not alone in their thinking. On a nationwide scale, the Netherlands is at the forefront of efforts to integrate transportation and ecological networks. Dutch planners can compare maps of the nation's road system and ecological networks such as large areas of vegetation, wildlife corridors, and wetlands. Where they show a bottleneck, roads intercepting key flows of water or wildlife, for example, they can change road designs, add culverts, or modify vegetation.

---

[13] http://www.csmonitor.com/World/Global-News/2011/0503/Italy-s-largest-animal-is-on-the-brink-of-extinction

Japan

In an article (Experimental study on the Mitigation of Ezo Deer Roadkill Accidents) reported in Conservation magazine and on the website[14]: "*While fences were effective at excluding deer from the road, the deer were able to enter the deer exclusion zone around the end of the fence and get between the fences. The experiments showed how installing the One Way Gate where the deer exclusion fence was shaped into a short V-lead, instead of installing it in line with the fence, enabled panicking deer to more easily find the gate to escape; and the Deer Guard (Texas Gate) for where footpaths cross the fence if longer than 3m, significantly decreased the number of deer intruding on roads.*"

Ireland

Quoting from a paper[15] in the proceeding of an American conference we find that: "*the number of crossing structures for wildlife on the Irish National road network has increased markedly within the last few years. The structures are targeted at protected species whose habitat is directly disturbed by road construction. These are otters (Lutra lutra) and badgers (Meles meles). However, structures have been put in place for red squirrels (Sciurus vulgaris); i.e., rope ladders linking trees on opposite sides of a motorway and the first structures for pine martens (Martes martes) and bats. Underpasses and overpasses (potential green bridges) have been constructed where farms have been bisected by new road schemes. These structures allow for the safe passage of domestic cattle, but may also be utilized by wildlife, e.g. red deer (Cervus elaphus) and other smaller wildlife species. Non-target native species which can utilise these structures are: red deer (Cervus elaphus), the indigenous Irish hare (Lepus timidus hibernicus), Irish stoat (Mustela erminea hibernica), fox (Vulpes vulpes), pygmy shrew (Sorex minutus) and field or wood mouse (Apodemus sylvaticus). Non-native species which could potentially utilize such structures include: Sika deer (Cervus nippon), fallow deer (Cervus dama), brown hare (Lepus europaeus), rabbit (Oryctolagus cuniculus), grey squirrel (Sciurus carolinensis), hedgehog (Erinaceus europaeus), brown rat (Rattus norvegicus), house mouse (Mus (musculus) domesticus), bank vole (Clethrionomys glareolus), feral ferret (Mustela furo), American mink (Mustela vison), and*

---

[14] https://ur.booksc.eu/book/69310088/268987
[15] http://repositories.cdlib.org/jmie/roadeco/Dolan2005a/ Lisa Dolan , Ecology and Plant Science, University College, Cork, Ireland Dolan L. 2006. Monitoring of wildlife crossing structures on Irish national road schemes. IN: Proceedings of the 2005 International Conference on Ecology and Transportation, Eds. Irwin CL, Garrett P, McDermott KP. Center for Transportation and the Environment, North Carolina State University, Raleigh, NC: p. 608.

domestic cats and dogs, amongst other introduced species. This is the first study to examine the effectiveness of crossing structures in Ireland. An initial pilot study monitoring the use of crossing structures in County Cork revealed encouraging results as mammal ledges in oversized arched culverts were used by: otter, fox, rabbit, pygmy shrew and wood mouse. The pilot study was expanded to monitor crossing structures on a national scale in order to examine: how much are they used by target and non-target species, whether a 600mm or 900mm pipe is preferred, and whether the presence of hedgerow planting enhance use of passage structures?"

Poland

Poland becoming a member of the EU required the preparation of environmental assessment studies both before and after road construction projects. Animal movements have become a controlling factor in decision making relative to new road construction and improvement of old roads. The rising collision risk and the 40 collisions in one month in 2003 on a 160km stretch of highway stirred society to initiate studies of animal movement patterns throughout the country. Besides large species that can cause the death of the driver when colliding with a car (such as elk, deer, and wild boar), several smaller animals (such as fox, badger, amphibians or reptiles) with vulnerable populations in the surveyed area were also studied, and the building of passages and bridges for wildlife became not only an obligation but also a necessity. Since 1997 ten underpasses and one overpass were built for large mammals. Unfortunately, many of the target species did not use the bridges due to their being too narrow, unscreened, with lack of vegetation and guiding structures to the crossings, and lack of fencing. Mitigation measures were improved and maintained better. For small mammals, amphibians, and reptiles, nine underpasses were built in 2004. The follow-up monitoring of these structures showed that the effectiveness of the tunnels with guiding structures was nearly 100 per cent for amphibians and reptiles and 85 per cent for small mammals.[16]

---

[16] Wildlife tunnels and fauna bridges in Poland: past, present and future, 1997-2013 Jadwiga Brodziewska, Towarzystwo Badan Ochrony Przyrody (The Wildlife Research and Conservation Society) Brodziewska J. 2006. Wildlife tunnels and fauna bridges in Poland: past, present and future, 1997-2013. IN: Proceedings of the 2005 International Conference on Ecology and Transportation, Eds. Irwin CL, Garrett P, McDermott KP. Center for Transportation and the Environment, North Carolina State University, Raleigh, NC: pp. 448-460.

Caribbean

On the island of Providencia (off Nicaragua) they close the roads; guards stopping people from driving when the black crabs are migrating down to the sea (mopeds do crabswerves to miss them) and again when the 1000s of young are migrating back up into the hills.

Tasmania

The Tasmanian Wildlife Roadkill Collective was set up in 2000 to look at ways of reducing the toll on native wildlife. In July 2006 it published its findings in a truly landmark document entitled: *Wildlife Roadkill Mitigation Information Kit. A guide for local government and land managers.*[17] The document covers 36 pages and can be seen on the website.

Roadkill in education

There have not been many studies conducted to measure the number of animals killed on the road over a long period. The RoadKill project[18] is designed to involve students and teachers with scientific monitoring of roadkill using the Internet and to increase participant awareness of the hazards to wildlife. Monitoring roadkill brings excitement and stimulating conversation to all. High school science teacher Brewster Bartlett (his students coined the nickname Dr. Splatt) has had students participate in roadkill censuses in March and April since 1993 beginning in New Hampshire and now extending to many other states. The unmotivated student becomes extremely interested in a gruesome subject. Students soon realize that there are many animals killed or injured by motor vehicles. Roadkills vary depending on the population of the community, the amount of traffic, and the type of roads. Migratory patterns of animals and habitat of the local area will also affect the number of roadkills, and they estimate that 250,000 animals become traffic victims every day.

"Students involved in the RoadKill Project adopt a road and keep track of the dead. From the smallest frog to stray dogs and deer, students dutifully record, but don't touch, what they see. Even the squishiest blob is recorded as an URP: unidentified road pizza. The students pose theories about their findings: Does the full moon bring out more animals? Are more animals killed on roads with higher speed limits? Is there more roadkill during the daylight-saving time because people are driving in the dark?

---

[17] http://www.davidpublisher.com/Public/uploads/Contribute/551109533b762.pdf
[18] http://roadkill.edutel.com/rkprotocol.html

"Daylight-saving had no effect on the roadkill count", Bartlett said, *"but the students did count more dead animals during the new moon than the full moon, perhaps because the animals were more freely under the cover of darkness. Roads posted at 35 mph have more creature carnage than highways because the slower roads are often winding and travel through rural or suburban areas."*

"A student in Florida found that there was more roadkill in places where people threw food out of the car", Bartlett said. *"Animals would scurry out to eat the leftovers and get run over, and then predators would rush to eat the roadkill, and also get hit."*

"The number of raccoon road fatalities plummeted in Massachusetts during the spread of the rabies virus in the mid-1990s. And leash laws throughout New Hampshire dropped the number of dead dogs to zero", Bartlett said. *"Meanwhile, more wild turkeys are being sighted, and smashed, because their population has come back, thanks to restoration efforts by the National Wild Turkey Federation"*. *"I've been doing this for many years, and it's interesting because it changes every year,"* he said.

"But some things never change. Skunks come out of hibernation in early spring, sluggish and hungry, and get run over. In March, squirrels and raccoons emerge hunting for food, and end up under tires. In April, the snakes, the turtles and frogs are out and about and become the victims of passing vehicles. Young beavers pushed out of their family lodge by the adults in March and April wander out looking for a new home and meet their end on a busy road. Robins chase each other during the mating season in the spring and don't notice they're flying into traffic. The slow-reproducing turtles doggedly make their way across roads, and their deaths mean the end of generations of turtles. The most noticeable roadkill are deer, which appear in spring and fall, at first hungry for food and later, for love. Without predators in congested little Rhode Island, the deer have flourished, doubling their numbers to an estimated 16,000 over the last decade. Hunters take 2,000 deer a year, but there are still so many that deer account for more than 1,200 vehicle collisions annually, even in the cities, said supervising wildlife biologist Lori Gibson.

"Deer are the only roadkill that motorists can take home with them, under state law. But people still try to scoop up the bloody remains of other animals they find on the road; 'finders keepers' will get you a fine."

But I ask *"Whatever for?"* What is so terrible about someone picking up a dead rabbit, mink or fox? If you can pick up deer, why on earth prohibit something else. With this kind of law, America is no longer the 'land of the free' but the land of the nanny state. It reminds me of the time I kayaked 50 miles around the Isle of Wight in a day. I stopped to rest before crossing back to Gosport, when a family arrived at the beach, the children jumped off the promenade and started throwing stones into the sea. Their parents arrived and shouted at them to come back and smacked their legs for being so adventurous. Silly leg-smacking nanny state!

School

My twin and I, having both passed the 11+ examination, attended Watford Grammar School for Boys, which is still a very successful grammar school despite the exterminating attentions of Tony Crossland, Socialist Education Minister and ex-public schoolboy who vowed he would close "*every f*****g grammar school*". Not very nice language from the grandson of a one-time leader of the Exclusive Brethren, and to think that my mother used to push him out in his pram and his cousin married my mum's older sister! Anyway, cycling to school one morning, I picked up a small hedgehog, thinking that it might interest some of my chums. During lunch break, I was showing it around in our classroom, which was the Geography Lecture Room and was the home of VIth Science C and VIth Science D, the two 'A' level years studying biology and chemistry. The lecture room was arranged with tiers of desks rising towards the back so that all could see the teacher and projection screen clearly. There was a strange black enclosure in the front right-hand corner of the room, which housed a defunct back-projection system. There was a large globe on the master's table. The door was on the front left-hand corner of the room. In the centre of the ceiling, there was a powerful extract fan, which was on. The hedgehog was not attracting enough attention, so it began to be tossed around the room at unsuspecting heads. Before long, my brother noticed the fan and threw the little beast at it. His accuracy was rewarded with the prickly animal being transformed into a misguided missile that whizzed round and shot down onto an unsuspecting group of boys. The roomful of boys quickly became a strange scenario. Everyone was gazing up at the ceiling and ducking and dodging every time the hedgehog was caught in the blades of the fan and flung down at random onto the boys below. It was inadvisable and possibly painful to not pay close attention to the hedgehog distributor in the ceiling. As few boys wanted to handle the prickles, it was mainly Dennis and I who were chucking it up into the fan. A guard was set up at the door to warn of the approach of staff or prefects. Suddenly the fan jammed causing it to whine alarmingly until someone dashed to the switch and turned it off. A window pole was fetched and after a bit of prodding the beast fell down onto a desk below. On the next throw, the hedgehog went right through the fan into the void beyond and there it remains, quite possibly until this day.

While talking of animals at school, I once took to school a weasel that I had removed from a gamekeeper's gibbet on the Westwood estate near Chipperfield. There were also a lot of tawny owls hanging from that gibbet. They had been trapped by a nearby pole trap, a circular gin chained to the top of a pole, which caught the owls by their legs. Birds trapped in this way hang and flutter upside down until the gamekeeper comes and despatches them or until they die a slow and agonizing death. Such traps had been banned in 1904, but have been and still are being used. (A gamekeeper in Norfolk was fined £1500 in January 1996 for setting such traps). When I reported this to the police back in 1953, they merely warned me that I might get prosecuted for trespass. So we went back, removed the illegal traps and added them to our museum. Such is the arrogance of the shooting industry that not only did they not feel obliged to obey the laws against killing predators, but they flaunted their disregard of the law by hanging their illegally taken kills on a gibbet. They were confident that neither their employer nor his guests or clients shooting those woods would report them for breaking the law. I believe that the disregard of the law on shooting estates is so widespread that the law should empower responsible persons to inspect all private land where shooting is carried on and they should be allowed to attend any shoot as an observer. If the shooting fraternity have nothing to hide they should concur with this provision. But again I digress. The weasel is a member of the *Mustelidae*, one feature of which is the possession of scent glands at the base of the tail. The weasel that I kept in my desk that day had an interesting aroma about it that was new and strange to the boys of Remove Lower B. It got passed around between lessons for anyone who dared to have a tentative sniff and declare it disgusting. I am sure the teachers were nonplussed when every time I was asked a question the cry would go up, "*Git yer weasel!*"

I regret to say that on another occasion involving a member of the weasel family, I endeavoured to discomfort a teacher and was myself discomforted. It was in the summer of 1956 and happened in the following way. I found a polecat-ferret (a ferret is a domesticated descendant of an albino polecat (*Mustela putorius*) and a polecat-ferret is a descendant of an escaped ferret that has reverted in the wild to something like the normal colouration), I found it floating dead in the canal. It was not roadkill; it had been shot. While skinning it with a view to stuffing it, I came across the rather potent scent glands located at the base of the tail. I realised that here was the very source of the expression, 'stinks like a polecat'. The opportunity could not be missed. I excised the scent glands carefully and, putting them in an empty medicine phial, I took them to school. They gave off a pretty niffy aroma of a musky nature. A tentative sniff at the phial resulted in immediate involuntary retching by almost all who tried it. The effect on my classmates was so good that I got carried away and, feeling that this unique opportunity should be exploited to the full, I smeared them liberally along the edge of the master's desk during the short interval between periods when we were waiting for the arrival of the French master. The real secretion of the glands was now for the first time released into the room. The effect astonished even me. Co-operative members of the class closed the windows to concentrate the smell for the master's enjoyment. The effect was to cause gagging and choking among the more sensitive children. The atmosphere was equally charged with the expectancy of an imminent and now unavoidable event of which they would be the immediate witnesses. I hurried back to my desk in the corner at the back, revelling in the spotlight of attention, but inwardly trembling that I had gone too far, the consequences of which I had not yet contemplated. I did not risk putting the incriminating phial in my desk but hid it on the dado rail behind the heating pipe in the corner of the room at the back next to my desk. The master due for the next lesson, who was to be the recipient of this olfactory reception, was our French master, H.E.Powell-Evans. A possible reason for his selection was that he used to have the nickname 'Polecat', but this had of recent years been replaced with the much friendlier 'Brumas'. (Brumas was the first polar bear cub in London Zoo [1949] and the first polar bear cub to be born in captivity). The classroom of Remove Upper B (O-level year) opened onto the back of the school hall. The boy on watch who could see the staff room door called out, "*He's coming*", and an unusual hush fell on the class. The door opened and Brumas entered. His face wrinkled and his mouth closed as if shutting out some unwholesome toxin. "*What's this smell?*" he demanded. "*What smell?*" innocently queried a few voices. "*Open the windows at once*", he ordered. "*Who is responsible for this?*" he demanded, obviously rattled at the complicity of the class. No one offered any suggestions. He ordered us to get on with some work and, after a minute or two, advanced slowly down the gangway in my direction. I kept my nerve and gave the appearance of diligently getting on with the translation he had set us. He reached the back of the class, turned around and stood beside me surveying the class from behind. With contrived nonchalance, I got on with my work. I heard a soft rustle from his tweed jacket and the eyes in the back of my head told me he was reaching behind me, he had found the phial, he was unscrewing it, he put it to his nose and, involuntarily jerking his head away, exclaimed, "*Is this your's Boy?*" "*Er, yes Sir.*" He said no more. The lesson continued without further reference to the matter.

For the class, the highly explosive incident had gone off like a damp squib, for me it had only just begun. Brumas left the room at the end of the lesson without saying anything. I leapt up and desperately mopped at the master's desk with my handkerchief, spitting on it and rubbing in an attempt to minimise the effects for any other staff visits. The door to the hall was left open to clear the air, which resulted in the hall also filling with the musky aroma. The headmaster was away and the second master was acting head, his name was Mr Lister, known to generations of boys as Fanny (he had been in the RAF in the war and treated school as if he were still on parade). To him, punishment should be swift, humiliating and savage. The sound of a plimsoll being vigorously applied to the buttocks of a bent-over boy would almost certainly indicate his whereabouts in the school. He was all for doing the same to me there and then. Alerted by P-E and enraged by the smell which now pervaded the whole school, he came marching into the class. *"Boyt"*, he barked, *"Where did this smell come from?"*, his little ginger moustache adding bristles to his question. *"It's the glands of an animal I found and I, er, opened the pot to let someone smell it"*, I offered hesitantly. I had admitted enough. No further questions were necessary. However, my form master, Mr Openshaw, was the person whose right and pleasure it was to discipline me. The second master knew quite well that Oppy would regard it as his prerogative. He was also aware that Oppy enjoyed disciplining boys. He could get quite nasty if he were robbed of that pleasure just because he happened to be away on the day of the offence. Fanny Lister could only fume and bluster, but for the moment I was safe, whatever might follow in the days to come.

Perhaps I should here say something about my form master. Mr Openshaw had more than one nickname. He was generally known as Oppy, but his real or imagined proclivities were reflected in the names Uncle and Shiner, and some I shall not mention. He was the cricket master and was in charge of the school's sports equipment, which was kept in a small room in the Pavilion, an old building which had been the clubhouse to the West Herts Golf Club before the Grand Union Canal was dug between it and the links. This room was known as the Inner Sanctum where, it was darkly hinted, only innocent and unfortunate boys allowed themselves to be trapped alone with Shiner. It was in this room, not the classroom, that Oppy had made an appointment for me to meet him there after school on the following Thursday when he would deal with me for my behaviour while he had been away.

I arrived in some trepidation at the appointed hour and was drawn in among the cricket pads, bats, stumps and other paraphernalia. The door closed ominously behind me. I could see Oppy was highly animated in anticipation of the duty that lay before him. I felt like a sacrificial lamb. I knew there was nothing to be said in mitigation of my actions, though I doubt the extent of my endeavours to make the classroom uncomfortable had been realised by the staff; if they had, I cannot imagine what my punishment would have entailed. I knew no argument or reasoning would alter the outcome. I endeavoured to maintain a penitent mien; I deserved some kind of punishment and I would try and take it like a man. It never entered my head to sniffle or blub to mollify what the master felt he ought to administer. I guessed I was going to get the whack in some form or other. I knew no one who had been selected for this type of tutorial who could advise me where and how it was administered. My only anxiety was that I had to keep a stiff upper lip whatever the severity of the treatment might be. I resolved to control my emotions. Oppy's rasping voice was telling me off, but I doubt whether what he said penetrated my brain; it has not penetrated my memory. His lined and haggard face was peuce with animation and his long red hands trembled uncontrollably. Unlike my mother about to administer punishment who used to say, "*This is going to hurt me more than it hurts you*", it was evident to me that this was going to be as great a pleasure to him as it was going to be painful to me. The cold hard rasping voice ordered me to let down my trousers. He groped in an umbrella stand full of cricket stumps and extracted a long thin cane. "*Bend over Boyt*", it was an expression quoted many times by my elder brother, John, who heard it when receiving a more conventional beating from the hands of the then headmaster, Percy Bolton. I felt it was in the family tradition to have it said to me. I bent over. His clumsy fumbling hands pulled down my underpants and lifted the tail of my shirt. He stood back. I heard a movement behind me…. a short whistle…. Whack…. an explosion of pain in my backside …. WHACK …. another explosion of pain…. I was keeping count…. **WHACK!**… Was that it? "*You may stand up now*". I stood up and quickly got my trousers up and secured my belt. Thank goodness it was over, I had survived. Then I felt what I had been warned to expect: Oppy's shaking hand began to gently rub the place he had just been beating. That was why he was called Shiner. More admonition followed which again left no lasting memory and I was allowed to escape. I examined the damage in the wardrobe mirror when I went to bed – there were not three weals, there were five. How did that come about? It was painful to sit down for a day or so, but then a deep-seated ache appeared and I became lame and could not run. This prevented me from competing for the school in an athletics match on the Saturday. Whether it was just a bad bruise or a haematoma I know not; I certainly did not think of seeing a doctor about it. I did not let on to my mother what had happened either. Had I done so, I should probably have been given a further punishment.

Foot and mouth disease

Let me ask an odd question or two: Is it possible for roadkill to benefit society other than by being eaten? Or to help in the war on an epidemic? Or to get the government off the hook? The answer is, Yes. This needs an explanation and to do so I shall need to start at the beginning of what is a bit of a long story, the foot and mouth outbreak in Britain in 2001.

On the 19th of February 2001, 27 pigs suffering from foot and mouth disease (FMD) were identified during a routine inspection of Cheale Meats abattoir in Brentwood, Essex. The pigs had come from Burnside Farm at Heddon-on-the-Wall in Northumberland owned by the Waugh brothers. When this farm was investigated on the 23rd of February over 400 pigs were found to be infected and had been for some time. These pigs had been fed pigswill containing waste food from restaurants, which could have contained infected meat that had not been subjected to adequate cooking. Two days later a suspected case of FMD was confirmed at Burden Farm, Highampton in Devon. This animal was from a flock of 40 sheep bought on the 13th of February at Hexham market in Northumberland by Willie Cleave, an animal dealer, and sent to Longtown Market, Carlisle, a holding centre, before being trucked to his farm at Highampton. These sheep had come to market from Prestwick Hall Farm, four miles from the Waugh's farm at Heddon-on-the-Wall. It was therefore considered likely that the infection arose from the feeding of infected animal matter to the pigs at Burnside Farm, whence it had spread by air to Prestwick Hall Farm, and sheep incubating the infection went to market at Hexham before the symptoms had become apparent. This seemed quite plausible until it came to light that a video, taken on the Waugh's farm in February, showed a dog tearing at a dead sheep on a rubbish heap; it was one of eight dead sheep brought onto the farm on January 24th - four weeks before the disease was confirmed at the farm. Mr Waugh said that the sheep came from land near Prestwick Hall Farm! The carcasses were hidden in a shed during an inspection by a MAFF vet and were then dragged out of the shed and burned. This seems to present evidence of a possible alternative mode of transmission. However, a more sinister possibility has been suggested. The Newcastle Evening Chronicle reported that scientists in British, American, Canadian and Mexican governments were all staging an FMD simulation exercise in October 2000. A spokesman for the Canadian Government said he was unable to comment on its FMD simulation exercise due to agreements it had made with the British Government. *"Due to the sensitivity surrounding events which have occurred since February this year, we are unable to comment further on the reasons or results of the November exercise"*, he added. Newcastle-based microbiologist, Dr Harash Narang, said: "*I firmly believe that the virus escaped from a MAFF experiment and had infected sheep as long ago as last October*". At the same time, the UK Government was preparing its own 'contingency plans' for a foot and mouth outbreak - even though the last foot and mouth outbreak here was in 1967. Was it purely coincidence that MAFF officials telephoned timber merchants in December 2000 asking if they could supply wood for pyres, should foot and mouth strike? Mike Littlehales, who ran a timber yard in Staffordshire said: "*I got this call from a lady who said: 'This is the Ministry of Agriculture. Would you be interested in supplying timber in case of foot and mouth?' The last time we received a similar call was during the foot and mouth outbreak in 1967*". Questioned about this in the Commons, Nick Brown said they did it every year to update their records. However the outbreak arose, it established itself in the shocking conditions at Burnside Farm and was rapidly spread by the trade and transport of animals around the country and abroad by businesses such as Willie Cleave's. The government was slow to act, no animal movement bans were installed for four days and no killing was begun until five days after the initial discovery. The army was not called in for 25 days.

Once the government had ground into action, a policy of slaughter within 24 hours of the herd in which the animal was found was implemented and culling of herds on contiguous farms up to three kilometres away was carried out to create a 'firebreak' around the disease, and no animal was to be moved without a licence. However, MAFF could not keep up with the volume of work; the disposal of carcasses, in particular, took longer and longer to carry out, and a huge backlog of decaying carcasses developed. Neither could MAFF cope with the paperwork for movement licences; animals suffered and starved, and lambs were born into mud and died. A farmer was fined £1500 because his sheep, which were starving due to the animal movement restrictions, broke out of their field to find something to eat. Nauseating smoke began to cloak the English countryside. Television news bulletins brought the scenes (but not the smell) of huge pyres of burning animals into homes throughout the land. Having spent 32 years of my working life in the world of fire: fire research, fire testing, fire protection and fire safety, I watched the first transmission of these images in growing disbelief. It was very evident to me that the specification for the fire was wrong in that the design could only allow for very slow destruction of the carcasses and hence the palls of smoke. I knew too that the job could be carried out much more quickly, more efficiently and with less pollution if the design of the fire were changed. So, being me and being bidden in two of the gospels not to hide my light under a bushel, on the 26th of February I wrote an email to the Ministry for Agriculture, Fisheries and Food (MAFF). Here is the email:

Dear Sirs

I have been appalled at the sight on the news today of the attempts to burn carcases of diseased animals. The fact that diggers have to go in and turn over the unburned carcases is evidence enough that the design of the fires is WRONG.

I spent 34 years of my life working in fire research. May I give you some advice on how to do the job faster, more efficiently and most importantly, more safely?

Combustion requires OXYGEN. A pile of bodies (largely composed of water) dumped on the fuel (as is being done at the moment) allows burning to take place only on the top and sides of the pile. This was in evidence in the pictures on the news - flames flickering around a pile of black bodies. The fire has to be burning UNDER the carcases for them to be consumed. This requires them to be placed ON a griddle or supported on a TIMBER CRIB. Unless the griddle resists heat it will collapse so a crib of timber (sleepers or tree trunks) is required. This allows the fire to burn under the carcases and bring about swift and complete combustion.

Has no one in MAFF seen an Indian funeral pyre? The body lies on a crib of branches and is burnt very efficiently (well, apart from feet sometimes falling off into the Ganges). If they burnt bodies in India as you are attempting to do here the Ganges would be choked with scorched meat and bones.

FIRE is a SCIENCE. It is horrifyingly obvious that MAFF does not seek advice from scientists acquainted with that discipline. Timber section, spacing and fire load are specific for the type, disposition and quantity of matter to be destroyed. May I suggest that you consult the Fire Research Station (part of the Building Research Establishment) at Garston, Watford?

I do not apologise for being outspoken, I live on the edge of an agricultural common in the midst of a farming community. If the overall measures you are taking to control this outbreak are as incompetent as your method of destroying infected animals, I tremble for the farming industry.

I look forward to your response.

Yours faithfully

Arthur Boyt

You will notice that I made a couple of jokes in the message, I thought they might appreciate that as I don't suppose many people were sending them jokes around that time. It was evident I was not touting for business since I was advising them to consult another government department to fill in the details of how to carry out my suggestions. I now realise it was a little insensitive of me to suggest, as I did, that they were incompetent; it might have made them reluctant to pay my message any attention. However, on the 5th of March MAFF phoned me up to thank me for my email and to say, Yes, they agreed with me, they were not completely burning the bodies, and they had contacted the Fire Research Station (FRS) for advice. I could not believe my ears, someone was listening to me. The caller offered to send me the Home Office specification for constructing a pyre. Wonderful, we were getting somewhere.

Five roadkill badgers © Arthur Boyt

During the 10 days after the outbreak of FMD I picked up no less than five dead badgers from the roadside. An account of the events surrounding the collection of one of those badgers is a little out of the ordinary. I had to attend a committee meeting of the Cornwall Orienteering Club (KERNO) at Victoria on the A30 west of Bodmin and about 15 miles from home. It was important for me not to be late as the Chair of the South West Orienteering Association (SWOA), Geraldine Gould, was due to be there and I happened to be Chair of KERNO. I set off and then remembered that there had been a weather forecast for snow and bad weather in the South. It crossed my mind that I might be ill-equipped to deal with a breakdown in the snow as I was wearing only open-toed sandals on my feet and had no rainwear; but too late to turn back now. Before long I spotted a familiar lump beside the road ahead of me. It was a dead badger and in good nick too. I jumped out, lifted it on board and was on my way. The Maxi skimmed along in fine style and I had just overtaken a long string of slow-moving vehicles on the narrow twisty roads when the car began to cough and despite all attempts to persuade it to continue it died on me. The symptoms of the engine's failure smacked of lack of fuel, but the fuel gauge was reading full. I had had trouble with the gauge before, so I got out and removed the petrol cap and rocked the car. No sound of sloshing petrol entered my ears. Just then a car stopped and a chap named James asked if I needed help. I gladly accepted a lift back to Longstone where I got a can of petrol. James, who lived at St Kew, kindly took me back to the Maxi. I tipped the juice in and spun the engine till the battery began to show signs of dying. It was evident there was an airlock in the system and when that happens there is only one thing to be done, suck it through! I pulled the fuel pipe off the carburettor and putting it in my mouth sucked. Suddenly my mouth filled with petrol. Ugh! Petrol is awful in the mouth! It evaporates rapidly filling your head with gas, you breathe in the fumes and it permeates its way through the skin. You cannot get rid of it by just spitting, but you have to do it anyway. Another try with the starter and Brrrrm! the engine leapt into life. I thanked James and tried to give him £10 for his help, but he would not take it. He explained he was a Jehovah's Witness and did it for the Lord. I raced off eager to make up time, but before I reached Bodmin, the engine was missing again. I stopped at Webber's coach garage for whom I occasionally drove a school bus and attempted to get in touch with the committee. I rang the hotel where the meeting was being held but only got the answerphone. I drove on gently. The meeting had been in progress for half an hour when I sneaked in and, as Geraldine was telling us that orienteering events were being cancelled up and down the country to prevent the spread of foot and mouth, no one really noticed my absence. We did not close the meeting till 10.30 p.m. and, having been so engaged with what was going on inside the room, we did not notice what was going on outside: huge snowflakes drifting past the window! Oh crumbs! Not what I wanted by any means.

I filled up with petrol to make sure there was plenty in the tank and set off for home in third gear, as it seemed to run better like that. Great heavy flakes blotted out the way ahead and the road became covered in a wet sloshy slush. About five miles from home the engine stuttered a few times, recovered, stuttered again and died. I got out into the slush in my sandals and for want of anything better to do sucked at the petrol pipe again and got another mouthful of petrol. Pteuoow! Then a chap in a minivan stopped and offered me a lift to the telephone kiosk at the Camelot garage where I rang home to ask Sue to come and tow me home. I could not take refuge in the garage and while away the time by reading the papers on display because it was now closed, so I had to wait in the telephone kiosk. These new phone boxes were not designed for people in sandals on a blowy day when it is snowing hard, only the back panel goes down to the ground, the side and the front have an air space at the bottom! I have no idea why they should have been designed in that way, I mean, if you dropped a £5 note it could be blown away and you never see it again. Perhaps it is to stop people sleeping in them, but then, if someone were stranded in one, miles from anywhere, they could freeze to death, and if they did would the designer be guilty of causing death by designing without due care and attention? As it was, my feet began to freeze. I managed for a time to wedge myself up off the ground and keep my feet out of the wind. A Citroen ZX drew into the garage. It must be Sue. I ran over and found, no, it was not. It was Tristan, a lad who had worked on our converted barn; his ZX was a Turbo! I sat in the car with him and chatted until we felt Sue was being a long time and drove off to meet her or find what had caused the delay. Going through Camelford she passed us going the other way. Tristan flashed his lights and turned and followed her. She didn't know who he was and got all nervous being pursued by a strange man flashing his lights at her in the middle of the night! She got really frightened when she stopped at the garage and the car stopped behind her and a bloke got out and came towards her! Then she saw it was me! She and I drove on to the Maxi. I didn't offer Tristan a tenner, he would have taken it; I never got round to asking him what he was up to driving around the place at 1 a.m. I hitched on a rope and Sue cleverly towed me down into Camelford and up onto the moor where the snow was lying an inch or so deep without our breaking the rope once or running into each other. And so it was we got the badger and the Maxi home, it was 1.30 a.m.! Next day I found that the cause of the gradual breakdown of the car was due to two broken spark plugs.

Encouraged by the positive response from MAFF to my letter, I decided to carry out a test burn to see if my ideas about carcass incineration stood up to experimental verification. I had been collecting scrap wood, as I do, whenever I came across any, and as they had been laying pipes for telecommunication purposes across the county I had plenty of opportunity to pick up the timbers used to hold the pipes in bundles. They measured 34in (86cm) and 49in (120cm) with a cross-section of 1.5 in (38mm) x 2.5 in (63mm). On Tuesday the 6th of March, I built a crib from these timbers measuring 3ft (914mm) by 4ft (1220mm) with a 2in (50mm) space between the timbers. I took two of my badger carcasses and laid them on the crib.

First badger fire test on small timbers before ignition © Arthur Boyt

I had cut off the heads as I collect skulls and did not want them destroyed. The two bodies weighed 21lb (9.5kg) and 26lb (11.8kg) and the fuel 140lb (63.5kg). I lit the fire with some kindling and diesel, and it burned well.

Badger test after ignition © Arthur Boyt

However, the topside of the bodies did not get direct impingement of flame and owing to a strong wind one side of one of them was also out of the flames.

Fire test with intense heat © Arthur Boyt

The wood was burned through before the bodies had been consumed, and at 20 min the crib collapsed. At 40 min there was only glowing charcoal left and although the smaller badger had all but burnt, there was still a lot of the bigger badger in the embers. The fire had not burned for a sufficient time to get the job done and the flames had been blown to one side. Now, the time a fire burns is dependent on the cross-sectional dimensions of the timber, not the quantity. Timber chars at a set rate, generally taken as 1in/hr (25mm/hr) for hardwood and 1.5in/hr (38mm/hr) for softwood. These timbers were 1.5in x 2.5in (38mm x 63mm). So would have burned through within half and hour which they did. To make the fire burn for longer I should need thicker timbers.

The day after my burn I skinned and cut the legs off two of the remaining badgers and put them in the freezer for eating at a later date. I cycled to Launceston that day and passed downwind of a burn at South Petherwin where 180 cattle and 600 sheep had been slaughtered and were now burning. The stench was choking and nauseating. A day or so later I received a letter from MAFF with the specification for the pyres drawn up by the Home Office. The specification was thus: Two lines of sleepers are laid on the ground and a layer of sleepers spanned across them 12 to 15 in apart (30 to 40cm). On this is laid two layers of pallets and on these a thick bed of straw. Finally, a layer of coal is laid at a rate of 4 cwt/cow (0.2ton/cow) (3 sheep = 1 cow) and the animals laid on the coal. The arrangement can be seen in the photo. Just prior to ignition gallons of diesel are poured over the whole pyre. Now I had the official specification for the cause of all the nightmares for people living downwind of

Cattle on MAFF pyre before ignition © Arthur Boyt

the pyres. No one who understood the science of fire would have specified a fire like that. It is in fact little different from a grand scale-up of a fire in your living room at home but without a grate. Whoever designed it knew little about fire and nothing about burning dead bodies. Perhaps it was a Home Office committee!

Pat Donohue, my old colleague from Fire Research Station days, and his wife, Veronica, came to dinner on the following Sunday so we had a good natter about the ridiculous pyres. I had got a bit of food out of the freezer in readiness two days earlier: a leg of badger in case they wanted to try something unusual (no, not the one leftover from the fire test), some Frankfurters (which needed eating up) and some roast turkey which was only seven years past its sell-by date! We also collected some mussels from Trebarwith Strand as a starter. Unfortunately, we forgot all about the mussels. Pat enjoyed a sample of the badger and they both said the turkey was very nice.

The farmers accepted that killing their flocks and herds was essential if FMD lesions were identified in any of their animals. There was, however, a growing uneasiness about the killing of contiguous healthy herds, particularly if there was no contact and there was space between the animals. In fact the government was exceeding the powers conferred on it by the Animal Health Act 1981 in ordering the killing of any animals other than those which showed signs of infection or had been in contact with those that did. Over 200 successful legal challenges were made against orders to cull healthy stock. This did little to stop the MAFF juggernaut, assisted often by armed police and soldiers, from illegally slaughtering the majority of the 7 million animals it destroyed in the contiguous cull. Farmers had to watch the killing of a life's (and often several generations') worth of breeding of invaluable and often rare stock. Not only was this illegal, it was pointless, as Elliot Morley, the Animal Health Minister, reported: 7549 premises were culled as contiguous farms of which ONLY 5 showed evidence of FMD! Although there were only 2030 actual cases of infection, six million animals were culled in an attempt to stop the disease spreading - at a total economic cost estimated at £5 billion. There were 4 million animals slaughtered for disease control purposes and 2.5 million whose welfare was threatened by the movement restrictions and surplus lambs which could not be exported because of an export ban.

The distress caused to farmers and their families was immeasurable. A number committed suicide and at least 60 deaths could be attributed to distress arising from FMD control measures. Many children were intensely traumatised by the events they witnessed. Noel Edmunds, set up the Heart of Devon campaign to fight MAFF's handling of FMD. His slogan "*Stop! You are destroying our lives*", summed up the feelings of the rural communities about Government policy. The Prince of Wales discreetly supported a campaign for vaccination against the government's policy, according to Sir Ben Gill, the outgoing president of the NFU. His action has been criticised as inappropriate for the heir to the throne, but I say "*Well done Your Royal Highness, that is just what we want to see from our future Head of State when the government's actions have become both illegal and inhumane*".

Three weeks passed and there was no change in the MAFF procedure for burning, so I rang FRS; the person I spoke to did not know if MAFF had been in touch with them and knew of no work having been done on the design of a fire on which to burn animals. This prompted me to write again to MAFF posting the letter on Saturday 31st March and offering to help and advise them and even carry out some tests. I outlined the means open to them to improve the burning of carcasses. The letter, was addressed to David Fields who had been so forthcoming over the pyre specification. On the Sunday we were entertaining our old friends Phil and Angie Barnes from Rilla Mill when the phone rang, it was Julie Dowton. She said, "*I am ringing to let you know that MAFF is proposing to build a huge pyre on Davidstow Airfield. They intend to start work tomorrow morning fencing off your side of the airfield so that you will not be able to get in or out.*" "*Good grief!*" I expostulated, "*since when has that been announced.*" "*Well, it hasn't. I don't think I was supposed to be told this but someone let slip that MAFF is proposing to bring contiguous cull animals here from the Canworthy Water incident and burn them down the length of the main east/west runway. There is going to be a public meeting on the airfield tomorrow morning at 9 a.m. MAFF is coming to tell us what they want to do and the commoners are going to try and stop them. Would you be able to attend the meeting?*" "*If it is at 9 a.m. I cannot be there*", I replied, "*as I am doing a school bus run, but I'll tell you what, I shall produce a flyer to hand to MAFF and anyone interested at the meeting, summarising the reasons why such action would be a highly irresponsible thing to do.*" It was pouring with rain on the airfield on Monday morning and the little huddles of people began to get wet. The chief vet for MAFF in Cornwall, Mrs Jan Kelly, made a plea to be able to use the airfield to dispose of bodies. Keith Goodenough, Davidstow Parish councillor and North Cornwall District councillor, and Julie Dowton, secretary of the Davidstow Commoners, spoke for the commoners and said that their solicitor, John McLachlan of Macmillans of Wadebridge, had taken out an injunction restraining MAFF from the use of the common for that purpose and that there should be a hearing in the police station in Launceston in two weeks time. I handed out copies of my flyer, but the ink had begun to run which made it look a bit amateurish. However, the owners of Cansford Quarry a few miles away offered MAFF the use of their quarry. No doubt a sufficiently attractive offer was made to stop them quarrying for a while and let MAFF onto the site to carry out a few attempts to burn dead animals. A few days later while work was afoot at the quarry in preparation of the pyres, I went along dressed in white overalls and attempted to get in, looking like an official, to get them to build a pyre following my design so that it could be demonstrated immediately as a better and easier way to burn carcasses. As I expected, I was turned back but not without giving Mr Kelly, the MAFF security officer, a copy of my letter.

I went around into the field above the quarry and looked down on the preparations going on below; a pyre was being constructed in accordance with the ridiculous specifications I had received a few days earlier. It made me so frustrated to be prevented from demonstrating how it could so much more easily and efficiently be done. On the following day, I again essayed to gain entrance to the site in my white overalls and again I was quickly shown the gate. The animals being brought in were from the contiguous cull, but even so, I was surprised that no disinfecting regime was in operation for vehicles coming off the site. Looking again from the field, I could see pigs being loaded onto the pyre below me. Smoke from the pyre at Canworthy Water 4 miles away drifted across the countryside. I understood the fire in the quarry was to be lit that evening, so returned later, but nothing was happening. However, I went to the quarry the next morning and from a distance I could see smoke rising! It had been lit late at night when the media had gone home. I looked down onto a smoky pyre burning around its edge; unburned pigs were rolling off it as it burned! What soon became obvious to me was that the pigs were not being burned they were being distilled into the atmosphere! The coal was hot enough to cook the animals but the temperature was too low for the gases given off to ignite and so the pall of smoke was not burned pig, it was gasified pig; the gases condensing into aerosols of fats and other products and drifting off downwind to coat the lips and lungs of all those unlucky enough to live to the lee of the pyre. While I was taking photos of the scene, the farmer appeared and raved at me for trespass and for taking photos. Buck Gilman, for that, is who he was, had apparently sold the right to take photographs from his field to someone else. I apologised for the trespass and said that my photos were not for the press, but were for me to monitor what was happening. I also offered to give the photographer the pictures if he wanted them. Buck calmed down after a while and I agreed not to take any more photos.

Two days later I met Simon Burt the photographer who took pictures of me looking down on the burning pyre and on a new pyre with 50 - 60 cows on. I watched as workmen poured 400 litres of diesel onto the cows and tried to light it. First, they took 10 mins igniting a pressurised flame gun and then a further 5 mins getting the pyre to catch fire using the flame gun. At last, it was burning and blazed merrily for a while, but it was only the kerosene burning and when that was consumed it reverted to a smoking smouldering heap with a little flame licking around the edges. The hair on the backs of the sheep that had been on a burning pyre for two and a half days was still not even singed! On the following day, the cows were not even beginning to be consumed and the three-and-a-half-day pyre still had hairy animals on it even though it was being stirred by a digger. What sort of lung problems are going to beset those digger drivers after spending so much time grubbing around unprotected in the smoke I don't know. I met Buck again and he invited me back to his farm across the road. We had some tea and reached an agreement that I could go on taking photos as long as I did not sell them to the press. Later I spoke to the headmistress of the school at Warbstow who said the school was closing because of the stench! I rang a crematorium and asked how long it takes to burn bodies, "*Seventy minutes is the average, but very heavy bodies can take up to 90 minutes*" was the reply. I then wrote a letter to MAFF, in which I said: "*I have tried to advise you that the burning can be carried out efficiently and quickly and with very much less impact on the surrounding populace and the environment. It is evident that MAFF is neither able nor willing to look at how this process can be changed for the better. I am now so concerned at what I have seen with mine own eyes that I believe it should be brought to the attention of the public at large. How many people are going to suffer serious illness because MAFF cannot take advice?"* Putting my words into action I wrote a letter to the Western Morning News (WMN), which was partly in response to a letter by Dr Milward and partly to draw attention to MAFF's incompetence. The following day I went out to the quarry and watched wood and coal being added to the pyre that had been smouldering for four and a half days now. Two days later I had a letter from MAFF in which Divisional Manager, Jan Kelly, dismissed my advice and offers of help with the statement that it would be counter-productive! Yes, this was the very same Mrs Kelly who threw the BBC film crew out of the DEFRA building in Truro. So here we are, over 6 weeks after my first contact, there are 150,000 carcasses rotting in West Country fields, and MAFF does not want to know about a quick way out of their problem. They desperately wanted to burn those carcasses less than a quarter of a mile from a food factory and half a mile from a reservoir for Camelford's water and fought a legal battle to do so, but could not pause in this mad rush to look at a better way of doing it! Funnily enough, the day after I received Mrs Kelly's dismissive letter I received a phone call from another MAFF office promising to look into my offer and come back to me. It was quite evident to me that the junior MAFF officers were doing their best to be helpful and make use of helpful offers from the storm of e-mails and letters they must have been receiving at that time, but this helpfulness did not get promoted or empowered by the senior staff. Two days later 60 or so farmers and others went along to the Intervention Board's hearing at Launceston where the use of Davidstow airfield was considered; only two were allowed in. I carried a placard for the benefit of the press, which read something like: 'MAFF threat to Bodmin Moor, a criminal act!' As Tony Blair had personally seized charge of MAFF at the end of March, I sent him a letter about the smoky pyres and the threat to Bodmin moor.

As the days went by the attempts to burn 4000 pigs, 500 cattle and 500 sheep at the quarry were stumbling forward with new pyres being built. Diggers were turning over the pyres and carrying smoking animals and hot coals around the site, a veritable Dante's inferno. When my face first appeared over the fence to witness the stoking of the pyres, the men below abandoned their machines and ran for cover and would not continue working while I was there, as if they were doing something illegal or immoral! What a performance! Were they under instruction to stop working and if so, what did MAFF have to hide? As it was evident nothing was going to come of my attempts to interest MAFF in how to burn carcasses, I got in touch with the army who had taken over control of the disposal of carcasses and were now co-ordinating the slaughter and disposal procedures. The whole business of slaughter and disposal was stalling because MAFF was unable to co-ordinate the arrival and departure of the right teams in the right order to the right place at the right time. What would have happened if it had been left to MAFF does not bear thinking about; as it was, carcasses were left for up to three weeks, rotting on farms and fields, the noxious trickle of fluid from decaying corpses running into ditches, across roads into watercourses and even into drinking water; the stench from the piles of bodies permeating the countryside; the smoky pyres smouldering for a week to two months. Even after the army stepped in the backlog for disposal continued to rise for another month. A huge pyre was prepared at South Arscott Farm, close to Holsworthy, on which it was intended to burn 1000 cattle and up to 15000 sheep. At last, I got a breakthrough, Major Belinda Forsythe, who was in charge of operations at South Arscott, invited me to do a demonstration burn. I went with her to a farm in Devon where a large flock of sheep had been slaughtered. On the way I discussed with her the matter of payment for what I was doing; she offered to cover my expenses and assured me I would not be out of pocket. When we arrived, the farmer told me that his farm had had no contact with the outside world until the day MAFF vets came to test his flock, two weeks later they came back to test again and found they were infected. He told me, "*At that point, the vets began to put on protective clothing, something they had not done before*", and went on, "*I have no doubt they brought the disease with them on their first visit.*" We found the sheep were to be taken away and not burnt on site, so I went home; on my way I bought the Western Morning News and found a headline in the letters section, the Western Morning Views, which read: '*Heaven help farmers facing pyre bungles*'. It was my letter. There was with it a picture of a pyre blazing in the darkness with cows' legs sticking out through the flames. It looked good but conveyed the wrong impression: it had been taken during the initial kerosene burn-off and was not how the fire would look for the next week or so. On the following day, I met up with Major Forsythe and was taken to another farm where a pyre was being constructed. We togged up in protective gear and walked up to where the pyre was being prepared. There was a gang of men doing nothing. They had run out of materials and could do no more until supplies arrived. Part of the pyre was finished and was loaded with cows. Then I noticed the timber that was being used for the pyre. It was oak! Great baulks of quality oak, to be used as firewood! This exemplified for me the profligacy of the government in its desperation to get rid of the excrement of its own misplaced policy. What added to the despair I felt was that these timbers contributed little to the fire. They often did not start to burn until the pyre had been turned over by the contractor after several days. However, when I got home I looked up the internet and found that old sleepers cost about £15, new softwood sleepers £20, and new oak sleepers £25; I was surprised there was so little differential between them. Another thing that bugged me on seeing this was that I had contacted several timber merchants and found they were prepared to supply lorry loads of off-cuts and scrap wood for nothing, and poor quality timber at very reasonable rates. They had not been asked by MAFF to supply anything even though I had phoned the information through to MAFF. As we could not do the burn here, Major Forsythe said we should have to do it at South Arscott, so after being disinfected I went home.

I rang my one-time colleague, Dr Richard Phillips, at the Loss Prevention Council laboratories at Borehamwood to ask if he had any ideas about the spacing of the timbers of the crib, which I considered would be critical for the success of the burn. You see, the burning surfaces in the crib radiate heat onto each other; if spaced close together the radiation is intensified and more gas is produced, but as it does not have space to burn on the surface it is carried up above the fire and burns in a tall flame above the fire; if the space is wide, there is less radiation and the gas given off from the burning wood has space to burn while still between the burning surfaces, which means the flames remain largely within the crib and do not reach much above the fire. The optimum configuration of the fire would be to have the flames reaching between one and two feet above the fire. Richard suggested 4in (100mm) might give the right answer, but went on, "*Why not cover the fire with some sort of lid to deflect the flames and hot gases down and across the bodies; if this were combustible it would also add to the radiation onto the bodies.*" This seemed an eminently appropriate suggestion and I thanked him for his advice. He wished me well in the venture. On my way to South Arscott the following day I managed to get a puncture, but it did not delay me for long; being able to mend a puncture in a cycle tyre in 12 minutes means that a wheel change on a car is child's play, I think that Formula 1 events would be much more fun if drivers had to change their own wheels and, what is more, using a scissor jack and normal wheel brace to boot! I am sure it would add a touch of comedy to what is otherwise a dreary procession of noisy machines with the occasional horrendous crash.

The site of the pyre was like Piccadilly Circus! Dozens of lorries delivering fuel and carcasses, bulldozers shovelling coal and straw and dead animals, lorries tipping hardcore and diggers flattening it. There was provision for ten pyres, each 120m long and 5m wide in various stages of construction. I sought out the farmer to ask where to do my burn. He seemed a bit unsteady, I think he had been at the bottle, but whether it was to celebrate what must have been a pretty persuasive payment to get him to give up his farm for this operation, or whether to drown his fear of what might lie ahead when he had to resume relations with his neighbours and the townspeople of nearby Holsworthy, I was not quite certain. The army were not in evidence, so after repeated phone calls and waiting for an hour I got on with building my pyre with the help of a contractor called Dave. I was to use materials available on the site, so I collected some pallets and about thirty baulks of softwood (sleepers) each measuring 94in x 9in x 5in (2.4m x 0.23m x 0.13m) I broke up the pallets as kindling and then constructed a crib with two layers of sleepers measuring 8ft x 8ft (2.5m x 2.5m) in area. Two sleepers (bearers), 8ft (2.5m) apart, laid on their broadside formed the base of the crib. A sleeper was laid on its narrow side on both these bearers and the space between them filled with kindling. Over the kindling was placed 12 sleepers laid on their narrow side and spaced equidistantly (about 4in,100mm) save that the centre two sleepers were placed side by side to form a baulk 10in x 9in (2540mm x 2286mm). Eleven more sleepers were laid across the others and spaced equidistantly. Four more sleepers were laid over these, two at the edge and two 2ft (0.6m) from the edge. Pallets were cut to fit between the four sleepers on the top of the crib. The next day I obtained help from a tractor driver to bring me some sheep from a great mound of dead animals to put on the crib and to load them onto it for me. Eight big ewes (said to be Suffolk x Mule) were laid in two rows on their sides with the heads of all but one in the centre and three lambs laid over the ewes' heads. Care was taken that the ewe carcasses did not touch each other so that flames could

My test burn of sheep without covering © Arthur Boyt

pass around each carcass. The operating principle in my pyre was that there was open access to air from below; the opposing faces of timber would generate an intense fire that would blast onto the underside of the sheep, pass around each body and, directed downwards by the cover, bathe the bodies in flame.

A double layer of pallets was laid over the carcasses and two sheets of 8ft x 4ft (2.4m x 1.2m) particleboard laid over the whole to deflect heat and flames onto the top of the pyre, intensifying the burning of the carcasses. It was intended that adjustments to the burning rate could be achieved by addition of fuel beneath the crib and between the sleepers. The cover was expected to burn off fairly quickly, at which time it was intended to replace it with sheets of corrugated iron. The next day was the London Marathon and I enjoyed watching the whole wonderful event. Having run it twice in the '80s I can relive the experience though not at the pace of the leaders! El Mouaziz won the men's race, Tulu the women's and Tanny Grey-Thompson the women's wheelchair race. I learned that the pyres were to be ignited in the evening, but as I wanted to be able to see what was going on I decided to leave my test to the morning, however, I went along in the evening to witness the lighting of the great pyres. When I arrived on site an army officer conducted me to the scene of action. It was then that I caught sight of Mr Kelly, the MAFF security man, then he caught sight of me. He hastened over, "*Mr Boyt, I am afraid that I am going to have to ask you to leave the premises at once.*" It took barely a moment's cogitation to formulate my rejoinder: "*And I am pleased to be able to tell you that I am here at the invitation of the army to witness this conflagration and to carry out a test of my own method of burning carcasses tomorrow. What is more, I should like to invite you to come and witness on behalf of MAFF my test burn tomorrow to see how it compares with your method of disposal.*" He looked at the officer and looked at me and, frustrated at his inability to turn me off the site, hurried away - as I expected he did not reappear on the morrow to witness my test. Hundreds of gallons of kerosene were poured over the pyres and at 10 p.m. they were lit. I took photos for a while and then left to get some sleep. I had phoned BBC SW to try and get them to record the test on camera but was not successful. Come the morning I got me out to the farm and walked around photographing the various stages of destruction that had occurred in the night. In places where the fire had been exposed to strong wind, the coal had burned well and actually got rid of almost whole sheep (12 hours after ignition). Owing to pressure from the populace in the neighbourhood, MAFF had relented and reduced the number of proposed burns to two, but in order to get the 14,000 to 15,000 animals they wanted burned, they had loaded double the number of animals onto some of the pyres they had ready to burn on the Sunday. This was counterproductive as it prevented those pyres from doing ought but smoulder in from the edges; burning of the animals themselves had hardly commenced 12 hours after the fires had been lit.

It was now that my moment had come, I was about to find out if my bold promise was anything more than just a blast of hot air. There had been heavy rain in the preceding days and the animals and the timber were saturated. I put in some new dry kindling, but it would not light the crib. Much to my annoyance I had to obtain some kerosene and slosh that onto the kindling, even that did not work. I then got more paper and kindling and, while lighting and sloshing kerosene, managed to set a glove alight! At this point, I was very glad I had not been able to get the attention of the BBC to film the proceedings! I flapped about and quickly pulled off the glove, but at least I had got the fire going. It began slowly, taking about 10 mins to dry the soaked timbers before really being able to take hold. However, by 20 mins the flames were coming through to fan out under the cover and in 5 more minutes flames were roaring all around the bodies, which were beginning to be consumed.

Test burn with covering at 25 minutes © Arthur Boyt

This was very impressive! By 40 mins the pallets and plywood cover had burned away, so I added more pallets and some sheets of corrugated iron. The heat radiating from the fire made that job painful and almost impossible. At 75 mins I added some 2 x 2 sections to prolong the fire, which was beginning to collapse. At 90 mins there were only small lumps of carcass remaining and at 2 hours there were only little fragments still unburned. The crib collapsed and by 3 hours there was nothing left of the animals in the hot bed of glowing charcoal. At no stage had there been any significant smoke production from the fire, no smell of burning flesh and the column of hot gases had been carried well up away from the ground once the fire had become fully developed. The only residue remaining after the fire was the two charred bottom bearers, wood ash and some bone fragments. The burn had been a success beyond my wildest dreams! Unfortunately, there was no one from MAFF or the army to witness my achievement, only the contractors tending the great pyres which had been all the while smoking and smouldering beside my experiment. The contractors were duly impressed and taking my advice to load pallets onto their ineffectual pyres produced a sea of flame instead of smoke and that is how I left the scene with quite a blaze going on behind me.

MAFF pyres after burning all night with my test fire after 30 mins © Arthur Boyt

The following day I wrote a report of the test and a 1000 word article for the Western Morning News and spent a lot of time on the phone telling people about the test. The article did not appear in WMN but there was a picture of me looking over Canford quarry with its collection of pyres smoking away below. The report is given in the Appendix; this is the first time it has been published anywhere despite my sending it to all and sundry. It offers a simple and effective means for burning carcasses quickly and cleanly on the farm. No movement of carcasses is involved with potential spreading of infection and no contamination of groundwater by burial. The farmer himself can carry out the work as soon as some timber is delivered. Two days later I took the film to Exeter to get it developed in an hour and I ordered 10 copies. When I collected them I found I had picked up the wrong film for developing and now had 10 copies of pictures of some flocks of starlings and the badger burn! I called at the National Farmers Union (NFU) HQ in Exeter to try to talk to Anthony Gibson, the SW Regional Director of the NFU, who had become a hero in the SW through his outspoken comments on Radio Devon and in his column in the Western Morning News. His statement: *"The contiguous cull is one of the most bloody, tragic and disgraceful misjudgements ever committed"* remains one of the tersest indictments of the government's handling of FMD. Despite this, he was awarded an OBE in the Queen's birthday honours, a deserving award. I was unable to see him and left a copy of my report. The next day I had the right film processed and was able to include some very convincing pictures with the report. I sent copies to the Prime Minister - Tony Blair, the minister for agriculture - Nick Brown, Major Forsythe, MAFF at Exeter and Truro, Col. Simon Bell in charge of operations in Cumbria and Bill Harper, the owner of the feed supplier of that name in Holsworthy, who had contacted me after reading one of my letters to WMN.

I received some acknowledgements but little in the way of response from anyone. Having got that far there was little more I could do. Those in charge had been given proof that my ideas would help them move the mountains of rotting animals piled around farmyards throughout the land. If Downing Street had had 200 dead, stinking cattle blocking the road for two weeks and Whitehall was downwind of one of those stinking pyres, you can be certain Tony Blair would have put an end to it in 24 hours. Instead, he chose to ignore what could have helped both him and the farmers out of the dreadful mess that government policy and government incompetence had got them into, and he and his useless ministry were quite happy to leave devastated farmers imprisoned on their farms with their yards and fields piled with the decaying corpses of their dearly loved animals and to subject the rural populations to months of having to breathe stinking acrid rotten air. They did not have the capacity to act as if they had any brains at all. As for me, I had shot my bolt. I gave up trying to communicate with those who had no wish to listen. I did, however, write to the press about the closure of footpaths and the need to get them reopened. There is a universally held belief that ramblers spread foot and mouth disease and that the total closure of Rights of Way is a necessary instrument to hinder them from doing so. That this belief has no rational scientific backing influenced neither the government when it amended the Countryside Act, nor MAFF when it advised local authorities, nor local authorities when they closed the Rights of Way. The government wanted to be seen to be doing something and this seemed like a good idea. A few walkers were prosecuted *pour encourager les autres* and as a result ramblers and tourists stayed at home, the rural economy was devastated, but the disease continued to spread. To close footpaths on coasts, moors and dales was an action that the rural economy could not afford. This was realised too late in the course of the disease. In one case, public access to Northam Burrows Country Park on the coast at Westward Ho! in Devon was restored at a cost of £14,000. MAFF would not allow the public onto the site while animals were there nor would it allow the sheep on the site to be removed alive so they were killed to make way for the public. The local council felt it was of more economic value for public access than for grazing.

The government's measures did not stand up to scrutiny. A member of the public who stepped off the road onto a footpath into the countryside may never have been near a farm animal nor their footpath go anywhere near one, nevertheless, it was an offence. However, it was not an offence for farm personnel (who actually touch animals) to visit other farms and even work with animals on several different farms, as long as they were not under Form A restrictions (site of an outbreak of FMD). They may have come from within an infected area and have handled animals during operations such as shearing, castrating, dehorning and milking; nonetheless, there is no offence committed. We have here an 'Alice through the looking glass' scenario in which a townie walking on a footpath 90 miles from the nearest outbreak was liable to a £5000 fine, whereas a farmer handling animals on 15 farms in an 'infected area' was in no way breaking the law. If the latter was acceptable to the Ministry then the use of footpaths was of far less risk and they should never have been closed. The greatest risk via a human agency (as opposed to natural spread via wind, deer, badgers, birds etc) was from MAFF's own vets who were moving from farm to farm inspecting and testing animals, particularly if they had the disease or were suspected of having it, and checking that healthy animals did not have it (a policy described by a Devon farmer, Margaret Stanbury, in a letter to WMN as *'foolhardy and dangerous'*).

Walking, cycling and riding on the moors were banned but driving across the moors was not. A rambler or tourist from an inner-city was not allowed to set foot on the moors (under penalty of prosecution) but a vehicle (possibly direct from an as yet unidentified infected farm) had free right of way. So it was OK for a tourist's vehicle (which may have driven past an infected farm) to be on the moor, but his feet, which were last lifted from suburbia, were not to hit the ground on the moor. However, the farmers around the moor with commoners' rights had unrestricted access to the moors. Which was the most likely to be in a position to transmit infection to the moors, the tourist or the farmer? It had to be the farmer, but it was not seen as advisable to remove his right to be there.

Tragic as the consequences of a foot and mouth outbreak were to the farmer, he was compensated by the government for his direct losses (the total paid in statutory compensation for slaughtered animals was £1,079,500,000), but the hotelier and other tourist-dependent concerns were not. The tragedy for them was that the measures responsible for their going bankrupt were unnecessary.

Dr Barry Groves in his website Second opinions[19] puts the case for vaccination very succinctly: "*Vaccination would have saved billions of pounds; it would have saved millions of animals' lives; it would have prevented bankruptcies in the farming community; it would have saved farmers from committing suicide; it would have saved the tourist industry; it would have saved people's livelihoods, it would have saved our reputation abroad. It wasn't done because a vaccinated animal could still be a carrier of the foot and mouth virus, the excuse given: it wasn't done because a vaccinated animal could not be exported and 'our export markets would have been harmed'*" according to the National Farmer's Union.

"*But this is a ridiculous argument that would have been seen through straight away if those in government had had any knowledge of economics and the countryside.*

"*Britain's meat and live animal exports were reputedly worth £507 million a year. It was solely to protect this that vaccination wasn't seriously considered. But this, surely, is bordering on criminal lunacy. £507 million may seem a lot but tourist and rural industries alone were losing that much every two weeks. And for what?*

Firstly, it didn't save our export industry — we couldn't export animals or meat. After the BSE scares, this foot and mouth fiasco has further damaged foreign confidence in our meat. But even if we manage to return to exporting £507 million of meat and livestock, it will take several years merely to recoup the billions this crisis cost.

"*Secondly, Britain exports 195,000 tons of pork to the EU — but we import 240,000 tons from them. Britain also exports 102,000 tons of lamb to the EU — but imports 125,000 tons from them. So why do we need to export pork and lamb!* "*The truth is that we do not need to export this meat and so the argument that vaccination would stop our exports was totally irrelevant.*"

There was a persistent outcry for a national public inquiry. David Hill, Devon chairman of the NFU said, "*Let those who ran the chaos face those who suffered from it*". The government refused to hold one. Instead, it set up the Learned Lessons inquiry, chaired by Iain Anderson, a former adviser to Tony Blair. This was the government's own inquiry, though one that fell short of what people wanted, since evidence was not taken in public. It records '*a catalogue of mismanagement*'. There have been a number of unofficial enquiries: by the County Councils of Devon and Cumbria, by the Royal Society of Edinburgh,

---

[19] http://www.second-opinions.co.uk/cjd.html#.YpIJ1ejMK5c

and by the Royal Society. I quote from the Oral Evidence given to the Cumbria FMD Inquiry, 8th May 2002.

Nick Green: "*Many businesses were wrecked both in tourism and agriculture; peoples lives destroyed and rural communities torn apart by an unscientific, bullying policy dictated almost entirely on political grounds. The loss of hundreds of years of breeding to some of the finest stock resources in the world has without doubt resulted in the worst tragedy to hit Cumbria this century. The decision to conduct the 3km cull was a purely political one. The policy had no scientific merit at all. It was a holocaust driven by economics and politics. The sole objective of Prime Minister Blair was not to upset his plans for the General Election and to conduct the election without controversy. To do this resulted in the biggest massacre of British livestock ever.*"

Dr Paul Kitching, ex Head of Exotic Diseases at the IAH Pirbright: "*The policy of culling within 3km of an infected farm was based on the wrong model and was introduced on the back of a fundamentally flawed prediction. Ministers were alerted to the wrong policy in March.*"

Dr Shannon, chief scientist at the Ministry of Agriculture and Defra: "*The committee that advised the Prime Minister made incorrect assumptions about the outbreak because it did not fully understand the disease, the food industry or farming practices.*"

Dr Alex Donaldson director of Animal Health Institute at Pirbright in Veterinary Record said infection by air could only take place within 200m from 100 infected animals.

Comments from submissions made to the EU Committee when they visited Knowstone in Devon, where 80 cattle and 200 sheep were chased around the countryside by men taking pot-shots at them with rifles. John Gouriet: "*The cruelty and the incompetence, the refusal to look upon other alternatives were a disgrace for any organisation let alone a national Government*".

Tina Jones daughter of Mr and Mrs Winslade whose 60 organic Charolais suckler cattle were culled despite being tested negative: "*This area is teeming with deer, so what is the point with culling the sheep and cattle if wildlife are carrying the disease anyway? Why do that? It makes the whole policy ridiculous. The amount of stress that people were put under has been completely underrated. The general public really don't know what has happened, the Government's very happy to bury this and the general public are not aware of what has happened.*"

However, the government shows no evidence of having learned anything. Instead they have passed the new Animal Heath Act 2002, described by Lord Moran as: "*a truly frightening piece of legislation which gives the Government the powers it did not have in 2001. In future, DEFRA officials will have the power to order any animal they wish to be killed, without having to justify their actions. It was designed to legalise and extend powers for mass slaughter, under which so many thousands of healthy animals were killed last year. It contained provisions of a positively Stalinist nature, such as making it a criminal offence, punishable by up to six months in prison, for anyone refusing to assist an inspector in killing an animal*". Stephen Smith QC said that it raised issues which are in breach of the Human Rights Act 1998. I believe the government should publish now, before the next outbreak occurs, their policy for dealing with an outbreak in the future; the scientific reasoning behind the policy and the measures needed to be put in place to effect that policy. That policy needs to take a look at the 100,000 tons of meat imported per year from countries where FMD is endemic and the present lack of controls over any meat coming into the country. If this were done, the public (who benefit or suffer from the policy) and the professionals (who are qualified to criticise such a policy) could express their opinions **before** an outbreak occurs and a consensus of opinion be achieved. Any Minister who fails to do this can be taken to be incompetent without an outbreak of FMD to prove it. The same holds true of government's response to the threat of avian flu. The government likes to appear to be taken by surprise and thus be able to take whatever action it fancies because of the need to be seen to be doing something.

I have shown I can burn carcasses quickly and cleanly. I am sure I could reduce the cost of incinerating, but I shall do no more as the government has taken no notice of what I have done and has refused to pay either for my expenses or for my time.

Other meals - Seal

On the evening of my first Christmas eve at home alone, ten months after I had been excommunicated from the Exclusive Brethren, the 'priests' who were handling my 'case' arrived at 10 p.m. They had been to see me after I had broken my arm while hang gliding ten days earlier and were now checking that the penitence and contrition I had shown then were real. I maintained my attitude of penitence and self-condemnation, answered all their questions truthfully and with humility, and felt that I had won their approval when they actually said "*Goodnight*" before departing. I was up early on Christmas Day in case they invited me to their meeting at 9 a.m. to express my repentance to the 'assembly'. I received no such call. I stayed around all day in case they came to bring me word that my case had been considered and I was to be restored to the fellowship. While waiting anxiously for them I took the opportunity to clean the kitchen and the morning room. I dragged out the washing machine and the dishwasher and washed the floor. I cooked a Christmas dinner of kidney, corn, potatoes and cabbage, with mince pies and custard for pudding. Although I had no Christmas card, no decorations and no celebration, this was not altogether unusual as Exclusives do not keep Christmas. And although the giving of presents was not prohibited, nor the consumption of a turkey and 'seasonal pudding' deemed inconsistent with our usual shunning of 'worldly' practices, I did not allow the lack of these normal Christmas Day comforts to impinge on my sense of well-being. I had long since come to terms with what I hoped and believed would be the temporary absence of my loving wife, but having neither radio nor television (in accordance with Exclusive rules) to mitigate the enforced solitude, I took care that I did not wallow in self-pity and introspection; cleaning the house was one way of distracting the mind from unavoidable ills. I moved the furniture around in the morning room and washed the floor and prepared an evening meal of soup, grilled cheese on toast and defrosted raspberries from the garden with cereals.

On the following morning, the reunion with my wife, friends and family, that I had dared to believe might occur, not having come to pass, I decided to take a trip to one of my favourite stretches of coast. It was a good job I didn't wait in for the priests, they did not get in touch for another three weeks. I had made as my motto a saying of an old family friend and member of the Brethren, Charles Middleton; it was '*What you can't avoid must be enjoyed*'. I packed a lunch and set off for Cley-next-the-Sea on the Norfolk coast. After three miles the oil warning light came on and I returned home to fill up with oil. I reached Cley in 3¼ hours, having picked up on my way two pheasants, one of which had been half-eaten by rats, and a song thrush. I parked at the car park behind the beach at Cley and visited the bird sanctuary before returning along the beach. I bumped into a couple whom I had met in the Spring while on a birdwatching holiday at Fair Isle. Then I spotted a large lump on the sand ahead of me; it proved to be a young common seal! It was dead and appeared to have been just washed up. Pups of the common seal (*Phoca vitulina*) are nursed by their dams until they are 20 – 30 kg in weight after 3 – 4 weeks; they then have to fend for themselves and learn to swallow fish or they will die. They lose a lot of their bodyweight while learning to feed and become vulnerable to chilling and pneumonia. Although this one weighed only 33lb at seven months of age, it felt as though it weighed a lot more by the time I had carried it back along the gravel beach to the car. I then walked the 3 miles along the beach to Blakeney Point.

This is a wonderful walk that I have done many times over the years. All kinds of seabirds can be seen offshore in the winter and there are always lots of dead birds washed up on the huge gravel bank. I have found dead long-tailed duck, a wryneck, red-throated diver and dozens of redwings that must have hit the water in a fog. Once, way back in the early '60s we found two live oiled guillimots, my brother Dennis having to dash into the breakers to rescue them. One died on the way home, but the other lived for quite some weeks, though its digestion never recovered from having eaten the crude oil while preening. We called it Moses.

Well, this visit was no less rewarding; I found a great length of rope, which I dragged back with me and managed to get tar onto my yellow anorak from it. I had to leave a 100-foot x 6 inch (30m x 150mm) marine hawser, it was too heavy to lift one end let alone drag it 1 1/2 miles. I came across a freshly dead fulmar (*Fulmarus glacialis*), which absolutely reeked of a sweet fishy oil. This smell is an oil they carry in the proventriculus (a chamber between crop and gizzard) which is believed to be used as an energy reserve, but which is also used as a means of defence; it may also be used for keeping the feathers waterproof. If threatened, the bird spits a jet of this nauseating and clinging liquid over its attacker. The oil contains liquid waxes akin to those found in sperm whales. The first four young white-tailed sea eagles (*Haliaeetus albicilla*), reintroduced from Norway on Fair Isle in 1968, started to feed on young fulmars. Three of the young eagles disappeared and one was found with its feathers glued together with fulmar oil; it was cold and wet and died shortly after being found. It is quite likely that the young birds, having no parent to warn them of the danger, got messed up with the fulmar oil and perished from losing the insulating protection of their feathers. It's a good job we are not endowed with such potent spit or vomit! Just think if you could spit at someone and they would go off and die! We'd all be wearing the chador with safety specs! It doesn't bear thinking about.

It was not until the next weekend that I got round to skinning the seal. I had to tidy my workshop and clear the bench to give myself room to operate. I measured the seal and took outline drawings just in case some time in the future I might have time to stuff it; it measured 4 ft from nose to tail. I hung the seal up and skinned it. It had a layer of blubber all over it and I tried to leave as much blubber on the body as possible to reduce the cleaning time on the skin. The pelt was so lovely that it made the job very satisfying, revealing this great rug of mottled fur. I brought the body in to cut up on the draining board in the kitchen. I removed the guts and found they were empty. So it had failed to learn how to catch and swallow prey and had weakened until it caught some disease. But it had plenty of blood….there was blood all over the sink, it sploshed onto the tiles on the floor, it oozed over onto the washing machine and sat in sticky great clots. And after all that cleaning that I had done the week before! I cut it up into meal sized chunks with an old carving knife, which improved dramatically with a bit of sharpening. I didn't wash any of it, but packed it away all gory in polythene bags and put it all down in the freezer except for the neck, which I seared in the pressure cooker and then, when it had sizzled all over, I added some water and pressure cooked it for half an hour. After adding potatoes and greens I came to put it out onto my plate. I poured off the liquid and there was a rich golden oil floating on the top. I spooned this off into a bowl; my first sample of rendered blubber. The meat was extremely tender and certainly did not taste of fish. If anything it had a faint flavour of blubber which hinted at rubber. Over the months I gradually consumed the whole lovely animal. There was usually a layer of oil to decant and when I boiled lumps of blubber on their own I was able to add quite a quantity of the oil to a pot I was using to store it. One interesting thing about it was that it did not solidify like lard even in the fridge. I used to oil my walking boots with this wonderful stuff and it certainly kept the water out, but I found I had quite a following of hounds sniffing round my feet whenever I went out in them!

Eleven years later I found the seal's head still waiting for me in the bottom of the freezer. This could be an interesting experiment, I thought as I prepared it for cooking. I gave it the usual treatment of half an hour or so in the pressure cooker and with a few vegetables all was ready. Well, the blubber had gone rancid and was bitter and awful, but the meat and tongue and things were as sweet and tasty as ever. It just goes to show that all these 'Sell by' and 'Best before' dates are just a ploy to make people throw food out and go and buy more, at least, that is what I think.

Other roadside treasure

Having just completed my morning school-bus run, I set off on my bike from the yard where Ron Hearn kept his coaches on Brockley Hill on Watling Street just below the Royal National Orthopaedic Hospital in Stanmore. I turned left towards London on the A40 and was cycling over the M1 bridge when I noticed a garment lying plastered to the highway. It was there again the following morning, but this time was closer to the kerb having been pushed just a little by every passing wheel. It was a sweatshirt, a sort of greeny-brown in colour, like a wine bottle made from recycled glass. It had an embroidered pattern around the chest. The following morning it had reached the kerb but its very existence in staying in one piece and enduring the constant pounding of weighted rubber gave it the air of a survivor; it seemed to me it had a will to live, a character, a life of its own. I had to pick it up. It was wet and heavy with sand and dirt. I gave it a good shaking and stowed it away as carefully as I would any other roadkill. A few rinses, a run through the washing machine and out came a beautiful garment that was, over the years to become a friend, in fact, a favourite.

Another garment I picked up from beside the road, which cannot be described as roadkill, was a pair of underpants. I call them my lucky pants and for why? Because I found them along with more worthwhile treasure - money! I had spent a morning conducting a survey of the birds of a tetrad (four square kilometres) in the vicinity of Chapel Amble when I had the opportunity to cut a long corner off my return to the car by cutting across a field where there was no right of way, i.e. by trespassing. I decided not to and went the long way round. Almost immediately, as if to reward my law-abiding action, I spotted a £20 note in the grass. No sooner had I stopped jumping for joy than I spotted another note, this one was a £5 note! I now began to search diligently in the whole vicinity and, sure enough, there was another - another fiver - £30! That proved to be the limit of my serendipity, but not entirely, for there was a pair of blue check pants about my size and with nothing worse than a small tear on the back. Although only from British Home Stores, it too has become one of my favourite items for daily wear. They were not the only pants I found that year. While cycling around the Venetian lagoon in Italy, I picked up a pair of natty swimming trunks. They were just the right size and can be used as running shorts when my regular shorts are in the wash or cannot be found. They were put to good use at once as I found a dead little egret by the road that was desiccated, empty, and ready for my museum. The pants made the perfect wrap for the legs, head and wings when pushed in with my sandwiches and warm clothes.

I also picked up a blue fleece from the A39, not two miles from home. It was stained a bit, so it may have had vomit on, but all that had weathered away and it only needed a trip through the washing machine to become another warm favourite. A garment with a history like that is a much more fun thing to wear than something you have bought (and the whole world can buy) from a supermarket. Baseball caps are another thing I occasionally find. I have specimens from the US, Ireland and lots from the UK. They come in useful when orienteering as they save me scalping myself as I collide with branches while reading the map.

The freezer

Although I used to come by roadkill once or twice a week and so maintain a steady supply of meat for my dinner plate, there were times when something big came along, a hare, a badger, a muntjac or even a fallow deer. Obviously, these could not be eaten all at once and so it would be frozen for lean times ahead or to supply the necessary for a party. I had a 21.7 cu ft (0.61cu m) chest freezer in my workshop. It was generally fairly full. Besides roadkill, it had to look after the superabundance of nutritious items arriving after a successful visit to the skips at the back of the local supermarkets. The freezer always seemed to be in need of defrosting. It also had a number of specimens not generally considered suitable for the table which were collected for the purpose of taxidermy, the art of skinning, stuffing and mounting to make the specimen survive in a permanent similitude of real life. However, small items in a freezer have a tendency to dry out and before long freeze-dry, in which condition they are neither usable for taxidermy nor suitable for eating. I had a weasel that was given me by some friends, Arthur and Chris Vince, in the hope that I might like to eat it. I had never tried one before and, despite its diminutive proportions, I decided to see what it was like. However, before I got round to eating it, it became something of a media star in its own right, appearing uncooked on a dinner plate in the Sun newspaper and other publications. When I got round to preparing it for eating, I put it in the microwave to defrost and after a few moments I heard a strange whistle emanating from the microwave - opening the door I could see steam coming from the weasels mouth accompanied by this eerie whistle. The little beast had almost dried out and the little moisture left in it was boiling off and so producing the noise. I decided not to go ahead with the eating experiment.

Another large bag occupying too much space in the freezer is a collection of skins judged too beautiful to throw away but not of sufficient interest or urgency for me to set aside my other pressing activities and do something about them. They comprise several hares and a number of cats of various colours. They would make such lovely gloves if I only had time to do something with them. One long-term resident of the freezer is a fallow buck's head in full antler. It has been there for 15 years at the time of writing and may well stay for another 15 before I get round to doing something with it; its pelt is also in there somewhere. Perhaps I should try and get that pelt cured. Will it be too late? Well, if the hair slips I could use the leather instead. Anyway, in addition to these esoteric items there were many pounds of good food stored there. One day I needed to use the socket into which the freezer was plugged to power some tool for use on a job in the workshop. I unplugged the freezer and... Yes,... you have guessed it, I forgot to plug it back in when I had completed the job. What is more, I then went away for a holiday for two weeks! When I returned and went to the freezer for my dinner....Oh Dear! It had defrosted! Some of the bigger bits were still a bit cold but the frost had all melted and now the freezer was awash with melt water. The bottom 6in (150mm) was a pool of murky red water. Everything has defrosted and the rule is that you do not refreeze such items. But I could not eat a whole freezer full at once and I certainly could not bring myself to throw away such a lot of treasure. To defer this difficult decision, I switched the freezer on again. When I next looked all was safely frozen again. I made my decision, I would eat some and see how I got on. The first item was a badger's leg and after my usual pressure-cooker treatment it was no less enjoyable than in the past (although perhaps my uncritical, easy-to-please palate is no judge in a case like this). I resolved not to waste the contents of the freezer, but eat my way through it. And this I did. When I reached the level of the frozen red lake, I had to get a hammer and screwdriver to chip my dinners out as required. These items seemed no less palatable than meals I had had before. It may well be that some faint deterioration could have been detected by a professional gourmet, but to my well trained palate there was no diminution of the enjoyment I had in the eating of it and by my continued state of rude good health and physical fitness, no reduction in the nutritive benefit I derived from its consumption. It became quite exciting as I got nearer to the bottom as long-forgotten cutlets reappeared for the first time for years. There was one unlabelled bag with a strange yellow hue to its contents, instantly recognisable as seal. Other items that had lost their labels were less easy to identify, but one rather green specimen was so strong and memorable, it had to be the badger from the bird-ringing hut in Ringshall coppice. Eventually I dug out the last grotty edible item and was able to defrost the chest and give it a good wash. So much for the danger of refreezing items in a freezer. I have no doubt there is the opportunity for bacteria to develop, but all meat has bacteria on it, and hung meat benefits from bacterial action. However, I believe in thoroughly cooking all such meat, and while some may regard pressure-cooking as a primitive method of culinary preparation, it does ensure that everything is well and truly dead.

Among the items in the freezer of interest from the natural history aspect, are various small birds such as swallow, robin, chaffinch, greenfinch, linnet, blackbird, wren, goldfinch and dunnock. When I see something dead by the road I have to stop and inspect it, it is always so interesting and so beautiful. Having picked it up, I cannot throw it down, I always want to get it home, skin it, stuff it and mount it. So, it goes into a pocket or cycle bag, I get it home and that is as far as it gets. There are several short-tailed field voles, a common shrew, a water shrew (caught in our garden, I regret to say, by Pansy, our young tortoiseshell cat), a slow worm and a pipistrelle bat. I used to have the skin of a greater horseshoe bat, cured and waiting in the freezer to be stuffed. Like the weasel, this too had acquired a certain celebrity status as it had appeared on television and in various papers and magazines. Perhaps the most frequently asked question during interviews with the media about my roadkill eating experiences was, "*What is the strangest thing you have ever eaten?*" My answer was always, "*A greater horseshoe bat*". The first time this question was asked was during filming for the 'Inside Out' series on SW Television. Russell Labey was the presenter and while were inspecting the bat's skin he asked, "*What does bat taste like?*" I immediately replied, "*A bit like a mouse*". To which he responded, "*Silly question*". Terry Wogan picked up on this a day or so later and quoted it on his radio show. However, you will have noticed that I said "*I used to have*" it. What has become of it? Well, one day after it had been got out for a camera crew to photograph, I left it on the kitchen table. When I came back into the room, I noticed two odd little broken bones on the table. Puzzled, I examined them. They were long thin humeri. Then I found a patch of the wing membrane of a bat and realised that the bones were a bat's wing bones. Pansy had eaten the rest of it!

Owls and buzzards are large birds often seen beside the road, usually a motorway, where it is impossible or inadvisable to stop. But sometimes one is able to pick them up and again these go into the freezer, and I now have quite a few awaiting my attention. I fear most will end up as dried wings and skulls, but should I be incapacitated by some unfortunate event in the future, I shall have plenty of material on which to improve my taxidermy skills and as therapy for any enforced immobility. I always say, "*Prepare for the worst and it is less likely to happen, and if it does, why, you are ready for it*".

One day, not long before this book was ready to publish, when the freezer was in desperate need of defrosting, I went to it with hammer and chisel to remove the incrustations of ice that were gradually pushing up the lid. I lifted the lid and gasped aloud….it had been partly emptied…..someone had been and removed lots of frozen meat….we had had the burglars! I rushed indoors to tell Sue and phone the police. I had to check from my diary when I had last looked into the freezer to give the police the time frame within which the crime could have been committed. Sue worried that they might have taken something else, so before informing the local constabulary, we examined the scene of the crime. Using a cloth to avoid spoiling the fingerprints, I lifted the lid to show Sue how much had gone. She immediately said, "*But it has defrosted.*" I looked again and sure enough, the ice around the top had all gone. A muntjac's head which had been on the top was still there. No one had stolen anything…..the ice had melted and allowed the meat packages to slump together and make it look partly emptied…..what a relief! But now I needed a new freezer, urgently. The old one had been running almost non-stop for 25 – 30 years, it owed me nothing. A replacement was needed before the contents spoiled. I hunted through papers and websites for days before locating a chest freezer of adequate dimensions that had not already been sold. I drove down to near St Ives to collect it and paid the lady £70. She told me how once she had a freezer break down and everything defrosted. She went to claim on her insurance, and they told her she could claim up to £500! The thought entered my head, could I claim for the contents of my freezer and put a price on for stuff that had cost me only time. I was beginning to think it would be a much-needed boost to our finances, when I remembered that I had declined to insure the freezer contents and so save on the premium! When I came to transfer the goods from one to the other, I found one roll of pork that was dated 1993, 15 years past its sell-by date! I put it in for it to mature a little more. The fallow buck's antlered head was transferred but its pelt was showing signs of ageing and I did not have room for so bulky an item. I salted it and posted it to the tanner. When it returned it was a beautiful white-spotted fawn rug with only a small patch where the hair had slipped where it had been pressed against the side of the freezer.

R. Dale Guthrie, of the University of Alaska, describes his inspection of 'Blue Babe', a 36,000-year-old frozen bison in 1979 in his book 'Frozen Fauna of the Mammoth Steppe'. The carcass still showed some red muscle so Guthrie along with several others had a go at eating part of the ancient bison. *"A small part of the mummy's neck was diced and simmered in a pot of stock and vegetables"*, Guthrie wrote. *"We had Blue Babe for dinner. The meat was well aged but still a little tough, and it gave the stew a strong Pleistocene aroma, but nobody there would have dared miss it."* It was considered to be 'agreeable.'

Freegan Activities

I know that there is food for free to be found in the skips and bins at the back of every supermarket, but you have to be fairly brazen (or discreet) to be skip-dipping in public. I remember one night being inside a large waste container outside the back of Sainsbury's in my home town. I was standing on pizzas, lasagnes, pasties and sausages, making a choice of what to take home when I heard a car draw up. I looked out and saw a blue light on the top, uh, uh, police. I lay low, but footsteps approached, and a torch flashed into the container. *"What's going on here then?"* came the ominous enquiry. *"Oh, hello,"* I answered cheerily in my best BBC accent. *"I am salvaging something for my meal tonight. There is some jolly good stuff in here. It is a wicked waste to let it go to the tip. Would you like to try this excellent pizza?"* And so saying I held out to him a perfect pizza all clean and in its original wrapper, with 'Special offer' stuck over the price label. *"Here give it a try"*, I urged. *"Gor blimey!"* said the copper, *"come on Bert, let's get out of here"*. And off they went, leaving me to make my selection undisturbed. I mean, I have a friend who is a GP; he picks up roadkill - no problem - but just imagine one of his patients coming by as he is head-first in a skip! I remember one day at the Fire Research Station in Borehamwood where I worked, where there was a skip into which they used to throw the leftover food from the canteen (sometimes there might be a sack of bread rolls, some of them might be buttered). I suppose I had a reputation for skip dipping and that day my attention was caught by a buttered roll sitting right on the top – like a lump of cheese baiting a rat trap. My suspicions aroused, I picked it up and examined it, it looked OK so I opened it, instead of jam there was a mixture of spit and sand. It was then that my attention was drawn to the window of a nearby building where the station workmen lived; the window was crowded with the expectant faces of the labourers who had set the 'trap' for me!

A case received widespread publicity in early 2011 when Sasha Hall, 21, from Great Baddow, Essex was given a bag of food worth £220 from a bin from *Tesco* which had been left out in the street. She was arrested, handcuffed and taken to the police station while her house was searched. She could have received a 7-year sentence but was given a 12-month conditional discharge. I must say I believe this to be an inane law and a waste of police time; to arrest someone for taking something that is going for landfill is ridiculous. In Germany there is an arrangement whereby people put out into the street furniture surplus to their requirements once a week/month; other people scavenge what has been put out and may well take home a three-piece suite that would, in England, go to the dump. This is an excellent arrangement and one which we could do well to do here. Which council will set the lead?

Is it dangerous?

In many parts of the globe there is malnutrition; meat is not generally available. But in other parts, where a lot of meat is eaten, other illnesses arise such as heart disease. Certainly, eating a lot of meat means ingesting polyunsaturated fatty acids and cholesterol, which are known to cause heart disease. Also, vegetarians are said to suffer less from cancer than meat-eaters. The question here is not, Is meat dangerous? But, Is roadkill more dangerous than meat from domesticated sources? The answer is No and Yes. No, because wild animals will not have been fed with unnatural and possibly harmful additives which might be the case with domesticated animals. But Yes, because there is a greater likelihood of contamination of meat with gut contents and you may not have the experience to identify diseased tissue which might be condemned during the normal butchery process. I have mentioned earlier the possibility of picking up a tapeworm from infected muntjacs – cook them well.

People often ask me how do I know the animal is not diseased? Well, for one thing diseased animals very quickly succumb and usually go away somewhere quiet and hidden to die. But rabbits with myxomatosis are seen occasionally as the disease moves around the country. I don't know if people ever eat these animals but I did make a meal of one myself once. I cooked it well as usual in the pressure cooker. It did not have any greatly different flavour but did taste a bit slippery. I can report that I had no negative repercussions. I once watched a myxy rabbit cross the M5 near Bridgewater. It bumbled blindly forward through the constant stream of vehicles that somehow did not hit it and reached the central reservation unharmed.

I had a girlfriend once who was a vet and she was certain that I had to be a carrier of TB as I had handled so many dead badgers without taking any precautions. Anyway no one near to me has ever caught TB, in fact, I know no one who has, so I suspect that the danger of infection in people's minds is greater than the actual risk. I once had a pigeon with a growth in the chest cavity, but I scraped it out and ate the rest, I did not notice any difference from the usual taste of pigeon. But parasites, that is a different question! Of these there are legion.

Salmonellosis

Salmonellosis, is a bacterial disease caused by a bacterium, usually *Salmonella entericus*. Infection can be caused by eating infected chicken, eggs or other contaminated food (including vegetables) not properly cooked, and by handling pets such as reptiles, baby chicks, ducklings and even a cat or dog. It comes from the faeces of the animals and contamination of their bodies. Edwina Currie, while Health Minister under Margaret Thatcher in 1988, said that most of Britain's egg production was infected with Salmonella. Chicken farmers were up in arms, and she had to resign. The risk of infection was said to be 200 million to one! Treat your roadkill with the same precautions – wash hands and cook well (the meat, not your hands) – and you are unlikely to be infected.

Weil's Disease

Leptospirosis, sometimes known as Weil's Disease, is a bacterial disease that affects humans and animals. The main risk to the roadkill eater is from handling infected rats. The bacterium, *Leptospira icterohaemorrhagiae*, is passed in the urine of infected rats and contaminates ponds and waterways, food, or soil. Again, as with salmonellosis, wash the meat well and cook thoroughly.

Liver flukes

One nasty you could get from a roadkill sheep or goat is fascioliasis. The liver fluke, *(Fasciola hepatica)* is a parasite that infests the liver and bile duct of humans and many species of animals. It belongs to the phylum *Platyhelminthes* (flatworms), class *Trematodea* (flukes). Its hosts include herbivorous mammals and it is found in 46 species of domestic and wild animals as well as man. However, infection by consumption of an infected animal can only be achieved by eating the liver raw.

The intermediate host is the *Lymnaea* snail which lives in marshy areas and standing water. The parasite produces cercariae which encyst on watercress and other aquatic plants. When animals or humans eat these plants, they become infected and the life cycle is repeated. I love wild watercress eaten straight from the water. But it is a bit risky unless you are eating from a spring or very close to one, or there is no sheep or cattle higher up stream. The safe thing is to wash it in a 6% solution of vinegar or potassium permanganate for 10 mins.

Worms

The roundworm, *Toxocara cati,* in cats or *Toxocara canis* in dogs presents a risk to humans giving rise to human toxocariasis. Their eggs, if swallowed, hatch in the stomach and pass through the gut wall into the blood where they travel around the body. These migrating larvae develop nodules in the liver, kidneys, brain and lungs, in humans they may settle in the eye and result in impairment of vision. The main source of infection in man is from contact with contaminated soil where cats have defaecated. Children are particularly at risk if they play where cats defaecate. Eggs can be present in cat meat if the intestine has been ruptured and gut contents or faecal matter has contaminated the meat. Adequate cooking should, however, eliminate this risk. Larvae can also be present as cysts in the meat of cats. Again, there is a possibility for human infection to occur if the meat is not properly cooked. Perhaps the most dangerous routes of infection are presented not by eating the cat, but by handling cooked meat or food after handling a cat that has recently visited its defecation area. These comments apply equally to infection by *Toxocara cani* from dogs.

Meat from infected cervids is suitable for human consumption but tissues or organs containing the cysts should not be eaten.

Cystic Hydatid Disease in humans can be a significant disease because of the mechanical and toxic effects of the cyst(s). The tremendous reproductive potential of the tapeworm as well as the sheer size of the hydatid cyst(s) can cause problems in the organs where they are lodged. If the cyst(s) bursts, the resultant toxic (anaphylactic) shock would probably be fatal. In Alaska and Canada most infections are benign, indicating humans are probably a less suitable host for the sylvatic form of *E. granulosus* than for the pastoral form.

Toxoplasmosis

Question: What caused Martina Navratilova to lose the US Open Tennis Tournament in 1982? Answer: According to the New York Times it was Toxoplasmosis. But did she catch it from a cat or from eating a cat?

Toxoplasmosis is caused by the protozoan *Toxoplasma gondii*. Infection is caused by eating raw or undercooked meat containing cysts from sheep, pigs, deer or rats. The cat is the primary host and touching cat faeces or anything that has come into contact with them and putting hand to mouth, or while preparing a cat for eating and contaminating utensils and dishes with gut contents can also transmit the parasite. Cooking above 150^0F (65^0C) for freezing for 24 hr will kill the pathogen. Acute toxoplasmosis has flu-like symptoms, but many people carry it without knowing. In Britain, one in five, and in France, two in five, are carriers of the disease. Until recently it was thought to be an insignificant disease in healthy people, but research has revealed that it has mind-altering properties. Dr Nicky Boulter of Sydney University of Technology writing in the *Australasian Science* magazine said, "*The effect of infection is different between men and women……it can make men behave like alley cats and women behave like sex kittens"*. (There could be exciting therapeutic possibilities here.) Studies have found that infection also changes the behaviour of mice which became more likely to take risks that increased their chance of being eaten by cats, which in turn would allow the parasite to continue its life cycle. Another study showed people who were infected but not showing symptoms were 2.7 times more likely to be involved in a car accident. Prevention: take care with raw meat and gut contents and cook everything thoroughly.

Giardiasis

There is a common protozoan parasite, *Giardia lamblia,* found in pets and wild animals that causes enteritis in man, the infection occurring as cysts picked up from faeces or eating uncooked meat, though it is usually caught by drinking or swimming in contaminated water (it is known as beaver fever in N

America).

Ticks

A disease which can be contracted after handling deer carcasses is Lyme disease. It is caused by a spirochaete bacterium, *Borrelia burgdorferi*, which is transmitted by the bite of a sheep or deer tick, *(Ixodes ricinus)* in Britain or Europe and a deer tick *(I. dammini)* in America. People are as much at risk just walking through undergrowth frequented by deer as by anyone handling a carcass. In fact, as an orienteer who regularly competes in areas where deer are present, I examine myself carefully to check for any little ticks that may have attached themselves to my person. They often do not become apparent until the next day when irritation and a red skin lesion draw attention to the tick. Ticks are best removed by gripping them firmly with tweezers as close to the skin as possible and pulling steadily; this often leaves the head in the skin, so I prefer to do it by partially asphyxiating them with a smear of vaseline for 10 min and then pulling them out with tweezers. Should the red area grow to 5cm (2in) in diameter, see a doctor. Other symptoms include: weakness, fatigue and pain and stiffness in the joints especially the knees (just how I feel after an orienteering race). If not attended to it can result in permanent disability and possibly, though rarely, death. A friend of mine, Mike Tween, picked up an infected tick while orienteering and became badly crippled as a result. He has since died.

Ixodes ricinus and other ticks also carry a number of other diseases which can be transmitted to humans: louping ill virus, tick-borne encaphalitis and Q-fever which is considered to be possibly the most infectious disease in the world, as a human being can be infected by a single bacterium *(Coxiella burnetii)*. This tick, as well as being a parasite on deer, is found on other farm animals, cats, dogs and rats. So treat all ticks with the utmost respect. Disinfect hands, tweezers and bites, and watch out for unusual symptoms in the ensuing days and weeks.

Bird Lice

I once picked up a dead crow from a quiet Cornish lane and carried it for about a mile to where I had left the car. I carried it by its feet and occasionally changed hands. By the time I was back at the car, I had developed a fierce irritation to the scalp where I had scratched my head while walking along. Something had crawled off the bird onto my hand and I had transferred it to my head. The irritation had become almost unbearable in the quarter of an hour it took to drive home. I dashed indoors yelling for my wife. Luckily, she was about and quickly got to work under a strong light picking off the little beasts with a pair of tweezers. What were they? Feather lice. They are small flattened and almost translucent. I knew of their existence and had seen them many times before, in fact, I had always called them (wrongly) feather flukes. They are flattened insects that feed on feathers and skin but not blood. They belong to an order known as *Mallophaga* or Chewing lice of the group *Pterygota* and cause irritation when feeding. Luckily they don't cause any diseases.

BSE and CWD

All animals are susceptible to infection by viruses and unicellular pathogens and to parasitization by worms and flukes. Thoroughly cooking meat will protect the eater from any transmittable nasties that may have been present in the meat. But would it protect me from mad cow disease? The question is, in a way, irrelevant because the chance of finding a roadkill cow must be pretty slim as I have never encountered any roadkill cow in all my sixty-odd years of noticing roadkill, and if you were to come across one, would you be able to get it into the boot of the car, or would you want to? But Top Gear, the mad British TV programme on motoring, purported to have found one once. Jeremy Clarkson and his cronies were driving across the States and were supposed to be living off roadkill. They had only managed to find a squashed squirrel when Jeremy drives up with a cow balanced precariously on the roof. Jeremy said he did not kill it but he did get help in putting it on the car. They got it off by reversing and swinging the wheel, so it was thrown onto the ground. It was a bit pathetic really because they did not make any attempt to cut bits off it and have a go at eating it.

But to get back to mad cow disease, a similar disease has appeared in parts of America in deer and deer are frequently picked up by roadkill afficionados. No similar disease has, as yet appeared in humans, but it is a possibility. Perhaps I should say something here about these diseases to put you in the picture. Mad cow disease is better known as bovine spongiform encephalopathy (BSE) and occurs, as its name implies, in cattle; it first appeared in 1985. A similar disease occurring in sheep is scrapie, which has been around for 300 years. Creutzfeldt-Jakob Disease (CJD) was first identified in 1921and occurs in humans at a rate of one case per million of population per year; it has three forms, sporadic CJD, genetic CJD (inherited from one parent) and iatrogenic CJD (caused by accidental medical transfer of infective material). A new form of CJD appeared in 1995, known as new variant CJD (vCJD); it was believed to be a human form of BSE. A similar disease peculiar to deer, chronic wasting disease (CWD), was first described in 1967. These diseases are not caused by parasites, bacteria or viruses but are considered by some to be caused by a form of protein known as a prion which is a self-replicating protein, which does not have a covering and is not considered to be a living organism; whereas a virus is genetic material contained in a protein shell and is the smallest living organism. It has been put forward by the establishment that feeding cattle with a high-protein product, derived from ground-up animals, and known as 'meat and bone meal' (MBM), in which some of the rendered sheep has been infected with scrapie, passes the disease on to the cattle as BSE. Likewise, it is postulated that humans eating beef from cattle with BSE can develop vCJD. Both CJD and vCJD are always fatal, but may take 10 – 30 years to develop. CJD takes 4 –5 months from the first symptoms and vCJD 14 months until death occurs.

Mark Purdey

While writing this book, I received a phone call from a chap called Andrew Tweedie to tell me that there was a dead badger by the road near to his home somewhere beyond Truro. It is amazing how complete strangers (as well as friends) will ring me to let me know about roadkill they have spotted. Wonderful! He also asked if I had seen a book entitled 'Animal Pharm' by Mark Purdey in which he thought I would be interested. He told me he had some copies and if I cared to call, he would be pleased to let me have one. I was down that way in the next day or so and I took the opportunity to pick up a copy of 'Animal Pharm' (the badger had disappeared). The book paints a totally different picture of the epidemiology of BSE to that generally held. Purdey contends that prions are not infective, although if they are injected the new host will develop the same syndrome. I have had to discard what the establishment preaches about these diseases. I am utterly persuaded that what Purdey arrived at which is recounted in the book, and which is rejected by the establishment is, in fact, the truth and is upheld by all the evidence. The book tells the story of an amazing worldwide hunt for the facts about the causes of the disease in both animals and man. Purdey was a Somerset farmer who was ordered by a Ministry of Agriculture inspector in 1984 to administer a toxic organophosphate pesticide (phosmet) twice yearly to his organic dairy herd. He refused, took the Ministry to court and won. Treatment with phosmet, which had been in use since 1972, was enforced on UK farmers from 1982. The first case of a new neurodegenerative syndrome, BSE, occurred in 1985, but it was not until 1986 after several hundred more animals had gone down with it that it was declared to be a transmissible spongiform encephalopathy (TSE) similar to scrapie in sheep. In 1987 Purdey postulated a link between the use of phosmet and BSE. In 1993 he treated a cow, that had developed the symptoms of BSE, with injections of magnesium sulphate (Epson salts) and it completely recovered (no money there for the big pharmaceuticals). He wrote to the Minister, John Gummer, who reiterated the government stance that it 'was caused by feeding meat and bone meal (MBM) containing material from scrapie-infected sheep to cattle'. Purdey published an article about the phosmet/BSE link in the Ecologist in 1994 and gave a presentation to MAFF about it. They refused to carry out any research *"because of the cost to the tax payer"*. The government continued with phosmet treatments until 1995. As to the infection of humans with diseased prions, Purdey has this to say: *"A global study of the most basic rudiments of the history of TSEs clearly demonstrates that this disease does NOT spread via animal-to-animal contact or via ingestion of the 'infected' by the 'uninfected'. For instance, when I was researching the most intensive global hotspot of sheep scrapie in the northernmost Icelandic fjords, I found that the Icelandic sheep farmers had adopted the custom of slaughtering any sheep the moment the first symptoms of scrapie emerged. This tradition had not evolved from any fear of the disease exploding in the sheep population - since scrapie has occurred at a consistent incidence rate for light years in Iceland – but was carried out because the hard-pressed farmers thought it best to eat the sheep (brains and all!) before the wasting symptoms of scrapie reduced the poor beast to skin and bones. So if scrapie or CWD can be passed onto humans via consumption - as the scientific authorities would have us believe - why have no cases of CJD erupted in these Icelandic sheep farmers? In fact, Iceland has only ever witnessed two cases of CJD in its entire medical history, and these victims had both hailed from the scrapie-free district in the far south of the country"*. He has amassed hard scientific evidence *"which indicates that both vCJD and BSE could result from separate exposure of bovines and humans to the same package of toxic environmental factors, ferrimagnetic metals and low frequency sonic shock, and not from the ingestion of the one species by the other"*.

Purdey applied his theory to CWD in deer and vCJD in humans. He travelled the world visiting sites where clusters of these diseases have occurred and formulated a theory as to how these diseases have arisen and what should be done about them. He noticed that CWD was first reported in deer in Fort Collins, Colorado, where trials had been carried out injecting deer with strontium 90 and cesium 134. He said of this: *"it is unlikely that the space/time correlation between these unique radioactive experiments and the emergence of a novel neuro-degenerative disease is a mere coincidence"*. With the assistance of his brother Nigel he conducted epidemiological studies of the disease worthy of several research teams. He has issued a warning on his website: *"hunters who are feasting off deer shot in CWD regions which have thrived off mineral licks/pine needles containing trivalent manganese, will, in turn, become contaminated with trivalent manganese themselves; and thereafter rendered hyper susceptible to the low frequency infrasonic shocks in their hunting environment (eg; natural infrasound, rifle shots, etc).The same eco-prerequisites that caused CWD in the deer are now primed and present in the human hunter. CJD could result".* So, if you live in a CWD-affected area and want to pick up roadkill you might be advised to take a copper salt supplement to protect your prions.

Purdey's quest to discover the truth was hampered at every turn by government bureaucracies and self-serving scientific cliques who sought to smear and marginalize him. Dogged by dirty tricks and forced to work alone as something of a scientific sleuth, he struggled to reveal hidden interests and dangerous secrets. His supporters included many members of the public, as well as Prince Charles and the poet Ted Hughes. The latter wrote to him expressing *"a million congratulations".* He died on 12 November 2006.

I would urge readers to get a copy of 'Animal Pharm' or borrow it from the library. If enough people learn the truth about what has been going on, maybe one day a Minister of State for the Environment, Food and Rural Affairs will be man enough to override his civil service 'advisers' and open the door to Purdey's work and the real truth about BSE and CJD.

All this reminds me of the sad history of Ignaz Semmelweis, the Hungarian physician who discovered, in 1847, while working in the maternity clinic in Vienna General Hospital in Austria, that if surgeons washed their hands after conducting *post mortem* examinations before dealing with mothers in childbirth, the incidence of puerperal fever, could be drastically cut. He was ridiculed and, what is more, was dismissed from the hospital. He was eventually forced to move to Budapest and was allowed to work in a hospital there only on condition that he did not tell surgeons to wash their hands! Semmelweis wrote angry letters to prominent obstetricians, denouncing them as irresponsible murderers. He was committed to a mental asylum in 1865 where he died at the hands of his guards two weeks later. Semmelweis was only recognised when Louis Pasteur developed the 'germ theory of disease' in 1864 which offered a theoretical explanation for Semmelweis' findings. Mark Purdey died a year before his book was published. As Semmelweis was then, Purdey is still regarded as a nutcase by the establishment.

Dr Barry Groves in his website Second opinions[19] upholds Purdey's theories and claims there is no evidence of BSE in cattle being transmitted to man. He writes: *"Clearly, the 'experts' need to be more open-minded and consider that they may not always be right. They need to listen to others outside their very narrow field. Mark Purdey committed the ultimate sin. He tried to tell them that they might be wrong. No 'expert' would listen to someone who was 'only' a farmer. Yet if Mark Purdey's hypothesis had been considered earlier, who knows how much grief it might have saved. It has still to be proven beyond doubt, but it is a much more likely hypothesis than that which the 'experts' have managed to come up with. Purdey went out and tried to discover the cause of BSE and CJD; the 'experts' merely sat around a table and discussed it."* I have to say I encountered the same blinkered attitude in my dealings with MAFF over the burning of foot and mouth carcasses. Let me give Mark the last word,: *"The BSE debacle represents the mere tip of the iceberg of Establishment ineptitude and socio-eco-irresponsibility. My book returns us to the lessons that can be learnt from the intuitive wisdoms of the people on the 'ground'. At the same time it will alert us to both the insidious and unscientific techniques which the incestuous clique of official experts employ to marginalize and discredit those who dissent from the totalitarian line. It will show us the ill-conceived basis on which the positions of the Establishment are truly based, along with the woeful degree of administrative complacency over issues which, in most cases, are matters of life and death for normal people".*

Motorways

I don't recommend collecting roadkill from the carriageway or central reservation of motorways and busy dual carriageways, it increases the chances of your becoming a roadkill specimen yourself, which would, admittedly, add a little humour to your demise. Stopping on the hard shoulder is hazardous unless you can get right off the road. But a stop to investigate a 'suspicious rattle' in an emergency or a 'possible puncture' just after you had passed a nice bit of roadkill would be one way of cloaking your actions with legality. I once spotted a dead buzzard on the central reservation of the M5 somewhere near Cullompton. It was too busy to stop when I saw it, but I had opportunity to return to the location a few days later. The bird was close to a junction, and I was able to see the bird from the road above. I almost parked right above the motorway, but decided to go a little further down the road and park on the verge. I then made my way on foot down the slip road and paced up and down the hard shoulder for what seemed like an age waiting for a break in the traffic to allow me to cross the carriageway and pick up the bird, which seemed to be waving its wings at me in the slipstream from every passing vehicle. At last, there was a sufficiently large gap in the traffic roaring by, I dashed over, grabbed the buzzard by the legs and scuttled back to the safety of the hard shoulder. It was a beautiful specimen. Its huge wings, soft feathers, cruel beak and razor-sharp claws held my attention as I walked back up the slip road. It was only then that I noticed a car parked over the carriageway just where I had decided not to park. Gulp! It was a police car! Oh dear! I slipped the bird into a plastic bag and sauntered nonchalantly towards the inevitable meeting with the law. I endeavoured to rehearse some plausible explanation for what they would doubtless regard as my foolish action. Could I blarney my way through what lay before me? I walked on. When I reached the roundabout in full view of the patrol car I turned left to get to my car. No one got out of the police car, no one shouted to me to stop, in fact, nothing happened. I couldn't believe it! They had not seen my rescue mission on the highway below, or, if they had, they had not deemed it necessary to take any action! I was still a free man!

Is it legal?

UK

Non-game animals

For most of us, finding something of value that does not belong to us, is more of a nuisance than a joy. We feel duty bound to try and reunite the item with its rightful owner. But I do remember the horror of discovering I had lost my wallet and the joy of meeting it again at the local police station. It had money in it and, of course, the finder was rewarded with thanks and a crisp piece of paper from the wallet. But a dead bird or animal, to whom does that belong? Does it belong to the person on whose land it is found? I am reliably informed that live animals and game belong to no one until they are dead. But the minute they hit the ground dead they belong to the owner of the land (unless they have been lawfully shot and fall in a neighbouring property, when they belong to the shooter, but he would be trespassing were he to enter the land – without permission – to collect it). Except in a situation where an individual has lawfully obtained possession of game by enclosing them and is caring for them as domestic animals, then they are his property. But if it is on or beside a road, what then? It belongs to the owner of the road, and to whom does the road belong? Motorways, trunk roads and some other roads belong to the Highways Agency, a government body; other roads belong to the local authority, which may be the county council. However, the surface of roads across an individual's land belongs to the local authority, but the subsoil belongs to the owner of the land through which it passes and would revert to him if the road were to be taken out of use. The Highways Act 1980 states that: "*(1) If any horses, cattle, sheep, goats or swine are at any time found straying or lying on or at the side of a highway their keeper is guilty of an offence; but this subsection does not apply in relation to a part of a highway passing over any common, waste or unenclosed ground*. So, farm animals getting out onto a road are the responsibility of their owner who would be liable were any damage to be caused by them. Cattle strayed onto the road between Camelford and Bude in foggy weather and a motorist collided with them and was killed. But farm animals grazing on unfenced moor land, commons or forests belong to the farmer, but the farmer would not be liable for any damage if they were involved in an accident. Just such an accident happened to me.

Game

There is a widely held belief that whoever knocks down game (hares, pheasants, partridges, red grouse, ptarmigan, black grouse, woodcock, snipe, deer and rabbits) is not allowed by law to pick it up, but whoever else comes along next may do so with impunity. The Game Act 1831 and the Game Licences Act 1860 as amended used to state that a motorist who accidentally killed game by running into it in his car might break the law if he took the bird or animal away with him. He would have been entitled to do so only if he had a game licence and the permission of the landowner. But from 1 August 2007, the Regulatory Reform (Game) Order 2007 removed the requirements for the game trade in England as previously set out in these acts; it was followed by similar legislation in the rest of the United Kingdom. The effect of this new legislation meant that it would no longer be necessary to hold a local authority licence or an excise licence in order to kill or deal in game. So, I have every confidence in saying that should you accidentally hit a rabbit or a pheasant you have as much right to it as the next person to come along.

Wildlife

The Wildlife and Countryside Act 1981 is the primary legislation which protects birds and animals, in the UK. Under this legislation all birds, are protected by law and thus an offence is committed if one:

Part 1 Section 1

(1) ..intentionally -- kills, injures or takes any wild bird

(2) has in his possession or control any live or dead wild bird, or any part of...a wild bird,

except where:

(3) the bird had not been killed,… or had been killed… otherwise than in contravention of the Act

Section 4

(2) (c) or the act was the incidental result of a lawful operation and could not reasonably have been avoided.

Subsection (1) rules that to intentionally run down a protected bird is an offence, and (2) to possess a bird procured in such a way is also an offence. But Subsection (3) and Section 4 Subsection (2) (c) rule that there is no offence if the bird was killed accidentally or as a result of a lawful operation (driving) and there is no offence to possess a bird killed in such a way.

The same legislation applies to bats, otters and red squirrels (which are included in Schedule 5):

Section 9

(1) If any person intentionally kills, injures or takes any wild animal included in Schedule 5 he shall be guilty of an offence, or

(2) has in one's possession or control any live or dead wild animal, included in Schedule 5 or any part of, or anything derived from such an animal, he shall be guilty of an offence, unless

(3) he shows that -- the animal had not been killed or taken, or had been killed or taken otherwise than in contravention of the provisions of the Act.

Section 10

(3) (c) or the act was the incidental result of a lawful operation and could not reasonably have been avoided.

The same arguments as given above for birds apply equally to wild animals.

Badgers come under the Protection of Badgers Act 1992 and offences are committed by:

1 Taking, injuring or killing badgers

(1) A person is guilty of an offence if, --- he wilfully kills, injures or takes, or attempts to kill, injure or take, a badger.

(3) A person is guilty of an offence if, except as permitted by or under this Act, he has in his possession or under his control any dead badger or any part of, or anything derived from, a dead badger.

(4) A person is not guilty of an offence under subsection (3) above if he shows that— the badger had not been killed, or had been killed otherwise than in contravention of the provisions of this Act or of the Badgers Act 1973

(c) unavoidably killing or injuring a badger as an incidental result of a lawful action.

Again, the same arguments apply to the accidental killing and the unavoidable killing of badgers and the possession of dead badgers and any parts or derivatives thereof where the badger had not been wilfully killed.

These offences are offences of strict liability, in other words the onus of proof is on the person in possession of the dead beast to show, on a balance of probabilities, that they have it lawfully. An offence is not committed if the creature was not killed, taken, or sold to them or anyone else illegally.

A letter appeared in the Guardian after there had been an article on me advocating the eating of roadkill and casseroling a badger in which the author claimed that casseroling a badger was against the law. I replied in the following vein: *"Ray Knagg (Letters, January 4) claims 'badger casserole is illegal. Under the Protection of Badgers Act 1992 it is an offence to possess a dead badger or any part of a badger'. But badgers accidentally killed on the road do not come under the provisions of the act by reason of the following clause: 'A person is not guilty of an offence ... if he shows that ... the badger had not been killed, or had been killed otherwise than in contravention of the provisions of this act or of the Badgers Act 1973.' This makes it quite clear that it is not against the law to remove a dead badger from the highway or the verge to dispose of the body, and if that disposal involves casseroling and eating it, the act is no impediment to such an action."*

Deer

Four species of deer come under the provisions of the Deer Act 1991, they are: the red deer (Cervus elaphus), fallow deer (Dama dama), roe deer (Capreolus capreolus) and sika deer (Cervus nippon). Two other deer have become established in this country: *the muntjac deer (Muntiacus reevesi) and the Chinese water deer (Hydropotes inermis)*. The muntjac is widespread in south and central England and Wales and is increasing in number and range to the Scottish border. It frequently comes into conflict with cars and always comes off the worst. The Chinese water deer is mainly restricted to Bedfordshire, Cambridgeshire and Norfolk.

The Deer Act regards removing a carcass from land as poaching, but it does provide a good escape clause. This is what it says:

1 Poaching of deer

(1) Subject to subsection (3) below, if any person enters any land without the consent of the owner or occupier or other lawful authority in search or pursuit of any deer with the intention of taking, killing or injuring it, he shall be guilty of an offence.

(2) Subject to subsection (3) below, if any person while on any land— (c) removes the carcase of any deer, without the consent of the owner or occupier of the land or other lawful authority, he shall be guilty of an offence.

(3) A person shall not be guilty of an offence under subsection (1) or subsection (2) above by reason of anything done in the belief that— he would have the consent of the owner or occupier of the land if the owner or occupier knew of his doing it and the circumstances of it.

This suggests to me that anyone accidentally killing a deer and picking it up, or picking up one killed accidentally by someone else is not running afoul of the law whether the deer lands on the road or staggers a few yards before dropping onto the surrounding land. I believe that the owner or occupier of the land would welcome my removing said carcass. We roadkill buffs don't mind such things. It could cost the landowner time and money to dispose of the carcass, whereas I would remove it at no charge. Certainly, if you want to be all clean and above board, and you know who the landowner is, call round or give him a tinkle to check that it is OK. I do not believe that this interpretation of the law is likely to encourage people (poachers) to drive about trying to hit deer on our roads as the outcome of such collisions is occasionally fatal to the driver as well. And let me say here that I am totally against the killing of any creature by means of a motor car anywhere and under any circumstances.

I came across the following on the blog of a survival website in which Scswampfox wrote: *"Fresh roadkill deer is tasty as long as the guts are intact. It is also illegal to remove it from where it lies...It comes under the stealing by finding laws."* So, what is this stealing by finding law? A lady was arrested for taking stuff from a bin outside a supermarket (see Freegan Activities). But this was for freegan activity, not for picking up roadkill. But to get back to the Survival School blog, a post onto another forum was posted onto the blog. It read: *"As a professional deer manager, a member of The Humane Slaughter Association and a marksman on a retainer to DEFRA, I would beg you all not to attempt to hit a deer in your car. At best your car will end up a write off, at worst you will end up dead (I think about 30 people lost their lives last year as a result of deer impacts).* He is right about the risk of death. *As a professional stalker,... we... know exactly where to shoot deer and with the correct weapons. This ensures a humane kill without damaging the gut. If the gut is ruptured, then the meat is contaminated and not suitable for human consumption. It is essential that the animal is bled and gralloched straight after death (no you don't hang it up from anything). The object of the game is to cool the carcass as quickly as possible (we have special tools to hold the chest cavity open to assist rapid cooling). Any deer that has cooled to, or near ambient temperature without being bled or gralloched is a health hazard and not suitable for human consumption."*

Such meat may not be suitable for human consumption as defined by the slaughter regulations, but, as far as its actual suitability for human consumption is concerned, damage to the gut or delayed gralloching do not make it unsuitable, provided these facts are duly taken into consideration when it is being butchered.

Does God allow it?

Christianity

I was brought up in a Christian household in the 1940s and we never ate black pudding or black sausages because they were made with blood. My parents followed the directions given in the Book of the Acts in the New Testament which is part of the Christian Bible. As the new gospel of Christianity spread from its origin in Jerusalem to Antioch in Asia Minor, some Jews from Judaea told the Gentiles, or Non-Jews, who lived in Antioch that they had to be circumcised and keep the law of Moses to be saved. This produced a bit of a row and Paul and Barnabas were sent to Jerusalem to get a ruling on the matter. A conference was held and it was determined that Gentiles did not need to be circumcised or keep the law to be saved. Paul and Barnabas with Judas and Silas were sent with a letter to give Antioch the good news that they did not need to book into the circumcision clinic, but there were four things from which they should abstain. This is the relevant passage (Acts 15 v 28 & 29): *"For it seemed good to the Holy Ghost, and to us, to lay upon you no greater burden than these necessary things: that ye abstain from meats offered to idols, and from blood, and from things strangled,:........ from which if ye keep yourselves, ye shall do well."*

A prohibition against eating roadkill could be read into the second and third items. As to blood, I know of no Christian who feels duty bound by this scripture to eat only kosher meat. I certainly have never had any conscience about eating meat which might have some blood left in its arteries, veins and capillaries. If any one were to be worried about it, careful washing might relieve that conscience. I believe that a serious Christian need have no conscience about eating roadkill on this ground. Then, as to things strangled: strictly, roadkill has not been strangled. Major trauma or a bang on the head are more akin to death by hunting, and that is not proscribed. So how does this leave the zealous Christian who wishes to avail himself of a free meal when he finds a rabbit, a pheasant or a deer, dead and bleeding beside the road? From one point of view, you could say God put it there for him to come across; it would save him money that could be used to help the poor and needy or finance some new outreach project. I think it is OK for him to eat it with a good conscience, but if his conscience is troubled by eating any blood, I am afraid that to be consistent, he must become a vegetarian. But that does not stop him giving it or feeding it to an unbeliever in keeping with Deuteronomy, Chapter 14 v 21: *"Ye shall not eat of anything that dieth of itself: thou shalt give it unto the stranger that is in thy gates, that he may eat it."*

Judaism

The Torah of the Jewish faith is also the first five books – the Pentateuch - of the Old Testament of the Christian bible. What may and may not be eaten is given in some detail in the book of Leviticus. In a copy of the King James' version of the bible that I have before me, which bears my grandmother's signature, Mabel Eyles (dated 1884), the date of the writing of Leviticus is given as 1490 BCE, the postulated year of the exodus of the children of Israel from Egypt. This is from Bishop Ussher's timetable of the chronology of the world derived from the dates given in the bible and cycles of the lunar and solar calendar. Historical and archaeological research place the date of the exodus as somewhere between the 16th and 12th centuries BCE; the Time-Life editors of the History of the World series have gone for 1230 BCE. Moses is the supposed author of the Pentateuch, but modern scholars attribute the content of all of the first four books of the Pentateuch to four different authors (unknown) and an editor, and Deuteronomy to mainly two different authors, however, I digress. According to the book of Genesis (ch 1), Adam and Eve were given only the plants for food, as were also all the animals, carnivores included! The whole animal kingdom was vegetarian! However, after the flood man was given a change of diet. Genesis Chapter 9 v3: *"Every moving thing that liveth shall be food for you; even as the green herb have I given you all things."* Nothing was prohibited, not even the poisonous tree frogs.

It was only after the Children of Israel came out of the land of Egypt and God entered into a covenant with them that He imposed some rules on their menu. The first restrictions on what they were allowed to eat were given to Moses on Mount Sinai in Exodus, Chapter 22 v 31: *"neither shall ye eat any flesh that is torn of beasts in the field; ye shall cast it to the dogs."* This could be stretched to include roadkill today, I suppose. This is developed in Leviticus, Chapter 3, where fat and blood are prohibited: v16 & 17 *"...all the fat is the Lord's. It shall be a perpetual statute for your generations throughout all your dwellings, that ye eat neither fat nor blood."* This is enlarged on in Chapter 7 and we have the penalty for eating fat or blood given: v22 - 27 *"And the Lord spake unto Moses, saying, Speak unto the children of Israel, saying, Ye shall eat no manner of fat, of ox, or of sheep, or of goat. And the fat of the beast that dieth of itself, and the fat of that which is torn with beasts, may be used in any other use: but ye shall in no wise eat of it. For whosoever eateth the fat of the beast, of which men offer an offering made by fire unto the Lord, even the soul that eateth it shall be cut off from his people. Moreover ye shall eat no manner of blood, whether it be of fowl or of beast, in any of your dwellings. Whatsoever soul it be that eateth any manner of blood, even that soul shall be cut off from his people."*

A lot more tasty and nutritious items were struck off the Israelite's menu in Leviticus, Chapter 11, where lists of the creatures that might and might not be eaten are given. This pretty much rules out most normal beasts, except for ruminants and pheasants, partridges and pigeons and v 39 seems to allow the eating of roadkill provided it is a clean animal, although there is a penalty of being unclean until even and having to wash and wash your clothes: *"And if any beast, of which ye may eat, die; he that toucheth the carcase thereof shall be unclean until even. And he that eateth of the carcase of it shall wash his clothes, and be unclean until the even: he also that beareth the carcase of it shall wash his clothes and be unclean until the even."*

Chapter 17 gives the reason for not eating blood and the code for hunting, and again the let-out clause for eating clean roadkill: v10 - 16 *"And whatsoever man there be of the house of Israel, or of the strangers that sojourn among you, that eateth any manner of blood, I will even set my face against that soul that eateth blood, and will cut him off from among his people. For the life of the flesh is in the blood: and I have given it to you upon the altar to make an atonement for your souls: for it is the blood that maketh an atonement for the soul. Therefore I said unto the children of Israel, No soul of you shall eat blood, neither shall any stranger that sojourneth among you eat blood. And whatsoever man there be of the children of Israel, or of the strangers that sojourn among you, which hunteth or catcheth any beast or fowl that may be eaten: he shall even pour out the blood thereof, and cover it with dust. For it is the life of all flesh; the blood of it is for the life thereof: therefore I said unto the children of Israel, ye shall eat the blood of no manner of flesh: for the life of all flesh is the blood thereof: whosoever eateth it shall be cut off. And every soul that eateth that which died of itself, or that which was torn, with beasts, whether it be it one of your own country or a stranger, he shall both wash his clothes, and bathe himself in water, and be unclean until the even: then shall he be clean. But if he wash them not, nor bathe his flesh; then he shall bear his iniquity."* Roadkill is really covered by both 'dying of itself' and being 'torn by beasts' as it can be viewed as having got itself under the car, and a car is a bit like a mindless beast, anyway it has the same effect.

The book of Deuteronomy repeats and expands the prohibitions and introduces a reward for keeping them , Chapter 12 v 25: *"thou shalt not eat it; that it may go well with thee, and thy children after thee, when thou shalt do that which is right in the sight of the Lord."* But it does allow the giving away and selling of roadkill, Chapter 14 v 21: *"Ye shall not eat of anything that dieth of itself: thou shalt give it unto the stranger that is in thy gates, that he may eat it; or thou mayest sell it unto an alien…….."*

There is only one record of people eating blood, that is in 1 Samuel, Chapter 13 v 32 where they seemed to get away with it: *"And the people flew upon the spoil, and took sheep, and oxen, and calves, and slew them on the ground: and the people did eat them with the blood."* So, the warning given before: *"for the life of all flesh is the blood thereof: whosoever eateth it shall be cut off"*, means nothing, the people violated the law and nothing happened.

However, the Talmud, a later expansion of the law given in the Torah, goes into great detail about the procedure for killing animals (shechita), which bits of the animal are suitable and how they must be prepared and cooked to make them fit to be eaten, or Kosher. Anything that is not kosher is tref. Roadkill has not been through the proper kosher procedure and is therefore tref. I do not believe that shechita killing and kosher washing and preparation, as practised by the most fastidious Jews, gets rid of blood and fat at the microscopic level. Microscopes had not been invented when the Talmud was written. If there is any blood corpuscle or a molecule of fat left in the meat then the object of the whole operation is null and void, it has not succeeded in getting rid of the blood and fat, and whoever eats it is eating blood or fat and by so doing is breaking the Law of Moses. OK, you may not be eating a cup of blood or a fat deposit. But then I am sure I should be told, were I to enquire, that following the procedures laid down in the Talmud is acceptable to God. This may seem at odds with common sense, but then common sense and religion rarely go hand in hand.

The expression, *"For the life of the flesh is in the blood"*, is not actually true. Yes, if you drain the blood out of an animal it will die, but only because the capacity to move oxygen from the lungs to the tissues has been removed. There are fluids today known as blood substitutes that are used in heart operations where the blood of the patient is removed and is replaced by a substitute which carries oxygen around the body and thus keeps it alive. The reason for doing this is because putting real blood through a mechanical pump damages the blood corpuscles and that releases toxins sufficient to kill the patient. Blood is a transport mechanism to get oxygen (and other things) to the tissues. It does it by means of haemoglobin, a red iron compound, found only in the red blood corpuscles, that picks up oxygen where the concentration of oxygen is high (in the lungs) forming oxyhaemoglobin, an unstable compound, and transports it to all parts of the body and gives it up where oxygen concentrations are low (in the muscles). At the same time, it picks up carbon dioxide where it is high (in the muscles) forming carbaminohaemoglobin, another unstable compound, this one is distinctly blue, and gives it up where it is low (in the lungs). Should carbon monoxide be taken up instead, a cherry red stable compound, carboxyhaemoglobin, is formed that prevents oxygen being picked up. The body is full of blood, but death occurs. The body may have every drop of blood it needs but take away the oxygen and it quickly dies. Brain cells die first, after 3 or 4 minutes. Muscle cells will live on for several hours, and bone and skin cells can stay alive for several days. Evidently no one had tried removing a heart, a liver, a kidney, or a brain, any of which actions would result in death.

Islam

In Islam food has to be Halal. This is very similar to kosher, but there are important differences, such as the blessing said before killing the animal. To be kosher a blessing is said at the beginning and at the end of a slaughter session. To be halal, a blessing must be said by a Muslim before each individual killing. This could mean that were a Muslim to run over an animal and say a quick blessing as he did so and then quickly bleed the carcass, it might qualify as halal. Otherwise, I think it is safe to say that for strict Jews and Muslims, roadkill is off-limits.

Buddhism

The teachings of Gotama Buddha are found in the Buddhist Pali scriptures. Part of those scriptures are the Dhammapada, or steps in the Buddhist moral and spiritual law. There are five 'Precepts' in Buddhism, rather like the Ten Commandments of Mosaic law. They are: "*He who destroys life, who utters lies, who takes what is not given to him, who goes to the wife of another, who gets drunk with strong drinks – he digs up the very roots of his life*" Dhammapada 246, 247. The first Precept about not destroying life is why most Buddhists are vegetarians. This is reinforced by other passages which shews that the precept about not destroying life applies to all sentient beings: "*All beings tremble before danger, all fear death. When a man considers this, he does not kill or cause to kill. All beings fear before danger, life is dear to all. When a man considers this, he does not kill or cause to kill.*" Dhammapada 129 – 130. And: "*He who has renounced all violence towards all living beings, weak or strong, who neither kills nor causes other to kill – him do I call a holy man,*" Dhammapada 405.

This could lead one to believe that, apart from deliberately killing something on the road, true followers of Buddha may, if they wish, eat roadkill. However, Lord Buddha is recorded as saying: "*There may be some foolish people in the future who will say I permitted meat-eating and that I partook of meat myself, but meat eating I have not permitted to anyone, I do not permit, I will not permit in any form in future, in any manner and in any place. It is unconditionally prohibited for all*". This does sound like the final word on the subject, but Lord Buddha[20] does preface those remarks with this: "*To avoid causing terror to living beings, let the disciple refrain from eating meat*". So there you have it! Those who strictly follow the literal words of the Buddha must eschew roadkill. Those who allow some thinking to govern their actions may believe that they are not out of keeping with the ethics of Buddhism by eating meat that was killed accidentally in circumstances never foreseen by the

---

[20] www.harekrsna.com/practice/4regs/vegetarian/ethics.htm

Buddha.

'Those that kill animals to eat their flesh tend to massacre their own,' quote from Pythagoras

Hindu

There are six reasons for not eating meat given in the Hindu religion:

Scriptural law. The Vedic scriptures make Ahimsa, the law of non-injury, the Hindus first duty in the fulfilment of his religious obligations.

Karma. If you eat animals in this life you build bad karma and will be punished in the future.

Spiritual consciousness. Your spirit takes on the feelings locked in the flesh of butchered animals. Vegetarians live in a state of higher consciousness.

Health. Many scientific studies have concluded that eating meat is bad for your health.

Ecological reasons. Deforestation for pasture, erosion, pollution, loss of species and despoliation of the planet can all be traced to man's desire to eat meat.

Economic reasons. Farming animals is an inefficient means of converting vegetation into human flesh. It takes 16lbs of grain and many gallons of water to make 1 lb of animal meat.

So it looks as if the only argument against eating roadkill is that meat is not as good for you as vegetables. If you don't mind that there seems to be no religious reason for doing so unless the animal suffered in its death in which case you could be ingesting those bad feelings.

To balance the assertions made here that humans don't require meat it needs to be born in mind that in June 2002 an Auckland couple who were vegans were each jailed for five years for the manslaughter of their six-month old son after he died of brain damage and anaemia. He was suffering from a vitamin B12 deficiency brought on by his mother's diet as he had only been breastfed; he had been removed from hospital by his parents.

Feeding pets

In an article entitled: '*Rendering: From Roadkill to Cat Food*', Rachel Naba exposes a little-known fact as to the origin of some pet food and animal feed stuff.

"A pile of dead animals covers the floor of the rendering plant, covered with maggots. The humming of the flies swarming around the bodies is mere background noise as mini-bulldozers gather the carcasses for processing. As the bodies are dropped into a large pot for grinding, their bones, viscera, eyes, brains, and fur or feathers become a giant mixture of 'meat product'. After the raw product is cut and shredded, it is loaded into a large cooking pot and cooked for anywhere between twenty to ninety minutes. The grease, often called yellow fat or tallow, is skimmed from the top of the cooked mixture, and the cooked meat and bones are processed further, dehydrated, and made into meat meal or bone meal.

"An estimated 100 million pounds of waste material are picked up every day by the rendering industry. Diseased, poisoned, and otherwise inedible livestock are freely put into the grinder without treatment - tags, hormones, antibiotics, pesticides, intestinal waste, fur - nothing is left out. Dicarded meat and seafood from supermarket freezers are added, along with the plastic wrapping and styrofoam trays. Dogs and cats are shoveled into mix with their tags and flea collars intact. The resulting soup is a concoction of meat, pesticides, hormones, drugs (the chemicals used to euthanize dogs and cats do not break down in the rendering process), disease, plastic, metal, insecticides... This is what our pets are eating, and this is what is fed to chicken, hogs, and other livestock. Pigs are eating pigs, chickens are eating chickens, dogs are eating dogs, cats are eating cats....and humans are consuming the livestock that eat this filth.

"Farmers rely on this industry to dispose of their livestock waste (down or dead cows, sheep, etc), and slaughterhouses rid themselves of parts considered inedible for humans (feathers, cow heads, hoofs, viscera, etc.), diseased meat, scraps, and contaminated products. Dead zoo animals and roadkill can also be found in the mixture, as well as euthanized cats and dogs from vet clinics and animal shelters. It is the rendering business, and it is one of the most behind-the-scenes businesses in the food industry."

Other points of view

While travelling by coach to an international orienteering competition in Germany, I was chatting to one of my fellow team members, Mike Murray, who told me about a pheasant he picked up off the road on one occasion. Mike, who has been top orienteer in his age class in Britain for many years, has his own company, Michael Murray Cabinet and Furniture Makers of Dorking. He and his crew were driving to Redhill to install a kitchen when the car in front of them killed a pheasant at a village called Leigh. The senior craftsman, Tony Winch said, "*Stop the car!*" Tony jumped out and secured the bird and on they went. The job they were working on that day was for a butcher named Michael May; Tony persuaded him to dress it for him. The bird was returned oven-ready after a few days and Tony cooked it for his family. However, when the family heard that it was roadkill they refused to eat any of it. Tony took the cooked pheasant to work with him the next day and, in their lunch break, shared it among his co-workers who found it a very pleasant addition to their usual regime of cheese sandwiches.

Jack Hutchison, an orienteering friend of mine from Southampton, told me that he once picked up a pheasant from beside the road and took it home. He cooked it and he and his wife ate it. While eating it they found there was lead shot in the meat. Had it been shot and fallen by the road, or was it carrying shot around and was actually roadkill? Anyway, they were both ill afterwards and put it down to the pheasant.

John Spence a doctor friend of mine who lives in the Chilterns picks up roadkill pheasants and puts them out in his garden for the red kites to come and feast on. This carrion bird food sometimes gets raided by foxes. Perhaps this could become a popular feature where these birds are becoming re-established and neighbours could compete for the attention of the kites by putting out roadkill regularly for their favourite birds. I myself put out smaller specimens of roadkill and badly damaged or old specimens for a fox who regularly comes to our back door every night in his daily search for food.

Family objections

There are reasons why it might not be in your household's best interests to start eating roadkill. If you have somewhere you can do the skinning and butchering, OK, but if you have to do it all in the kitchen and your partner is not so imbued with the sense of economy and opportunity that you are, you may run into a little domestic friction that would be best to avoid. I mean, not everyone's spouse or partner likes to see a bloody badger sprawled out on the kitchen table being skinned and cut up with blood everywhere and fleas hopping about all over the place. OK, OK, I know you have got newspaper down and are taking great care, but that does not wash from the back of their eyeballs the image of mayhem taking place in their kitchen. I mean, here is an example of what I am talking about. I had picked up a freshly killed badger while driving the few miles to our friend Colin Middleton who then lived at Hornacott Manor and had hung it for four weeks (bit too long to be quite honest) before I got round to skinning it in the workshop. I had removed the skin and the badger was hanging while I jointed it. As I cut off one of the front legs, a great gush of blood poured out all over my hands and up my sleeve; it went everywhere, a great bloody sticky mess. Anyway, while Sue, my good wife, was upstairs at the computer, I washed the joints of meat in the kitchen sink. I cut off one of the badger's feet and threw it in the kitchen rubbish bin. Sue then went out to the Otter Sanctuary with her sister-in-law and nephews while I stayed at home and prepared cutlets from two pheasants, I had had hanging up for three weeks. I threw the feet into the bucket for composting, meaning to empty it before Sue came home. I forgot. When Sue came home it was not long before she took the compost bucket out to empty. She came back with a complaint about the feet, *"What were those feet doing in my compost bucket?"* she asked. I could see no harm in putting pheasant's feet in a compost bin, surely that is just the sort of stuff you want in the compost. Well, that blew over, but a little later, when I was upstairs in the bedroom getting changed to go for a run, there was the most terrible scream from below. My mind leaped into the kitchen and envisaged some badger steak accidentally put into the biscuit tin - no, that did not register; a badger ham left in her best milk saucepan - no again, that had not happened; so what could it have been, perhaps a mouse in the tea caddy? No, it was the badger foot in the rubbish bin! She had dipped her hand into the bin thinking the black thing she could see was a ball of screwed up black paper and pulled out the badger foot! No wonder she screamed! But what was she doing grubbing about in the bin for a ball of screwed up paper?

I am trying to say that if your partner is dead set against eating roadkill you are going to have to be very diplomatic to start something you have not tried before, unless you want an even bigger change in life.

Death on the road

For there to be any such thing as roadkill, two things are required, a road and a vehicle, and the vehicle needs to be travelling along the road. While a primitive wheel, a log as a roller, could have been used towards the end of the paleolithic era (2.6 million to 10,000 BC), the first real wheel was probably invented in Mesopotamia (Iraq) about 4000 BC. The earliest wheel found dates to about 3500 BC. Man, who had been eating horses for 50,000 years, discovered, with the invention of the chariot, that they could be put to good use pulling him around, particularly into and out of battle. The first mention of the wheel in the bible is of pharaoh's chariots when they came to grief in the Red Sea, when, it is said, Jehovah took off the wheels of the chariots and then drowned the occupants, which according to Bishop Ussher occurred in 1491 BC. It was not until about 1000 BC that people found they could get on the horse's back and the cavalry was born. Whether horses or oxen were the first to be used as draught animals we do not know, but oxen were mentioned first in the bible in that capacity (1 Sam. 6) when the Philistines made a cart (in 1140 BC) and tied two oxen to it to see if they would carry the ark of God back to the children of Israel, they did. One hundred years later the children of Israel made another cart to bring up the ark of God. Oxen were again used to pull it and Uzza and Ahio the sons of Abinadab who had been looking after it drove the cart. At one point the oxen stumbled and Uzza tried to steady it. God did not like this and struck Uzza dead. We are not told exactly how God struck him, could he have actually fallen under the wheels and become the first road accident victim? God moves in a mysterious way. The Romans, who made the sport of chariot racing a form of mass entertainment, became the world's first great road builders to provide quick access for men and goods to the farthest corners of their dominions and some of these roads are still in use today.

For the first 5000 years of their history, vehicles were drawn by horses. In Victorian times it seems that some considered it of little consequence to kill someone with their carriage as is portrayed by Charles Dickens in '*A Tale of Two Cities*' (1859), in which one of the aristocracy in his carriage runs over and kills the son of a peasant to whom he throws a gold coin as compensation. The peasant that night gets revenge by murdering the man in his sleep. A course of action not often followed by the relatives of victims in this day and age. The vehicle or the road are often regarded as being the cause of the 'accident' as if they had acted maliciously of their own volition. Of course, you did not have to be killed outright by a carriage, you only needed an open wound to get an infection that would very often kill you. A broken bone with an open wound usually resulted in gangrene; this would be fatal unless an amputation could be performed. To prevent further gangrene the stump would be cauterized by a hot iron or by dipping in hot oil or tar. Remember, there was no anaesthetic in those days and such operations, although conducted at high speed, must have been somewhat painful; it was not until 1846 that Sir Robert Liston used ether as an anaesthetic for the first time and in 1847 James Simpson discovered chloroform that was neither an irritant nor inflammable as was ether.

But still patients continued to die from gangrene, fever or blood poisoning. They had evidently never heard of the employment of the industrious little maggot! Richard Hollingham, in his book '*Blood and Guts: A History of Surgery*', recounts how Joseph Lister, alerted by the experiments of the French chemist, Louis Pasteur in 1864, and by the success of the Carlyle sewage authority in reducing the stench from the cities drains and cesspits with the use of carbolic acid or phenol, used for the first time a solution of carbolic acid as an antiseptic and as a dressing after surgery in 1867. His patient was a boy, James Greenlees, who had been run over by a cart and had a compound fracture of the leg with an open wound. Thanks to Lister and his 'antiseptic', James, instead of becoming a delayed roadkill victim, made a full recovery; antiseptic surgery had been born.

So, how fast did horse-drawn vehicles go? While we humans have two gaits, walking and running, horses have four: they can walk, trot, canter and gallop. Horses, like us, walk at 2–4 mph, but they trot at 8-9mph, canter at 12-13 mph and gallop at 20-25 mph with a top speed touching 50mph. Usain Bolt can run 200m at 23 mph and Roger Bannister held a speed of 15 mph when he did the first 4-minute mile. Horses can maintain a gallop for 3 miles or more. Carriages would normally have travelled at a trot and the Pony Express at a mixture of canter and trot. If you slipped and fell under the wheels of a carriage you would probably die at whatever speed it was going. Fire engines hauled by horses ran at a gallop and, no doubt, were a thrilling spectacle as well as a real danger to everything on the road. Five tons at 25 mph on iron tyres is not easy to stop. But did anything apart from children and old people get killed in these days of yore? People were certainly killed in considerable numbers by carriages in crowded cities (ca 140 per million population in GB in the mid-19th century). Domestic animals like dogs, barking round the horses hooves, must have been always getting under the wheels, and as Oscar Hammerstein put it in the musical Oklahoma!:

> *"Chicks and ducks and geese better scurry,*
> *when I take you out in the surrey*
> *with the fringe on top".*

A vehicle does not need to be going particularly fast to kill something; recently I watched two young pheasants get run over by cars going at no more than walking pace, the drivers having seen the pheasants were proceeding slowly yet, nevertheless, managed to get two birds under the wheels.

There were hardly any speed limits for horse-drawn vehicles. The first speed limit law I have been able to find was made in 1652 in New Amsterdam (later to be known as New York after it was seized from the Dutch by the British) it stipulated that no waggon, cart or sleigh should be driven at a gallop within the city and drivers should walk and lead the horses. This obviously did not apply to horseless carriages, but even before the first speed limits for motor vehicles, it was possible to go to prison for speeding, as a cabbie, Jacob German, discovered when he was arrested and jailed in New York City in 1899, for driving his electric taxi at the 'breakneck speed' of 12 mph. This seems a bit unfair as that is the speed of the canter and cantering was permitted in New York at that time.

So I think we can take it that roadkill of wildlife really only began with the advent of mechanically propelled vehicles. Nicolas-Joseph Cugnot, a Frenchman, is credited with building the world's first self-propelled mechanical vehicle in 1769. It could haul loads at 2½ mph but crashed into a wall in 1771. The first mechanically propelled vehicle to carry passengers to be used on the road was Richard Trevithick's steam road locomotive, Captain Dick's Puffer, but which was known by the locals as 'Puffing Devil', and which, like Cugnot's machine had only three wheels. In 1801 it made several short journeys through the streets of Camborne in Cornwall, climbing 250ft (76m) in a distance of about a mile from Rosewarne to Camborne Beacon at a speed faster than a walk. Trevithick's cousin, Andrew Vivian, was at the controls and they gave free rides to seven or eight friends. This event is celebrated in song and the Loveny male voice choir, with whom I used to have the honour of singing, always give a spirited rendition of it between the bar and the buffet after every concert. It goes:

Going up Camborne Hill coming down,
Going up Camborne Hill coming down,
The horses stood still,
The wheels went around,
Going up Camborne Hill coming down.

In 1802, Trevithick and his cousin built another locomotive with a stagecoach mounted on three-wheels, called the London Carriage. They drove it the 60 miles to Plymouth and shipped it to London where it ran around the streets at a speed of 6mph before it too had a crash. Trevithick gave up the idea of road vehicles and concentrated on railway locomotives. Steam road vehicles developed throughout the 19th century, largely being used for haulage and agriculture. Electric vehicles also made their appearance but were used more for carrying passengers. We have no record of roadkill during this period, but there were a lot of people killed on the roads every year. Gerald Cummins in 'The History of Road Safety' records 1,589 fatalities, mostly involving horse conveyances of some kind in 1875.

But with the advent of steam and electric vehicles, the UK government began to set speed limits for mechanically propelled vehicles with the Locomotives on Highways Act 1861 which set the limit at 5 mph (8 km/h) in towns and 10 mph (16 km/h) elsewhere. This was soon replaced by more restrictive legislation in the Locomotive Act 1865 which was known as the 'Red Flag Act' which reduced the limit to 2 mph (3 km/h) in towns and 4 mph (6 km/h) in the country. In order to enforce the limit, it stipulated that self-propelled vehicle should be accompanied by a crew of three: the driver, a stoker and a man with a red flag walking 60 yds (55 m) ahead of each vehicle to warn horse riders and horse-drawn traffic of the approach of a self-propelled vehicle. The Locomotives on Highways (Amendment) Act 1878 reduced the distance of the pedestrian ahead to 20yds (18m) and the flag became optional, but the 4 mph limit remained. The Act also allowed county councils to issue licences to every vehicle entering the county at a cost of £10 a time! That certainly hindered the development of motorised transport. We have no record of any reductions in fatalities brought about by the reduction in speed, but they probably did not run over many rabbits or badgers with that man out at the front! But now something appeared over the horizon that was going to alter this safe and tranquil scene: Karl Benz in 1885 invented a three-wheeled petrol-engined car and in 1889, Gottlieb Daimler and Wilhelm Maybach put an engine into a carriage and produced the first four wheeled vehicle powered by an internal combustion engine. A certain William Thomson had first patented the idea of an inflated rubber tube as a vehicle tyre in 1845. Unaware of this, John Boyd Dunlop a veterinary surgeon working in Ireland in 1887 came up with a similar design and patented it in 1888. Dunlop fought a legal battle with Thomson and won and so it is Dunlop who is credited with the discovery. I mention this because it is the combination of pneumatic tyre and motor car that is so successful (and comfortable) and yet has become such a slayer of wildlife, leaving a trail of blood and battered corpses wherever wildlife tries to cross the hallowed strip of tarmac, concrete or stone.

On 28 January 1896, Walter Arnold of East Peckham, Kent became the first person in Great Britain to be successfully charged with speeding. Travelling at approximately 8 mph, he had exceeded the 2 mph speed limit for towns and had been caught by a policeman on a bicycle. On 10 September 1897 - The first drink-drive conviction in Britain was obtained, George Smith, aged 25, drove his taxi onto the pavement and into the front of 165 Bond Street, London. He worked for the Electric Cab Company of Hackney, London. He admitted *"having had two or three glasses"*.

In 1896, Parliament was eventually persuaded by the motoring lobby to relax the law and the Locomotives on Highways Act, was enacted which did away with the man out at the front and made a distinction between vehicles of less than 3 tons unladen weight and those over that weight; and it permitted the lighter vehicles to travel on the highway at a speed to be set by the Local Government Board up to 14 mph; the Board set the limit at 12 mph. The 'Keep Left' rule of the road was also established. This Act became known as the 'Emancipation Act' and to celebrate, a rally was run from London to Brighton that year. The London to Brighton Veteran Car Run, for vehicles built before 1905, has now taken place almost every year since 1927. The speed limit was raised again by the Motor Car Act, 1903, to 20mph. When this act was repealed by the Road Traffic Act 1930, all limits were removed for cars and motorbikes. However, the Road Traffic Act 1934 quickly re-imposed a limit of 30 mph in built-up areas, which remains to this day; it also introduced a requirement for a driving test. Outside built-up areas there were no limits until 1965 when a 70mph restriction for all roads was introduced. In 1977, the speed limit for cars and motorbikes on single carriageway roads was set at 60mph. The Isle of Man and the Indian state of Uttar Pradesh are the only places in the world that do not have a general speed limit and in Germany, 57% of the autobahn system remains free from a speed limit.

Speed has a direct bearing on the risk of death to humans. It something like 1 in 40 at 20 mph, 1 in 5 at 30 mph, 50/50 at 35 mph and 9 in 10 at 40 mph (90%). A vehicle striking a bird at those speeds would probably result in a higher mortality rate as they don't have ambulances to rush them to a Tiggywinkle's hospital. But Chris Mead wrote an article, I remember, urging drivers not to exceed 45 mph in country lanes as birds are programmed to react to aerial predators attacking them at that sort of speed.

The first U.S. state law regulating the speed of motor vehicles was passed in 1901 by the state of Connecticut with a speed limit of 12 mph in cities and 15 mph outside. How people knew whether or not they were exceeding the limit is a mystery because, although a speedometer had been invented by a certain Charles Babbage in the mid-19th century for trains, the first motor vehicle to be fitted with a speedometer which was patented by Otto Schulze in 1902 was the Oldsmobile.

Washington State introduced a speed limit in 1909 of 12mph in 'thickly settled areas and business districts', and 24mph elsewhere. These early speed limits were enacted to prevent pedestrians being killed in towns and cities, i.e. preventing human roadkill, and preventing casualties among the occupants of vehicles that might collide on the highway. Each state set its own upper limits and in the 1930s it was between 35 and 45 mph while at that time some cars were capable of travelling at 100mph. During WWII a federal limit of 35 mph was set to save fuel. By 1972 the majority of states had a limit of 70mph, with lorries, minor roads and night-time driving on lower limits, while Montana and Nevada had a 'reasonable and prudent' limit without defining what it might be. During the fuel crisis in 1973, the US government, unable to impose a limit on the states, made a 55mph limit a condition for the continued funding of their highways programme. It was adopted by all states by March 1974, but Montana circumvented it by handing out speeding tickets of only $5 for those who broke the 55mph limit. In 1987, under mounting public pressure, the limit was raised to 65mph. Following the increase, fatalities on roads with the increased limits went up about 30%. In 1995, the US Government withdrew the national capping of the speed limits and many states reverted to their earlier limits. Montana reverted to its 'reasonable and prudent' limit in 1995 but was challenged in its courts in 1998 and had to impose a fixed upper limit (75mph). Maximum speed limits now range from 60mph in Hawaii, to 80mph on some roads in Texas.

The design of the front of a car also has an effect on the mortality of pedestrians struck by the car. The use of shades fitted to headlights, no, not dark glasses, but a shade like the peak of a cap to cut down on glare to the driver in a fog were found to be just the right height to damage a person's kidneys when hitting them from behind. They became known as 'kidney cutters' and were banned. Rigid metal bull-bars, fitted to 4x4s and vehicles used off-road, began to kill pedestrians, and by the year 2000 some 2,000 deaths/year and 18,000 serious accidents/year occurred in Europe. The sale of metal bull-bars was banned by a European Union Directive in 2002. When I mentioned kidney cutters to my wife, she thought I was referring to pedestrian slicers, which I discovered were the front number plates of motorcycles. These were obligatory at one time, as I found to my cost when I was fined for not having one on my

Mobylette moped. But apparently although they were not banned, they were no longer a requirement to display. Someone on a blog referred to a 'possum dicer' but I have not found out what such a thing is.

What is the first record of wildlife killed by traffic? Roger M. Knutson, author of '*Flattened Fauna: A Field Guide to Common Animals of Roads, Streets, and Highways*', sites John Tjostem, one of his colleagues at Luther College in Decorah, Iowa, who found an entry in his grandmother's diary of 1897 of a snapping turtle *(Chelydra serpentina)* having been run over by a waggon in 1897 in North Dakota. Could that be the first record of wildlife roadkill? As far as horses are concerned, I came across a record on a website[21] in which an electric tram, powered from an overhead cable, suffered brake failure on the steep descent of Fore Street in Exeter in 1917 and collided with a horse and cart, killing the horse; a woman passenger on the bus was also killed when she was thrown off and the tram overturned, crushing her to death.

So who has the dubious distinction of being the first person to be killed by a motor vehicle? It is Mary Ward of Ireland who on 31 August 1869 was travelling at Birr in County Leinster in a steam carriage (invented by her cousin). The carriage hit a bump and she was thrown out and run over by one of the wheels. Her neck was broken and she died at the scene. People must have been more wary of steam vehicles as I can find no record of any pedestrians being killed by one. It is not until 1896 that a Mrs Bridget Driscoll (44) of Croydon was hit by a Roger-Benz car being demonstrated at the Crystal Palace in London on 17 August that gives her the dubious distinction of being the first roadkill victim in the UK.

In 1899 Henry Bliss (68) became the first human roadkill victim in America when he stepped off a trolley bus and was knocked down by an electric-powered taxicab; he died the next day. The first person I knew to be killed on the road was the man next door, a Mr Hugo (father of Brian and Mercia) who was run over by a bus in London in the 1940s. I also learned that death was a solemn affair when, the next day while my brother and I were making a row in the garden, Brian looked over the fence and put his finger to his lips. George Easterbrook writing in the Los Angeles Times in Aug 2007 said that 245,000 people had died on the roads of America in the six years since 9/11. In the year 2006, 42,642 Americans died and 1.2 million people are believed to have died on the world's roads.

In England collisions with deer have been blamed for 42,000 road

---

[21] www.exetermemories.co.uk

accidents each year and the loss of 15 human lives at the cost of £10.2 million. The total population of deer in England is thought to exceed 300,000 in 2012 and 2 million in 2022. Herds have grown in many areas because of restrictions on hunting with hounds, and the dwindling number of shooters who hunt deer.

The world record for roadkill on one journey was 598 rabbits in 1933 near Boise, Idaho over a 50-mile two lane road.

In my teens, when I began picking up little birds and animals found by the road, their bodies were needed for my hobby of taxidermy. When setting off from Norwich early in the morning to cycle back to our home in Watford, my pockets would fill with the warm bodies of house sparrows, chaffinch, dunnock and anything else that sacrificed itself on the road before us to supply material for my hobby. They were duly skinned and as the skin came away, I could see where subcutaneous bleeding indicated the region of impact. Most often it was contusion to the head, or internal bleeding after disruption of the vessels to the liver or heart. Birds kill themselves by flying into windows at speeds of between 10 and 25 mph so it does not take any great speed to kill a bird with a car. People finding a bird freshly killed by a car or a window notice how loose the head appears to be and say, "*Oh, it has broken its neck*". But the neck is not broken, the muscles are all relaxed, that's all. If the blow is sufficient to break the neck it would probably take the head off as well. If a car passes over a bird standing or running in the road, and it passes between the wheels it usually gets hit on the head (which kills it) or a wing gets broken and it flutters off to be caught by a predator, or wander back onto the road for something else to administer the *coup de grace*. Small animals get squashed or escape, but the larger they get the greater the chance to be knocked down rather than run over.

So what actually causes the death of animals that become roadkill? Sometimes small birds and animals manage to get right under the wheels of vehicles so that they are totally flattened. Like the crossbill that I ran over once. Death is here, I think, unquestionably instantaneous. Usually there is nothing the driver can do to prevent it, unless the beast in question is sitting still in the road when a quick swerve may avoid it. But if a hedgehog appears in your dipped headlights at 70 mph (you doing the 70 mph not the hedgehog, idiot) you will not have time to react before you have felt the slight knock as the tyre hits it. Likewise larger animals that have their heads run over die immediately for obvious reasons. A bang on the head also causes brain damage that results in a cessation of breathing or heartbeat. A severe blow or a crushing of the chest will rupture blood vessels and organs that allow blood to flow into the body cavity even if it does not puncture the skin and bleed onto the road. This reduces the oxygen to the brain and the heart, either of which will result very rapidly in death. Most of the small birds I have picked up appeared to have sustained no injury. Opening them up reveals either a haemorrhage inside the skull or a lacuna of coagulated blood in the body cavity, or both. We rarely see those creatures that are just injured and are able to get away from the road. Animals and birds can survive a broken leg, but they would be more susceptible to predation. The most likely outcome is that they die a slow and lingering death.

Natural decomposition

When something gets killed on the road, what happens to it? There are four possibilities:

1. It is squashed on the road and run over by every subsequent vehicle to pass that way, its body and guts being mashed up and rolled out thinner and thinner until only the skin remains to identify what had just been a live and beautiful beast.
2. Scavenging mammals, birds or reptiles eat it there or carry it away and eat it.
3. Somebody picks it up, takes it home, feeds it to their cat/dog, or prepares it, cooks it and eats it.
4. It lands in the gutter or on the verge which allows a sequence of events to occur over a long period of time in which a succession of organisms take up residence in it and consume it until there is nothing left but the skeleton.

Let me take you through the fourth option and discover what is going on there on the verge beside our roads in many thousands of places even as you are reading these words. But first, a phenomenon known as *rigor mortis* sets in which later goes off and while this is happening digestive juices and bacteria begin to decompose the body; meanwhile insects arrive, in wave after wave of flies, beetles and moths attracted by the different aromas that emanate from the corpse over the ensuing days, weeks and months.

Rigor mortis

If you don't know what *rigor mortis* is (Latin: *rigor* = stiff, *mortis* = of death), then let me explain. When an animal dies it is relaxed and floppy for a period and it then goes stiff. I was first introduced to this phenomenon in my early teens when an old lady in our meeting, Mrs Palmer, died in her bed and Miss Wickens, who lodged with us and was a District Nurse, was collected by the lady's grandson and driven furiously in his aunt's pre-war Chevrolet (a rare sight in post-war Britain) to enable her to lay out Mrs Palmer before *rigor mortis* set in. Well, as the years went by, I became familiar with this, but I always used to think that this rigidity was caused by the blood in the muscles clotting and causing a sort of large muscular blood clot. However, I find that this is not the case. The muscles actually contract, as though they were alive, by biochemical reactions that result in cramp which will last for hours or days, according to the size of the animal and other factors, until the muscles begin to autolyse and decay. Let me see if I can elucidate this phenomenon. A muscle consists of many fibres. Each fibre contains two proteins, actin and myosin. In life, the brain sends an electrical impulse down the nerves to the muscle, where it causes the release of acetylcholine, which allows sodium ions to enter the muscle fibres, which in turn triggers the entry of calcium ions into the fibres from the fluid surrounding the cells, causing the actin and myosin filaments to pull towards each other and shorten the fibre; this effects the contraction of the muscle. To end the contraction, a substance known as adenosine triphosphate (ATP) is created that pumps out the calcium ions and causes the muscle to relax. It requires energy to maintain this calcium differential. ATP is created from three sources: aerobic respiration, phosphagen and glycogen. When death occurs, aerobic respiration ceases as breathing stops and the heart stops pumping, cutting off the supply of oxygenated blood to the muscles. The phosphagen process lasts only for a few minutes. The glycogen process is able to operate for some time but produces lactic acid; it is the inability to synthesize ATP and a build-up of lactic acid that governs the time to onset of *rigor* for, as the ATP is used up, calcium ions flood in to cause the muscles to cramp. The muscles stay cramped and the body stiff until the acid builds up and the cell starts to autolyse or digest itself. *Rigor mortis* may set in within minutes in a small animal to perhaps 3 to 12 hours in a large animal (like a human), depending on a number of factors, especially temperature. It can also be accelerated by exertion (prior to death – obviously), strychnine poisoning or local heat. *Rigor mortis* begins to pass off after 36 hours but it may take three days for a large animal to lose its stiffness. This phenomenon can be used forensically as an indicator of the time of death. The onset of *rigor mortis* does not cause post mortem movements because the adductor or flexor muscles act in opposition to the extensor muscles, in other words, the muscles act in equal measure against each other which prevents corpses from wriggling and waving their arms and legs about.

A phenomenon known as cadaveric spasm or instant *rigor mortis* has been described in which people who have died of asphyxia by drowning or strangulation seize upon some object in their dying moments and continue in death to grasp the object seized. The spasm is different from *rigor mortis* in that usually only one group of muscles is involved; it persists into normal *rigor mortis*. It is also said to occur when death has resulted from a fall from a height. I have never encountered it with roadkill, something frozen say, in the act of leaping across the road; I am keeping a look out. Dr Baden says that oxygen depletion by strenuous exercise at the moment of death is the cause of cadaveric spasm. Now you would think that in a sport which has old people regularly flogging themselves in a sprint finish after a long race, as is the case in orienteering, there would be regular occurrences of people dropping dead gasping for oxygen and freezing with a cadaveric spasm in some extravagant running posture! Well, after 30 years of competing as an orienteer and thrashing myself into the finish I have only seen two people who had just died in an orienteering race but neither of them was other than flat out on their backs. But David Southwell and Matt Adams in their humorous yet frightening book, '*1001 ridiculous ways to die*', quote the case of a certain Malcolm Hardee (55) who fell into the Thames in London while on a drinking spree. The police diver who recovered his body three days later said that he was still clutching a bottle of beer in his hand!

Autolysis or self-digestion

Enzymes in the individual cells begin to act on the walls and contents of the cell which results in the gradual decay of the muscles and organs. The salivary glands, the stomach, the liver, the pancreas and the small intestine secrete enzymes, acids and alkalis which enable food to be digested. In a living animal the stomach and intestinal walls are protected from the actions of these fluids by a layer of mucus. Death stops the secretion of mucus and that allows the digestive juices to get at the gut and stomach walls. Perforations appear in the intestinal tract allowing autolysis to proceed into the body cavity. The body them begins to digest itself from the inside out.

Bacteria

Our intestines are full of bacteria and this army of unicellular creatures is known as our intestinal microflora; it is a balanced ecosystem of 400+ different species of bacterium. Bacteria are unicellular organisms surrounded by a cell wall which encloses only a strand of DNA and contains no organelles. There are bacteria in the mouth and these, along with ingested bacteria, pass into the stomach where the acid kills many of them; very few bacteria live in animals' stomachs except in the *Ungulata*; most of our bacteria are found in the lower intestine. There are more bacteria living in our intestines than the total number of human cells in our bodies. Our guts are like a grand hotel where the visitors outnumber the staff! The bacteria living in the small intestine are generally of benefit to their host in combating adverse bacteria and in actually digesting food that then becomes available to the host. Bacterial enzymes recycle liver secretions and others provide essential vitamins to the host. When you are ill, antibiotics administered to remove toxic bacteria kill off the beneficial bacteria as well and so destroy this beneficial action. After a course of antibiotics it is sensible to eat plenty of yogurt to replace the friendly bacteria such as *Lactobacillus acidophilus, L. delbreukii ssp bulgaricus, Streptococcus salivarius, Bacteroides fragilis,* and *Escherichia coli* (which comes in different strains, some good some bad).

It is worth mentioning the immune system here. This deals with viruses and bacteria that manage to get into the body through wounds, insect bites, our mouths or other orifices. Its agents are the phagocytes, white blood cells produced in the bone marrow, which circulate in the bloodstream and attack and eat bacteria and other micro-organisms. Death interrupts this arrangement and introduces a unilateral ceasefire in this battle, all the bacteria, good and bad, instead of calling a truce, go on the rampage literally devouring the hand that fed them. So, cellular enzymes, intestinal juices and bacterial secretions begin to breakdown the proteins and fats of which the body is made. This is known as putrefaction: the flesh changes colour, the abdominal wall first turning slightly green and becoming darker while the rest of the body adopts that greenish hue. The body begins to smell. The green becomes blue and changes to purple, brown and black. Gases are evolved that cause the body to become distended and make it smell very nasty. Anaerobic bacterial respiration produces gases such as methane (CH_4), ammonia (NH_3), sulphur dioxide (SO_2), putrescine ($C_4H_{12}N_2$) and cadaverine ($C_5H_{14}N_2$). What delicious names these last two compounds have! I would love to know what each smells like on its own.

Freezing conditions prevent the decomposition of bodies. Mammoths have appeared (and still do) at the foot of glaciers in such a condition that their meat can be eaten. Climbers lost on Everest still lie where they died, dressed in the clothes of their day. Mallory is there and a climber's body known as 'Greenpants' is to be found in a little cave high up the mountain. Scientists are now saying that DNA recovered from these mammoths could be used to clone the mammoth and bring it back from extinction! Presumably the same could be done to Mallory and Greenpants, but the big question is, although they might look like their predecessor and have a desire to climb mountains, would they remember the way down? The acid water of a peat bog also preserves bodies where they become tanned and mummified. Even burial in wet soil can prevent decomposition when the fatty parts of the body change into a yellowish waxy substance known as adipocere or grave wax that inhibits the growth of bacteria and preserves the body for centuries.

Insects

Autolysis and putrefaction are not the only thing happening to our item of roadkill. It is also receiving the attentions of a series of visitors interested in investing in its immediate future. There is such a host of insects that make use of the corpses of dead animals that whole books could be written on the subject. So, I shall have to be very cursory and cover only a few of the many insects which infest dead bodies.

Flies and Maggots

Wombat with maggots © Arthur Boyt

When something dies, the store of protein and fat in its body becomes available for recycling; they are valuable commodities and there is a good bit of competition for them which comes in the form of a number of species of true flies (*Diptera*) and beetles. The flies belong to the family *Calliphoridae*, the blow flies, of which the flesh fly *(Sarcophaga carnaria)*, the bluebottle *(Calliphora vomitoria)* and the greenbottle *(Lucilia sericata)* are common examples. While the fox may count it a bonus to come across a carcass and enjoy an easy meal, these insects have to find a dead body if their line is to be continued for another generation. To this end they are adapted to recognise the whiff of a body as soon as it is dead and home in on the source of the smell and there lay their eggs. They are said to be able to locate a corpse from 12 miles away. In fact, these flies are attracted to living animals as well and would lay eggs at any suitable orifice if they were not brushed away by the animal under attack. Some of the greenbottles e.g. *L. cuprina* and *L. caesar*, succeed in this attempt to jump the gun and lay their eggs onto a living animal into a wound or onto wool where it is matted with faeces around the anus or on the tail. The eggs hatch into larvae (maggots) and attack the living animal itself; this can result in serious injury if not attended to and is known as 'strike'. I watched amazed when my neighbour, Margo Goodenough, attended to a soiled ewe in the field next door to us and cut into the tangle of wool and faeces round its back end to reveal a handful of maggots which would have shortly broken through the skin to feed on the living flesh of the unfortunate ewe. In Australia the eastern golden-haired blowfly *(Calliphora stygia)* also feeds on living sheep, but only where *L. cuprina* is already at work. Bluebottles are known in Australia as blue-arsed flies.

The house flies *(Muscidae)* also go for carrion, but can equally enjoy other rotting matter; they and the blow flies are the first to arrive at a carcass and are known as 'pioneer' flies. The flesh fly (*Sarcophagidae*) may not be the first to arrive, but its maggots have a head start in the race to eat the carcass because the female lays larvae not eggs. The smell of maggots doing their work added to the aroma of decaying meat is a powerful attractant to all flesh-eating flies and the body is quickly converted into masses of white shiny wriggling maggots. In Australia, one of the late arrivals is the green hairy-maggot blowfly *(Chrysomya rufifacies)* which likes to eat the maggots that are already established on the corpse; they have a tough skin which protects them from other predators. Because the larvae of this species pupate on the ground, they in turn are parasitised by a wasp of the *Pteromalidae* that lays its egg in the pupa. Up to 12 larvae consume the contents of the pupa, pupate inside it and emerge from it as adults. Another Australian parasitic wasp *(Brachymeria calliphorae)* lays only one egg in a larva and when it hatches it eats the larva from within. There is a less common green bottle, *Cynomya mortuorum* which has no common name but sounds as if it could be a problem in mortuaries.

The website of the Australian Museum Online[22] has a fine description of maggots with accompanying photographs and a short video of wriggling maggots. This what it says: "*The larva, or maggot, is the main feeding stage of*

---

[22] https://australian.museum/learn/science/decomposition-fly-life-cycles/

the fly. On hatching, first-instar larvae are roughly 2 mm long, growing to about 5 mm before shedding their skin. The second instar larvae grow to around 10 mm before they shed their skins to become third-instar larvae. Third-instar larvae grow to between 15 mm and 20 mm before wandering off as pre-pupae.

"Maggots are remarkable eating machines. Their front ends are armed with mouth hooks with which they rake in decaying flesh, shredded from the corpse. Their rear ends consist of a chamber, in which their anus and posterior spiracles are located. (They also have anterior spiracles). Spiracles are used for breathing, and the possession of spiracles in a posterior location means that maggots can breath feeding 24 hours a day.

"Between their heads and their tails is a muscular, segmented body, a simple intestine and a pair of very large salivary glands. They wriggle easily through a corpse, secreting digestive enzymes and spreading putrefying bacteria which help create their soupy environment.

"Maggots are gregarious animals and travel around in 'maggot masses'. Their digestive activities are so intense that the corpse heats up in the vicinity of a maggot mass, sometimes reaching 53°C It can get so hot inside a maggot mass, that centrally located maggots have to migrate to the edge to cool down. However, the heat is a bonus, because it increases the rate of putrefaction, and the rate of digestion.

"Maggots moult twice during their development and can grow from 2 mm to 20 mm in length in four days. Having acquired the necessary nutrients to make a fly, they retire into their puparia where the transformation occurs.

"A female blowfly lays up to 300 eggs at one time, and with numerous females visiting a corpse, the number of maggots can be immense. For example, 48,562 maggots were found on a 156 g piece of meat after 24 hours exposure. However, because this was insufficient food to sustain them, only 231 flies finally emerged. In warm weather, conducive to fly growth, maggots can consume 60 per cent of a human body in less than a week."

During the later stages of decomposition (20 to 50 days) when most of the flesh has gone the body dries out and develops a cheesy smell due to the formation of butyric acid. This attracts another insect, the cheese skipper *(Piophila casei)* the larva of which feeds on fermenting fatty residues. The larva has the extraordinary ability to jump 15cm (6in) when disturbed! This is where it gets its name. It achieves the skip by grabbing its tail end with its mouth hooks, tensing the body and letting go. This fly is used in the production of an alarming kind of cheese in Sardinia: casu marzu. The wikipedia entry[23] for casu marzu gives: *"Derived from Pecorino Sardo, casu marzu goes beyond typical fermentation to a stage most would consider to be decomposition, brought about by the digestive action of the larvae of the cheese fly, Piophila casei. These larvae are deliberately introduced to the cheese, promoting an advanced level of fermentation and breaking down the cheese's fats. The texture of the cheese becomes very soft, with some liquid (called 'lagrima') seeping out. The larvae themselves appear as transparent, white worms, about 8 mm (1/3 inch) long. When disturbed, the larvae can jump for distances up to 15 cm (6 inches), prompting recommendations of eye protection for those eating the cheese. Some people clear the larvae from the cheese before consuming; others do not."*

When these larvae are consumed with the cheese they can cause enteric myiasis because they survive passage through the stomach and can bore through the gut walls with very nasty consequences. The moral here is: when eating casu marzu chew it well. The cheese fly can also emulate another notable body eater, the coffin fly. The coffin fly *(Megaselia scalaris),* a member of the *Phoridae,* is quite a small fly and it is able to burrow down to bodies buried 6ft (2m) down. They can even continue breeding underground.

I once had an interesting experience of the sequence of smell changes that accompanies the natural destruction of a corpse. I was working in a temporary building, which used to house the drawing office of the UK Fire Research Station but which was then serving as the office accommodation of the Fire Insurers' Research and Testing Organization. One day in the office my nose told me there could possibly be a dead animal somewhere about. It was strongest in a small room used as a store. I could find no body in the room and so assumed that there had been a death under the floorboards. Over the next few days, the stink grew so much that it was hard to believe there was no body in the room. I thought it must be one of a number of feral cats frequenting the premises. As the days went by the smell mollified and changed and eventually went away altogether. Some years later when the building was demolished to make way for a new laboratory/office block, I climbed among the ruins to see if an answer to this old riddle could now be solved and there, sure enough, under where the floor of the storeroom had been, was the skeleton of a fox and, what is more, almost completely cleaned up by the creatures I have detailed above. There was one thing though that seized my attention: the foxes head was twisted round and thrust between its front legs as if it had died in the throes of some terrible and inescapable pain. Perhaps it had eaten rat poison. Although we have a cat that

---

[23]https://en.wikipedia.org/wiki/Casu_martzu

sometimes sleeps like that, so let us hope it had just gone to sleep. Its teeth were all very loose in its skull but whether this was due to it being young I don't know. It affected me deeply to think of this poor animal coming there to die in agony and alone. But I have got away from the subject and that was maggots.

But what happens if the maggots get into something you want to consume? This has happened to me on an occasion or two and I have endeavoured to get rid of them before committing the meat to the cooker. However, on one occasion in which a partridge was left hanging for a while some maggots appeared when I washed it but a number appeared later on when I served it up on my plate! I decided that as they had been well cooked, I might as well eat them, they were after all made up entirely of what they had just been eating. They swilled about in the gravy like little noodles with a black dot at one end. I found that they could be pressed between tongue and teeth where they would burst like a small balloon. No great sensation of taste either good or bad accompanied this exercise and I suspect that they could be highly nutritious. In fact, I wonder that we don't use the clever maggot in the same way we use pigs e.g. feed them on carrion and harvest them. They would be so much cheaper to house than pigs and would not attract DEFRA round to lay charges of overcrowding or their not having enough space in which to turn round. I am sure if Jamie Oliver turned his attention to improving the image of the humble maggot, we should see maggot recipes beginning to wriggle into recipe books everywhere. I can imagine quite a simple production line consisting of an inclined pipe into which you put roadkill at the top end and have a bowl to catch the final instar of the larvae as they leave their dining table to look for somewhere to pupate at the bottom. Maggots usually crawl away to pupate remote from the carcass.

It has been estimated that 60 people die in Britain, alone and unfriended every year. The bodies of some of these lie undiscovered for weeks. When the mess is cleared up maggots and pupae are found under carpets and even in rooms remote from the scene of death.

Maggot Debridement Therapy

Maggots are wrongly categorised as always something disgusting; they can save lives. Having maggots develop in their wound, intentionally or otherwise, has saved the lives of people with gangrenous wounds. Soldiers trapped on no-man's-land in the First War and explorers in the bush or up mountains have emerged with wounds that would otherwise have killed them had they not been infested with maggots. In fact, maggots are now being used as a therapy for gangrenous conditions where other treatments have failed or are inappropriate. Necrotic tissue and the bacteria that go with it are the cause of death; what the maggots do is dissolve dead tissue by secreting digestive juices and then ingesting the liquefied tissue and bacteria. Native tribes in Australia and the Maya Indians used maggots in wounds from ancient times. Ambroise Pare seems to have been the first to note their beneficial effects on wounds after the battle of St Quentin in 1557. JF Zacharias (a surgeon in the Confederate Army) may be the first to be recorded using maggot therapy. Dr William Baer made the first scientific study of the use of maggots after noticing the clean wounds of soldiers trapped on no-mans-land for seven days in WW1 (1914 – 1918).

Their use as a form of medical therapy was reported by Brian Handwerk in National Geographic News for October 24, 2003 in an article entitled: '*Medical maggots treat as they eat*'. He quotes Ronald Sherman, a doctor at the department of pathology at the University of California at Irvine (UCI)[24]: "*After two or three failures of conventional medical or surgical therapy, maggot therapy should be considered for non-healing wounds, especially those which are infected or contain dead tissue [gangrene].*" He reports a case Sherman saw of a woman with perforation of the bowels and an infection that had spread through the abdomen, causing death (gangrene) of her bowel wall and peritoneum. Because it became necessary to remove dead tissue every other day in a risky surgical procedure, the attending physician decided to try the maggots. "*Two thousand of them were sprinkled over her open abdomen, and then covered with a dressing,*" said Sherman. "*Two days later the maggots were washed out, revealing no more gangrene. She healed well, and the abdomen closed, without the need for any further intra-abdominal surgery.*" Most patients feel nothing during treatment, but some do feel tickling or itching, like a crawling on the skin. "*A few patients have described discomfort or outright pain once the maggots become large, probably due to them crawling over nerves or squeezing into tight crevices,*" Sherman said. "*Pain is controlled with simple pills, or the maggots can be removed early and the pain disappears immediately.*" By the second and third day the wound oozes, becoming a bit sloppy and smelly. However, the process never lasts more than 72 hrs. There are some wonderful (some might say gruesome) pictures of what the Americans call Maggot Debridement Therapy in the raw on the UCI web[25]. John Church, an orthopaedic surgeon and modern maggot-medicine pioneer in the United

---

[24] http://www.ucihs.uci.edu/som/pathology/sherman/home_pg.htm
[25] Maggot debridement therapy. An alternative treatment for nonhealing ulcers - PubMed (nih.gov)

Kingdom, says "*There is still an art to medicine, and there's very much an art to using maggots, you must have a happy, hungry maggot or you will get no results. The environment on the wound must be what they would naturally seek out in nature.*" Edgar Maeyens, Jr., a doctor in Coos Bay, Oregon, who employs maggot treatment said, "*I call them microsurgeons, they can do what we can't do with scalpels and lasers. The maggots are marvellous.*" Wounds commonly treated include foot and leg ulcers, burns, and post-operative wounds that have become infected and re-opened. So, there you have it, the very cutting edge of biotherapy.

I ought to make a caveat here as it is possible to die from an infestation of maggots, in fact, that ancient tome of natural history, the Royal Natural History (Ed R Lydekker, 1893 - 96) which formed the main database to my own initial education in the subject, records that a gecko that fed on bluebottles became distended and died; "*...on dissection its intestines, lungs and liver were found to be almost entirely destroyed by maggots, whose presence was naturally attributed to eggs from gravid female blue-bottles, which had been swallowed as food. In another case, some lizards fed on the living maggots of the blue-bottle died in consequence of the attacks on their internal organs by their intended food.*" But more importantly it goes on, "*Far more important are the cases of infection of human beings; the resulting sickness, which often entails great suffering, and may end in death, being known as myiasis.*" so don't do this at home without medical supervision and if you must eat uncooked maggots, chew them well.

Beetles

Flies are not the only insects with an interest in fresh roadkill. There is a family of beetles, the burying beetles or *Silphidae*, which is very interested in winning the race to gain possession of a corpse. They are also known as sexton beetles (the sexton was a church officer responsible for the fabric of the church, ringing the bells and, more pertinently, digging the graves); some species have distinct orange bands on the black elytra (wing cases).

Sexton beetles at work, Biodiversity Heritage Library - Edward Step, Marvels of insect life

Illustration shows banded Sexton beetle (*Nicrophorus investigator*) at work. A lone male with a corpse will release a pheromone to attract a female rather like a female glowworm attracts a male with her light. They also display parental care of the young in the provision of food and also in chewing and regurgitating it for the young. Their stratagem is to move the carcass out of the wind in order that no others can smell it so that their larvae have the body exclusively for their own benefit. They dig the ground from below the body which falls into the hole where they cover it so that it is in a crypt. They also secrete antibacterial and anti-fungal compounds onto it to delay decay and reduce the smell that would attract the competition. It is amazing how quickly they can effect the disappearance of even quite large bodies like a rat or squirrel. A tv programme on decay at the end of 2011 showed a speeded-up film of a rat being buried by a pair of sexton beetles; it disappeared from view inside 12 hrs. Funnily enough another rat subjected to the same treatment merely moved about on the surface and was not buried at all, maybe the beetles were novices. Depending on the size of the body, the adults will fight others of the same species (males fighting males and females females) The adults and larvae feed on the carrion and also on the larvae of other scavengers. One interesting thing about the burying beetles is their habit of culling their own young to suit the size of the carcass; limiting the number of children to the amount of food available so that the family consists of a few children, well fed and developed, rather than many small weak and underdeveloped. I can't see this catching on in the human population even as the world becomes more and more populated. The strategy employed by barn owls is another way of reaching the same conclusion. Plenty of food allows the mother to lay more eggs, but unlike normal birds where the incubation of the eggs is delayed until the last egg has been laid to have a nest full of same-age nestlings, incubation begins with the first egg so that the chicks hatch in succession, so should food become scarce the older chicks consume their siblings beginning with the youngest. Another interesting phenomenon seen with burying beetles is that of phoresis, a form of symbiosis in which a mite, possibly *Poecilochirus* sp, hitches a lift on the back of the beetle to its next feast, which is fly eggs. The mite gets carried to the food and reduces the competition for the beetle's young.

Another instance of phoresis is where some species of *Nicrophorus* dislike the ammonia given off where maggots are thriving and carry on their backs mites which feed on fly eggs and so make the corpse atmosphere tolerable to the beetles.

Another beetle family attracted to corpses is the *Staphylinidae*, the rove beetles; they have short elytra and powerful jaws with which the larvae are also equipped. They look more like earwigs than beetles. The jaws enable both adult and larva not only to attack the carrion, but also prey heavily on the maggots already infesting the corpse. There are two British species, *Creophilus maxillosus* and *Staphylinus caesareus*. There is a member of this family that is commonly found on corpses in Australia, the devil's coach-horse beetle, *(Creophilus erythrocephalus)*. The eggs of this species have delayed emergence, so they are latecomers at the feast, however, they not only eat the larvae of other insects, but can munch their way into the pupal cases as well. This insect, as its Latin name suggests, has a red head. The devil's coach-horse found in Britain *(Staphylinus olens)* is not a carrion feeder, but hunts slugs and other invertebrates at night. One member of the *Histeridae, Hister 4-maculatus,* which is coloured rather like a burying beetle also preys on maggots, while another member, the genus *Saprinus* found in Australia, confines its attentions only to fresh pupae. Then there are several dung beetles (Scarabaeini) which are attracted to large carcasses, where they are interested only in the intestinal contents of herbivorous mammals. Dung beetles make balls of dung and roll these to where they have laid some young nearby.

Dung beetles moving dung, Biodiversity Heritage Library, Edward Julius Detmold

When all the flesh has been converted into nice new clean grey, blue, or green flies or beetles of various sorts, and they have flown away, the carcass has a different smell. This new smell attracts a new squadron of clients: the larder beetles or *Dermestidae*. The larder beetle *(Dermestes lardarius)*, which always reminds me of Belted Galloway cattle because of the pale band round its otherwise black body, eats any dried flesh remaining (it is also known as the bacon beetle).

Larder beetle,
Biodiversity Heritage
Library, E.W. Janson

The hide beetle *(D. maculatus)*, and the appropriately named *D. cadaverinus* are only interested in the skin, tendon or bone for their larvae to feed on. The remaining hair or feathers of the deceased attracts two more Dermestids, the fur beetle, *(Attagenus pellio)* and the carpet beetle and moths. The carpet beetle, *(Anthrenus verbasci)*, is a fairly well known diminutive little beetle, which has proved to be an unwelcome tenant in houses with fitted carpets and central heating. Its larvae are known as 'woolly bears' and eat their way slowly but surely through keratinous roadkill remains and posh woollen carpets alike. A colourful member of the Cleridae (the ham beetles), *Necrobia ruficolis,* also turns up in the later stages of a corpse's history to eat dried fat; they pupate inside the empty pupal cases of flies, sealing the opening behind them with silk. Another family of beetles found in Australian are the carcass beetles (*Trogidae*) of which, *Omorgus candidus* is a typical member commonly found in the arid parts of the country. They are large dark beetles with thick exoskeletons and are among the last beetles to inhabit a dead animal feeding on dried skin and ligaments, though they will consume a fresh carcass when they get the chance.

Moths

The last in this army of recycling specialists are the moths. By this time the smell is greatly reduced but what there is attracts a further wave of hungry insects, this time little moths, at least one of which is familiar to us all, the common clothes moth and the brown house moth. They graze on hair. These are my favourites, not because of the damage they do but because of their scientific names, respectively, *Tineola biselliella* and *Hofmannophila pseudospretella*. How poetic and beautiful are the names of these insignificant little moths! They just eat the hair which has been left by all the flesh eaters. My first job was working in an entomological laboratory where we had a culture of clothes moths. We fed them on kersey, a form of matted woollen cloth, but they would not eat it unless it was dirty, so we had to soil it with fish meal. The soiling effects of the myriads of insects pattering and oozing about on the corpse would doubtless make it very palatable to the fussy clothes moth larva.

Mites

There is a group of beasties that feed on corpses that I have already mentioned – the mites. Mites belong to the group *Arachnida*, they are very small and sport four pairs of legs unlike the *Insecta* which have three pairs. Thousands of mites feed on a corpse during its decomposition. *Macrocheles* species are common in the early stages while *Rostrozetes* mites feed on dry skin in the later stages of decomposition.

Collections of mites leaving dead mustelid © Arthur Boyt

So you see there is a whole economy of life out there depending on death for its very existence. If you or I pick up roadkill we remove that source of nutriment from the environment. But if we leave it lying in the road it gets flattened and dissipated along the surface of the road and nothing gets any benefit from it. If you don't pick it up and take it on with you, at least heave it off the road so that others can benefit from it. If I see something in the road and have no wish or need to take it home with me, and can safely stop, I do so and chuck it over a hedge so that a member of another set of scavengers we have not yet mentioned can feast on it safely, the foxes, buzzards, ravens, crows, magpies, and gulls.

Forensic science

The preceding paragraphs outline a lengthy process which can be used for determining the time or date of death of human bodies. This branch of forensic science is of sufficient importance for the police force in the North of England to set up a body farm where pigs (we are very like pigs) are laid out and the processes recorded at different times and temperatures. A similar exercise is being done in America where the University of Tennessee Forensic Anthropology Facility, better known as the Body Farm, was started in 1971 by anthropologist William M. Bass[26] as a facility for study of the decomposition of human remains. It is located a few miles from downtown Knoxville, Tennessee, USA, and consists of a 2.5-acre (10,000 m^2) wooded plot, where human cadavers are laid out in various conditions of being wrapped or part buried to gather information on decomposition under different conditions; something Sherlock Holmes never thought of doing. One aspect of this is that body juices change the conductivity of the soil into which they leak, and these changes in conductivity can still be detected hundreds of years later. This presents a tool for finding buried victims, mass graves and even old cemeteries.

Roadkill in the news

Wednesday the 12th of March 2003 dawned bright and fair. A mistle thrush was piping his favourite tune from high in a leafless sycamore, 28 chaffinches were feeding in the yard while a pair of robins hopped importantly among them. On a day like this I just had to go for a run before breakfast. I headed out onto Bodmin Moor across Davidstow airfield, built during WWII, now deserted and derelict. Brown Willy, Cornwall's highest mountain, beckoned from three miles away. Herds of hardy cattle and stocky ponies graze the barren grassy expanse that enhances the isolation and grandeur of Brown Willy and its more rugged and picturesque neighbour, Roughtor (pronounced to rhyme with doubter), but there is precious little wildlife to keep them company. While I was on the moor I heard one skylark and saw but one meadow pipit. Two hours of exercise certainly sharpened my appetite for a rather late breakfast.

While Sue was out, I invited the guests in our self-catering cottage to come in for a cup of coffee, it was then that the phone rang. A lady introduced herself as a friend of a friend and wanted to talk to me about eating roadkill. I had to let my guests depart and then learned that she was a columnist for The Times and her name was Lucy Pinney. Could she come and have an interview? *"Why certainly"*, I replied, *"and would you like to have a taste of badger or something when you are here?"* *"Well that would be very nice,"* she said. *"OK, when would you like to come?"* said I, turning over the pages of my diary. *"Could I come this evening?"* *"What, today?"* I exclaimed in surprise. Today would be a bit difficult, I had no fresh badger, and it was getting late to dig something out of the freezer and cook it. Sue was out and I could not clear it with her before making a decision; we had had six visitors only the night before, Sue would not be keen on helping with a meal without warning, especially if it was meat and, worst of all, badger. *"Tonight is not very convenient,"* I ventured,

---

[26] https://en.wikipedia.org/wiki/William_M._Bass

"I have nothing ready and I am off to Holland on Friday, what about sometime next week?" *"Well, I should be most grateful if I could come today as I have a column to do for Saturday's Times and tomorrow would be too late."* I know what it is to leave things to the last minute and anything I could do to get this lady out of her difficulty, of course I would oblige. *"Er, OK then, make it tonight."* We agreed on 8 p.m. as a suitable time to give us space to talk and eat. I dashed over to my freezer, which is kept in the workshop, as there is no space for it in the house (it would not be allowed in if there were, not with what it contained). I found some badger's hind legs, which looked as if they had been removed while the animal was fairly fresh, in other words they did not look green. My regular way of cooking roadkill was to do it in a pressure cooker for half an hour, this was quick, economical and made sure the meat was really dead without any nasty parasites surviving. However, it does tend to fill the house with steam with a rather interesting aroma. To add a touch of excellence I used to marinade the joints in cider and, rather than throw the cider away (heaven forbid), I would cook it in the cider. This distillate of cider and badger would quickly permeate the house and tended to make Sue call the fire brigade. For this reason I had begun to put my meat into a casserole and cook it in the AGA so that the smell was confined to the oven, or went up the chimney. However, there was no time for making a casserole, this had to be cooked pretty quickly.

I defrosted the meat in the microwave and browned it in oil in the pressure cooker with chopped up onions and a few cloves of garlic before bringing it up to pressure. I thought I might as well give it that touch of finesse and used cider instead of water. Thus, it was that, just as the house was redolent with the wonderful and unique smell of badger, garlic and cider, Sue came home. When, on top of this she learned that I had invited an unknown woman in for a meal with me, no, no, an unknown woman had invited herself in to have a meal with me and talk about roadkill…I leave you to imagine the effect on my eardrums; perhaps I should have called the fire brigade. Anyway, with an appropriate slamming of the back door (no, the glass did not fall out), Sue went out intending to stay away until the lady had gone and the whole unsavoury episode had ended. I dashed about getting things ready. I found some of the fish pie we had had the evening before and warmed that up in case Lucy did not eat much badger. Some frozen peas added a touch of green to the menu. It was 8 p.m., all was ready; the lady had not arrived.

The phone rang: it was Lucy; she was lost. I told her to stay put and went out to find her and lead her in. I located her in the mist on Bodmin Moor and guided her to the house. While I was serving the meal, Lucy produced a notebook and wrote something down every time I opened my mouth. This I found a bit disconcerting, as most people pay no attention when I start to speak. In her book, *A Country Wife,* published in the following year, she wrote of her arrival thus: "*There was a strange, intense aroma in the air as I took out my notebook. It would have reminded me of farm slurry, if it hadn't been so hot and steamy. Perhaps it was lightly boiled horse-droppings.*" She described me as 'cadaverous', an adjective appropriate to my line of interest if not my appearance. I found Lucy to be a very pleasant person, but, for a columnist of world renown, whose humorous anecdotes and comments are a pleasure to read, she seemed rather quiet and unassuming, in fact, almost shy. I managed to serve the meal without any mishaps and watched to see what Lucy's reaction would be to her first mouthful of badger. She speared a piece of badger on her fork, studied it carefully and then put it in her mouth. Her head jerked forward an inch or two as if she were going to be sick, but no, I was mistaken, she chewed it slowly and finally swallowed it. She described the taste as: "*a powerful mixture of kidney and liver, with a dash of concentrated musk.*" I couldn't have put it better myself, but she said the meal was '*execrable*', to me it was delicious. Lucy had set up a tape on the table to record the interview and the rate at which we ate was considerably affected by continuous questions and answers. Time was slipping by, and I became increasingly apprehensive that Sue would return at any minute. At 10.15 p.m. we were still busy talking when I heard the sound of the diesel engine come up the drive. Lucy jumped up to go and I quickly got a doggy bag and tipped the uneaten remains of the meal into it for her to take home with her and enjoy at her leisure. The door burst open and Sue came in, I recognised the look on her face, it warned me that anything could come out of that dear mouth of hers. It was at times like this that her relationship to her famous (or should that be infamous) sister, Annie King, came to the fore, who made sure her point was heard on one occasion by abseiling down into the chamber of the House of Lords and on another by handcuffing herself to the Alistair Witchell news desk when the Six O'clock News was on the air. I tried to put her off, "*Hello Dear, allow me to introduce you. This is Lucy Pinney from The Times.*" It was no good, she had to get it off her chest: "*This is a fine time for an interview!*" Getting that out seemed to draw her sting and Lucy was able to get away without any further welcoming remarks. She kindly did not put any of that in her article in Saturday's paper, but allowed herself to go into more detail in her book, *A Country Wife,* which, by the way, is a jolly good read and would be worth getting even if her visit to me were not mentioned in it.

A lady named Cathy appeared on Weakest Link once and, under questioning from Anne Robinson, revealed that she picked up roadkill to feed her 43 cats. Anne made her put down her board and demonstrate how she would stop the van, get out, pick up the rabbit, dump it in the back of the van and drive on. As if this was something out of the ordinary! Poor Anne, her protected celebrity lifestyle has robbed her of all the simple pleasures of life.

Media attention

In the spring of 1979 I cycled from Land's End to John-O-Groats via the Lizard (most southerly point), Cape Wrath and Dunnet Head (most northerly point) via the three peaks, Snowdon, Scafell Pike and Ben Nevis (up which I did not take the bike), 1240 miles in 12 days. Returning south on the train, the subject of eating roadkill badger came up in conversation with a group of my fellow travellers. As a result, I gave an interview for an article, which appeared in the Junior Telegraph and was followed up by a letter saying eating roadkill badger was not a good thing. This in turn resulted in an interview for radio, which went out on the John Dunn show and was partly repeated on Pick of the Week, but as I did not possess a radio I did not hear the broadcast at all. Stephen Beard, an independent reporter, heard the programme and asked to come round for an interview. I suggested he share a roadkill meal with me so he could get the taste of roadkill for himself. He duly came round bringing with him a lady who also worked for the Canadian Broadcasting Corporation (CBC). While we were dining on a hedgehog, I had picked up that week, he asked me if I could tell whether my meals were free of disease. I recounted how I once had enjoyed a wood pigeon from the chest cavity of which I had scraped out a large cancerous growth. Maybe it was this sort of comment that, as Stephen told me a few weeks later, resulted in the CBC switchboard being jammed with callers protesting at the content of a broadcast that was put out at breakfast time. How squeamish these hard backwoods people have become. Again, I never heard this broadcast go out. However, in 1981 I was sharing a room in a Kathmandu hotel with a guy from Perth, Western Australia, who started telling me about this roadkill chap from Britain that he had heard on the radio in Australia. I said, "*OK, OK. No need to tell me anymore, I know the chap very well, er, he is in fact in the room with you now!*" Then in 1983, having cycled from New Orleans to Winnipeg, I stayed at the home of my cousin, Paul Cavenagh, with whom I had had no contact for 36 years. He told me that he had heard the broadcast and reckoned that the subject of the broadcast must be his cousin.

Daily Telegraph

In 2006 I had a request for an interview from a young lady, Elizabeth Day, who wrote for the Daily Telegraph. I suggested she came here and join me in a roadkill dinner while we were talking. I duly collected her from Bodmin Parkway station, and we managed to pick up a few items on the way home across the moor. She told the story of her visit in an article entitled '*I'll have a badger with flies please*'[27] She phantasizes about my love of dogs: their moist noses, their wagging tails and their glossy coats, but above all what they tasted like after an hour in a pressure cooker. We picked up a pheasant which would make a good meal later. I had made a badger casserole which we now had for dinner. She sliced off a tiny piece of meat and managed to swallow it without throwing up.

Badger head for dinner © Arthur Boyt

The Times

The following article appeared in The Times on January 31, 2006 after a phone conversation. '*Fed up with Jamie? So try roadkill - rat or badger*'[28] By Valerie Elliott, Countryside Editor. She wrote saying I compared eating roadkill to eating windfall apples or gathering beech masts. She did write down that my favourite meal was the complete head of any animal as it has five different types of meat: the masseter muscle that closes the jaw, the tongue, the salivary glands,

---

[27] https://www.telegraph.co.uk/news/uknews/1510249/Ill-have-a-badger-with-flies-please.html

[28] https://www.thetimes.co.uk/article/fed-up-with-jamie-so-try-roadkill-rat-or-badger-xf2sjtjwl5q

the eyeballs and the brain.

The price of fame/notoriety

I have no objection to talking to interested callers on the phone, but not at 2a.m. on a Sunday morning. Which is the time a few failed comedians chose to give me a call and, as I am fast asleep in bed, pour their humour into the answerphone. Pretending to be a puppy or rabbit that I have killed (they havn't cottoned on to the fact that I am against killing animals) they demonstrate their upbringing by pouring foul and abusive language down the phone. Actually I find it slightly humorous but it frightens my wife and has resulted in our having to go to the expense of barring calls from them and all unidentified numbers.

Once I had a call from a chap with a strong Glasgow accent. We had a chat and I told him I was writing a book and he could see a picture of me in 'Ripley's Believe it or not 2008 The remarkable revealed'. Random House Books. He rang back after a few minutes and asked if I would put his name, Paul Meeong, in the book and his friend's name, Jonathon Leonard. After a few more minutes he rang again and said he had a badger could I tell him what should he do with it. A question or two from me about the animal he claimed to have found revealed that his badger was either imaginary or a species new to science. Undaunted, he asked for another friend's name, Shaun McMillan, to be included. If it means they will buy the book to show mums and girl friends, why, of course I will put them in, and with my best wishes.

I get calls and visits from journalists and TV presenters who sometimes stay for a meal of badger or something. Film crews want to tape me 'finding' some roadkill, skinning it, cutting it up, cooking it and finally eating it. This means that I must be able to produce suitable roadkill on demand. I have a wide circle of friends who are always telling me they thought of me when they saw some roadkill, so I engage their services to keep a lookout for me and I will end up with something to put before the camera. I have entertained crews from Germany, Sweden, Belgium and, of course, the UK and from the National Geographic Magazine. One chap said he wanted to do a film of the 'real' Arthur Boyt, not just the man who eats badgers. I agreed on condition he allowed me to put over the case against the shooting of snipe and golden plover on Bodmin Moor. To this he agreed and we spent many hours filming in the neighbourhood. He became very excited when I played him the answerphone tapes. I was invited to see the film before its release and was amazed and horrified to discover that the whole programme about me was hung on those disgusting tapes, even to the extent of putting on subtitles of the bad language to make sure we did not miss any of the filth. I protested for an hour or so to no avail that I was not happy with what was proposed. Also, there were now three other men (who had had failed marriages) on the programme, and what I had been told would be an hour's coverage of my life now became 14 minutes of a one-sided programme making us all out to be lonely jerks - and no mention of the shooting of snipe. Live and learn.

Can Roadkill save the planet?

The Sunday Observer of 7 September 2008 ran a frontpage headline: '*UN says eat less meat to curb global warming.*' In a special report by Robin McKie and Caroline Davies, the UN's chief climate expert called on everyone to give up meat for one day a week to reduce climate change. The Worldwatch Institute warned that "*the world's demand for beef is the driving force behind virtually every major category of environmental damage now threatening the human future: deforestation, erosion, fresh water scarcity, air and water pollution and climate change, biodiversity loss, social injustice, the destabilisation of communities and the spread of disease*". There is more to it than just the fact that each bovine farts 100kg of methane per year and 36kg of CO_2 into the atmosphere for the production of 1kg of beef. So how can roadkill affect that? Were people who find it impossible to give up their daily helping of meat to turn to roadkill instead, the demand for meat would be reduced without the anyone giving up meat! In fact they would realise the enormous economic benefit of eating roadkill every day of the week and so combine the saving of the planet with a growing bank balance.

Wasted food and roadkill

Tons of roadkill are collected from the roads of the USA and much of it is incinerated. Why, oh why, is this good food destroyed like this? It ought to be made available to the public for human consumption. Highway departments that currently bring in lorry loads of fresh carcasses should allow any impoverished members of their communities or any members of their communities, come to that, to take them away for free, or for a nominal fee to cover collection costs and so kill several birds with one stone, as it were, feeding the hungry, tidying the highways, protecting waterways and saving the planet! In any case, in a matter of a few years' time, I am sure it will be considered a moral crime to leave roadkill where it is. Richer nations will be obliged to send these thousands of tons of roadkill off to those parts of the world where food is so scarce that people, far from turning up their noses at roadkill, will be fighting to get to the front at the roadkill distribution points. Today we roadkill eaters are in the forefront of the battle to save the planet and save humanity. We shall be looked upon as the great pioneers of the movement that set the world aflame (a poor metaphor just here) and turned the tide of global warming! So get to it, jam on the brakes the next time you see some roadkill, and do your bit to stop global warming!

Roadkill in art

An exhibition of photographs of roadkill or the use of freeze-dried roadkill specimens as sculptures may seem bizarre in the extreme, but they have occurred and exist to this very day. In 1972, almost 20 years before Damien Hurst hit the headlines (and the jackpot) with his dead shark in a tank of formaldehyde, Stephen Paternite, an art student at Cooper School of Art in Cleveland, Ohio, exhibited a roadkill opossum in a students' show. The opossum was spreadeagled and tied down by leather straps to each paw. Paternite said of the display: *"It was a very strange and thought-provoking piece. I remember opening night of the show, receiving very strong reactions to the piece from near orgasmic to absolute nausea. The piece was definitely the talk of the exhibition and the beginning of a whole new avenue of thought for me."* It did not have the same effect on its viewers as Hirst's shark which was sold to Charles Saatchi for £50,000. Saatchi later sold the work back to Hirst who sold it on in 2004 to Steven A. Cohen for $8 million. Stephen Paternite applied for and was granted an award from the National Endowment for the Arts in Washington, DC to pursue his unique art form; government-funded 'roadkill art' had arrived. Despite a lot more skill going into their creation than into any of Hirst's bodies in formalin, he has never actually sold any of them, obviously, he does not get the right people to visit his exhibitions. Exhibitions of sculpture and roadkill photographs followed in 1975 and 1976 in Cleveland and Akron. Paternite was awarded another grant in 1987 from the Ohio Arts Council for his work. He held an exhibition the following year in Canton, Ohio, featuring 21 hybrid roadkill sculptures entitled 'Creature-Nites of Ohio' using parts of freeze-dried animals with doll parts and other things. One of these was a Siamese cat's body with a baby doll's head, another was the doll's body with the cat's head and tail, and another a kitten's head and tail added to the body of a rubber dragon. Three days before the exhibition opened to the public some elderly ladies walked through and stirred up the media resulting in a nation-wide frenzy of interest, criticism and opposition, particularly that such work should have been funded with tax-payers money. There is a video entitled 'Creature-Nites of Ohio'[29] which covers this interesting exhibition. Paternite has gone on

---

[29] https://www.youtube.com/watch?v=cSlr6Ft-Rv0

to create a new series of exhibits entitled '*Road-kill Radials*' in which animals parts and roadkill images are mounted in and around a tyre and a circular saw. His collection of sculptures can be seen on his website[30]

In an interview with Jeanie M. reported in '*One Inch Off the Pavement*', 1994, issue 2 and available on the website, Paternite told how he came to be interested in such an unusual artform. He said that when he was 7 or 8 years old. Ginger, their family dog, was hit and killed by a car at the end of their street. When his father came home from work, Ginger was retrieved and buried in their back yard in a make-shift grave. Many years later he picked up a beautiful hen pheasant that had been hit by a car. He took it home and had it mounted at a local taxidermy shop. He said his first trip to that taxidermy shop changed the direction of his life. He went on, "*I remember being absolutely speechless upon entering the shop. I had never seen such a vast array of mounted creatures in my life, from small birds to big game heads and everything in between. I knew at that point, taxidermy was something for which I had a keen interest and strong desire to learn*". This experience stimulated Paternite to enroll in a correspondence course in taxidermy from the Northwestern School of Taxidermy in Omaha, Nebraska. In his second year in art school in Cleveland, Ohio that he realized the possibilities of incorporating mounted animals in three-dimensional design sculptures and so opened the door to his rather unusual career.

During the interview, Jeanie M asked him if he had any memorable experiences collecting or finding roadkills? Stephen replied that he had an experience in 1975 of a huge, long-haired white cat which appeared to be in excellent condition. The traffic was heavy and he knew he would have to move quickly, so he grabbed the cat by its hind leg and flung it into the van, without ever releasing his grip on the cat's leg, but it shot right out of his hand into the van and exploded, projecting juice, meat and maggots all over the inside of his van.

Paternite is offering roadkill placemats which he describes as: "*Ideal for holidays, birthdays or that special gift for any discriminating gourmet*". Perhaps not to everyone's taste, these 12in x 18in (30cm x 45cm) hand-coloured photos might result in a diminution of appetite; I must say have seen more appetising pictures of roadkill.

In the Mail online '*Roadkill as art - yours for £35,000*'[31] Adam Morrigan

[30] https://www.virtualgallery.com/galleries/stephen_paternite_a3949435
[31] https://www.dailymail.co.uk/news/article-461310/Roadkill-art--35-000.html

from Horsley, Gloucestershire, teaches leather work at Ruskin Mill College, Stroud. He has a 'roadkill hotline' for people to call when they come across any roadkill. He collects it, skins it and, depending on what he has found, eats the animal, before using their hides for his sculptures. He says that badger tastes like pork, and that squirrel is quite nutty. "We're told these things are not edible because we're conditioned to think of them as vermin." One of his four exhibits - entitled *Road Kill (Absolution and Redemption)*' features a dead hare and a fox held in a frame made out of man-made fibre. 'I ate the hare but not the fox - it's very bitter - and turned them into leather.' The work is on sale for £35,000, but Mr Morrigan insists he is not interested in money and his work is more about provoking a reaction.

I came across a beautiful set of roadkill photos on Joy Hunsberger's website [32]: '*Entitled Roadkill Manifesto*' it shows a number of photos of different animals killed on the road. She has the following to say about her art: "*A lot of people don't understand my art. They think I'm trying to shock people, or that I'm romanticizing death or dark ideals. None of these is the case. My work is actually a very deep, ancient conversation. My obsession with taking pictures of roadkill is rather complex. In its simplest, most intentional form, it is a deeply spiritual ritual that pays homage to our four-legged ancestors, a practice in compassion, and also a raw energetic connection to the natural world. It is also a critical dissection of our/my place in the current world, and an apology for our/my disruptive unnatural influence upon it. Documenting roadkill is a way for me to honor the dead and heighten consciousness It is a feeble apology to all my ancestors who were run over in the name of 'progress', and a shrine to their perfect spirits. It is also a reminder of modern man's priorities, and the shrinking timeline for his existence, if he continues to ignore his place in the circle. If things do not change, one day, he too, will be run over by his own progress and lie flat on his back in the sweltering sun, festering and smelling like garbage*". I rather like her image of what we are likely to become if we do not change.

Media

Film

A 1977 American film entitled 'Joyride' was released in Australia and the UK under the title 'Roadkill'. It was remade and re-released in 2001, starring

---

[32] http://joyh.com/PHOTO/ROADKILL/body_roadkill.html

Paul Walker, Leelee Sobieski and Steve Zahn. It tells the story of how two brothers, driving across America to pick up the girlfriend of one of them, play a trick on a lorry driver by pretending to be a woman on their CB radio. The lorry driver discovers who it was and pursues them relentlessly in his lorry to a frightening crescendo. It is termed a thriller movie, I would call it a horror film. Don't watch it if you are of a nervous disposition and live alone..

Roadkill teddies

A soft toy designer has come up with a macabre new range of roadkill teddies[33][34]. The first to be launched is Twitch the Raccoon which comes complete with its own body bag to keep the maggots out, reports Metro. Twitch also has an identity tag stating that it had been "*run over by a milk float last Thursday, near the Hangar Lane Giratory system in London*". A zip on each side of the toy allows the owner to remove Twitch's innards and stuff them back in again. A tyre print runs across its back. Creators, Compost Communications, style themselves 'toy terrorists' and according to their website: "*We squash and burn and bludgeon and maim. But we're also toy fanatics like you. We love toys.*" Toy creator Adam Arber, 33, from London, said: "*I got the idea from looking at my mother-in-law's dog which is quite ugly and I thought it would make a great toy. A friend of mine had taken some pictures of roadkill and the two things gelled into one idea. He said he thought the toys, which cost £25, would appeal to people with a sense of humour and 'probably not anyone easily upset*'". The range of collectibles started with Twitch the Raccoon. To which has been added a cuddly toy, *Grind,* a teddy that's been squished flat. Other teddies are Splodge the hedgehog and Pop the weasel.

How to do it

Although I nearly always pick up roadkill with my bare hands, my advice is to always have a workman's glove with you under the front seat of the car, or the light plastic gloves available at filling stations for use when serving yourself with diesel, then if you need to lift a smelly badger into the boot you won't have a smelly/bloody hand all day to contaminate everything you touch. Have two gloves so that you are well protected if you are lucky enough to come across a deer. Have the floor of the boot ready covered with cardboard and it is always sensible to have a plastic sack or two in the car, it keeps any body fluids from making the boot and anything in it stink for a few months, and keeps any parasites from crawling around and eventually crawling or hopping onto you.

[33] https://technabob.com/blog/2009/11/06/road-kill-stuffed-animals/
[34] http://www.roadkilltoys.com/

Of course, if the badger smells that bad it is probably not worth the olfactory discomfort of having it with you in the car unless you are short of food, are hungry, or have visitors coming and you have not enough food to go around, or, like me, you collect skulls and bones and are loth to see some lovely specimens left by the roadside. If they have been dead for 24 hrs in the sun the belly will have gone a bit green, but in the winter they could be still OK after several days or even weeks. You just have to give them the sniff test. Putting it in a plastic sack does not alleviate the pong unless you can seal it well. When you get home, hang birds up by their heads or by their feet. Pheasants usually improve with a bit of hanging as it makes them more tender and adds to the flavour. The length of time to hang them depends on the temperature. Some say they are ready when fluid begins to drip from the beak. I usually go by the smell. Rabbits and hares should be gutted as soon as you get them home (by the road if possible) as they have a lot of busy bacteria in that huge caecum. I try not to leave them too long before skinning and butchering as once you have opened them they are more prone to attract bluebottles and begin to ooze with maggots. Deer that have been shot would be gralloched out on the hill. This saves the meat from being tainted and reduces the weight. But on the roadside, unless you have a sharp knife handy and don't mind gawping passers-by, I would get the beast on board quickly and do it, as they say, in the privacy of your own home. Opinion is divided as to whether venison should be hung and if so for how long. Some say butcher it fresh, others leave it till *rigor mortis* is over, others for a few days and still others hang it for 14 days. Butchers usually hang their carcasses in a cold store for 10 – 14 days.

I came across the following advice from a hunter and reproduce it here: *"I have seen and heard of folks throw out perfect meat. Since I started hunting I have done the following and have never had a bad incident.*

- *I wash the internal cavity out very well with cold water prior to hanging.*
- *I hang the deer/bear etc.. whole with the hide on (keeps from drying out too much)*
- *Depending on the temp is how long it hangs - but the evenings get cool during the season so the deep meat temp stays perfect, even in warm day temps if it is kept out of the sun. I average about 10 - 14 days*
- *I check it every day and butcher it when I see the following:*
  - *a) The internal cavity (ribs etc..) have a slight coating of mold beginning - this is wiped off with vinegar (I use quality cider vinegar)*
  - *b) The odor in this cavity has a hint of sour.*
- *I know this sounds bad but ask anybody from the deep woods or depression*

times. None of the meat is spoiled. No, you won't make jerky from the rib meat and will lose a thin covering from the rear (exposed meat) from drying. When I butcher it the internal meat is still very cool. The meat melts (even old bucks) and is cut with a fork. Yet nothing is spoiled. The only waste I have is bone and hide. My dog takes most of the cut scraps. Try it and ENJOY.☺

OK, the ageing of meat, I don't care if it is beef, venison, or goat, and how long it hangs is dependant [sic]on the conditions you have to leave it hanging. Meat should age at a tempature [sic] of between 35 and 40 degrees. If the meat freezes, it's not ageing. If the meat goes above 40 degrees it is a bacteria farm. The proper hanging time is 10-14 days, depending on what you like. I prefer 10 days for my farm animals. Because I don't have a walkin freezer, my wild game hangs long enough to let the rigor mortis release. I have seen people let a deer hang for 10 days in their yard at 50 degrees and the only thing they have after is the head mount."

Fresh or hung, you now have to butcher your animal. Let us use a rabbit

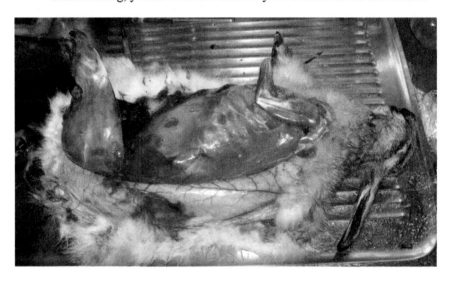

Rabbit being skinned © Arthur Boyt

as an example. You should have an incision from the rib cage to the vent. Separate the skin from the muscle layer beneath and peel it back. If it is a male this is the time to rescue the testicles. Make an incision down each hind leg from the centre-line of the belly to the ankle and peel the skin off the legs and cut off the feet.

The rabbit's skin is very loosely attached to the body but it is tightly connected on the back of the hind legs. Use a knife to separate the skin if need be, you will have to when you get to skinning almost anything else. Cut down to the vent and then cut through the rectum close to the vent, cut through the tail at a joint and the hind end of the rabbit will come free. Grasp the animal by the hips and pull the skin forwards in one movement to the shoulders. (You can pull it right up to the neck and off the forelegs). Make an incision to the front legs to the wrist (as you did to the hind legs), skin the legs and cut off the feet. Pull the skin forward to the ears. Feel for the point where the ears are attached to the skull and cut close to the skull. A strong pull will now separate the skin from the body, but if you want to keep the skin, ease it forwards cutting the connective tissue as the skin peels away. Separate the skin from the lips and nose and the job is done. If you are planning to stuff the animal you must take care around the eyes and lips not to cut off any skin. This same procedure is carried out whatever it is you are about to skin, but bigger animals are best hung up by a hook in the pelvis to allow you to work your way around the animal more easily than when it is lying down. And as I say you will need to cut your way between skin and body for everything bigger than a rabbit.

Lay the body on a clean surface, remove the heart, lungs and liver, identify and carefully cut out the gall bladder and with the lungs throw it out. Press the hind legs apart and cut down into the hip joint, then cut the legs off. Take the forelegs off at the shoulder joint and then separate the shoulder blade (scapula) from the body. Now chop the body up: in front of the pelvis, at the bottom of the rib cage and at the top and bottom of the neck. You now have 11 pieces of meat. I usually take the muscles off the rib cage and throw the cage out for the foxes. The legs can be divided at the joint if you wish. If gut contents have got on the body wash them off and wash out the mouth, otherwise don't wash them at all, leaving them full of their natural taste.

A simple recipe,

Quickly done and put into the lower oven of the AGA for 4 hours.

Badger Casserole

Ingredients

1 badger	3 spuds	4 cloves garlic
1 carrot	Plain flour	Cube of stock
2 onions	Seasoning	

Method

Gut and skin the badger and cut it into manageable joints, slice onions and garlic, roll joints in seasoning. Fry the onions for 5 mins add badger bits and fry together for 5 mins. Add garlic, carrot and spuds, and enough stock to cover. Bring to the boil and cook in lower (AGA) oven for 4 hours. Serve with a glass of red wine. I fished the head out first and dissected all the tasty titbits, masseter muscle, tongue, salivary glands, eyes and lastly, with the handle of a teaspoon, I dug out the brains! It was delicious. I heated the pot again two days later for some bits of foreleg and again after a weekend away to finish it all off. A very worthwhile bit of butchery.

Game Soup

by Mrs Beeton, Serves 8, Preparation time less than 30 mins, Cooking time 1 to 2 hours

Ingredients

2 partridges or 1 large pheasant	2 onions, shredded	1 turnip
3 slices of lean ham	1 head of celery	a small lump of sugar
55g/2oz butter	1 large carrot	salt and pepper, to taste
		2.26litre/4 pints stock

Method

1. Cut up the partridges, and braise the pieces in the butter until tender, then take out the best joints and set them aside.

2. Add to the remainder the onions, the celery, and 3 pints of the stock.

3. Simmer slowly for 1 hour, strain and take the fat off as clean as possible; cut the flesh from the parts saved in neat pieces, and add with the sugar and seasoning, give one boil and skim again to make sure it is quite clear.

4. Simmer the carrot and turnip, cut up in the remaining pint of stock, and when quite tender, add to the soup. Bones and trimmings of game and the inferior parts of birds can be used to make more economical soup.

Roadkill recipe for a Valentine

Any twerp can go into a shop and buy a valentine's card full of other people's soppy sentiments and think they are going to win the attention, if not the heart of their beloved. What is needed to mark your claim to the object of your desire is something unusual, something different, something revealing a brain between your ears and something that will mark you as competent, resourceful, enterprising and, above all, as one who is not going to dissipate the family budget on trivia. I can think of nothing more suitable to accomplish this than a meal of delicious roadkill served by you in your own home where you have control of the atmosphere, the ambience and all the romantic trimmings. So what is it going to be? I could suggest that if you fail to come across any roadkill you could get one from the butcher and if your sweetheart encounters a bit of shot you could say that a lot of wildlife does carry shot about with them as there is so much careless shooting going on in the countryside today. OK, so rabbit and pheasant it is to be. Here is my suggestion as to what to do with them.

Rabbit

Ingredients

Rabbit	Celery	2 Stock cubes (Oxo,
Onion	Garlic clove	oxo vegetable or Knorr
Red pepper	Water (3/4 pint)	basil cubes)
Potatoes	Carrot	

Method

Skin and gut the rabbit. Save the heart, liver and kidneys. Carefully excise the gall bladder and wash the liver. If the guts or stomach have burst, wash carefully, also trim off any torn muscle. Cut off the legs and separate the shoulders, chop off the head and neck, the back at the bottom of the ribs and at the pelvis, then chop the neck, the chest and the lumbar back each into two joints, this will give you 14 joints plus the heart etc. Wash the mouth out.

Slice the onion into a pan, scrub enough potatoes for two and cut into large lumps. Cover the onion with alternate layers of meat and potato, seasoning each layer sparingly with salt and pepper. Slice and add the garlic. Crumble the cubes onto the top. Add enough water to cover. Heat gently and simmer for two hours, stirring occasionally and checking that it is not boiling away. Test that the meat is tender (is it falling off the bone?), cook longer if necessary. Pour off some of the stock into two soup plates, extract the heart and liver from the stew, place the heart in the centre of your guest's plate and the liver in yours, pour a ring of fresh cream around the meat, sprinkle with chopped parsley and serve as a starter. Put out the nicest joints for your guest and pack it out well with the potatoes. Provide a side salad of sliced red peppers, sliced carrot and the centre of celery with heart and tender leaves.

Pheasant

Ingredients

Pheasant	Potatoes	Turnip
	2 Stock cubes (Oxo, oxo vegetable or	Carrot
Onion	Knorr basil cubes)	Water (3/4
Red pepper	Celery	pint)

Method

Cut the breasts and legs from the pheasant, gut it and save the heart, liver and gizzard, remove the stone bag from the gizzard. Cut the meat (not the giblets) into strips and roll all in seasoned flour. Put oil or fat into a casserole pan and fry the meat and sliced onions till brown. Scrub and cut the potatoes, carrot and turnip into chunks and add to the pan. Whisk some flour into 3/4 pint of water and crumble in the stock cubes. Pour over meat. Bring to boil and simmer in a cool oven for two hours. For starters fry an egg (easy or soft) and fish the heart from the casserole for your guest (and the liver or gizzard for you) and settle in the centre of the egg - yum, yum! Sprinkle with chopped parsley. If your guest is still with you, serve the casserole generously and provide the sliced pepper and celery as a side salad.

Set the table with a clean cloth, table napkins, wine and glasses with candles set to one side of the table (there is nothing less romantic than gazing at the object of your desires and being dazzled by a wretched candle flame). Start the proceedings with the opening of a bottle of elderflower champagne. It is the ideal introduction to a roadkill meal. However badly you cook the rest of the meal the elderflower will be remembered.

Should your valentine ever come back for another roadkill special in the weeks to come, be sure to add a wild vegetable like ground elder, hogweed, nettles or comfrey. A chef who can introduce you to a new and exciting taste, at no cost whatever, is someone whose company should be cultivated - you may be on to a winner.

Roadkill Christmas dinner 2007

Badger casserole

2 Badger hams	Carrot	Parsnip
Potatoes	Tomatoes	Flour, salt, pepper,
Broccoli	Blewits	spices
1 Big onion, sliced	Cooking oil	

Method

The great thing about roadkill is that you are getting meat without the guilt of killing an animal or having one killed on your behalf; a situation much more in keeping with the spirit of Christmas. It is all very well celebrating goodwill to all men if we are showing just the opposite to the turkeys.

What you have for Christmas depends very much on what you find by the road in the week or so beforehand (unless you are like me and keep a good supply of all kinds of roadkill in the freezer). Rabbits are always getting killed on the road and they make a very tasty and nutritious meal for at least four people. The pheasants that have survived three months of shooting go on getting themselves killed on the roads without a shot being fired. They may, however, be carrying a few bits of shot so be careful how you smash your teeth on them. Badgers are heavy with fat by now and are out and about as usual until the cold really sets in. So, lucky you come across an unlucky badger and you are set up for a thoroughly enjoyable and exciting Christmas. If it looks reasonably fresh don't worry about how long it has been dead as in this cold weather they will last for weeks unless its skin comes off in your hand when you pick it up by the back leg, in which case it may be too strong for any palate but that of the connoisseur. Skin it in the garage as this stops the fleas that have been its close companions from getting all around the house. Take off the hind legs with as much back muscle as possible and this will give you two good hams weighing around 3 lbs. The hams will have a good covering of fat and this will serve to baste the meat during cooking. If you are having a big crowd to dinner, add the forelegs, shoulder and, if need be, the neck as well. To add to the sense of economy find some blewits in the woods (Brock will feel very much at home with them) and make a sauce to go with the badger. Blewits are a safe toadstool because they are a pale blue/mauve above and below, are about in early winter, have no poisonous lookalikes and are really nice to eat.

Dredge the hams in seasoned flour, put a little oil into a casserole dish and lightly fry the meat on both sides. Remove the meat and fry the onion until it is golden. Slice the spuds and parsnip put them on the onion and chuck in the tomatoes. Put the meat on top and pour on a cup of cider/wine/stock with the remains of the seasoned flour. Bring to the boil, cover and simmer for 5 minutes. Place in a hot oven for 1.5 hrs, alternatively, you can put it in a slow oven or the bottom of the AGA for 3.5 hrs and go out for a good walk to work up an appetite. Add the chopped-up carrots and put it all back in the oven for half an hour. Cut up your blewits and cook them gently in a light sauce. Boil a pan of broccoli (or greens of your choice) for 5 minutes. Spoon off any fat or oil from the casserole and serve the meat on the bone with the sauce. The family will be amazed and there will be no tyre mark on the meat!

Other recipes you might like to try

1. Poached Pheasant in a Star Anise and Chilli Broth with Bok Choi and Udon Noodles[35], by Rick Stein, from Food Heroes
2. Maureen's Game Pie[36] by Christopher Sykes from Upper Crust
3. Roast Grouse[37]
4. Pan-Fried Grouse with Skirlie and Glazed Beetroot[38]
5. Roast Partridge with Bacon, Garlic and Thyme[39]
6. Braised Partridge with Cabbage[40]
7. Salmi of Pheasant (or Partridge, or Guinea Fowl) with Roast Chestnuts[41]
8. Game Pie[42]
9. Hare and Chocolate Sauce[43]
10. Royal Hare Stew[44]
11. Game Terrine[45]
12. Pan-boiled fox[46]

---

[35] http://recipe-finder.com/recipe/14004819472926020766
[36] https://bakerrecipes.com/maureens-game-pie-recipe/
[37] https://www.greatbritishchefs.com/how-to-cook/how-to-roast-grouse
[38] https://www.countrylife.co.uk/food-drink/glorious-grouse-44959
[39] https://baconshow.blogspot.com/2006/11/543-roast-partridge-with-bacon-garlic.html
[40] https://www.blackface.co.uk/braised-partridge-with-cabbage/
[41] http://beebrecipes.co.uk/recipe/salmiofpheasantorpar_14228
[42] https://www.bbc.co.uk/food/recipes/gamepie_8555
[43] http://letseatmarbella.com/2018/09/09/hare-in-chocolate-sauce/
[44] https://app.ckbk.com/recipe/floy06262c04s001r006/royal-hare-stew
[45] https://www.bbcgoodfood.com/recipes/game-terrine
[46] http://getknowedillustration.blogspot.com/2008/05/challenge_14.html

Literature

History

It came as a surprise to me to discover that a great deal of research has been carried out on the subject of roadkill and not a few books written on it. I am indebted to Henri Seibert and James Conover (who carried out the first survey of roadkill that included invertebrates) for their review of earlier work on the subject in America in 1991. The first study of roadkill anywhere in the world was of red-headed woodpeckers by H.S. Sharp in 1930. This was followed by a paper by Cottam in 1931, again dealing with birds. Work on rabbits was reported by Gordon in 1932 and Sperry in 1933. The first work on wildlife in general, was by Stoner in 1936 followed by Scott in 1938. Possibly the first book published was '*Feathers and Fur on the Turnpike*' in 1938 by James Simmons. This work was celebrated by Roger M. Knutson when he founded the International Simmons Society which oversees biennial counts of road victims; the Labor Day and Memorial Day counts neatly coincide with the most abundant presence of animals and highest traffic totals. The first publication in the UK seems to have been '*A survey of road mortality in mammals*' by Hodson in 1966, although I remember participating in a survey in 1958/1959 in which records were sent in of all roadkill seen over a regularly travelled stretch of road. Roger M. Knutson[47] in his interesting book, '*Flattened Fauna: A Field Guide to Common Animals of Roads, Streets, and Highways*', 1987 depicts many commonly found specimens of birds and animals in America as they look when flattened on the highway. It is a semi-humorous guide for people carrying out surveys of animal mortality and for the interest of travellers in general. Since then he has heard from flattened fauna fans, amateur and professional, from every continent except Antarctica, the only continent where roadkill is not a big issue. It offers tips on identifying even the most flattened of flattened fauna for all major groups from snakes and birds to mammals and reptiles, and how to, for example, tell a flattened muffler from a roadkill armadillo or a hubcap from a painted turtle. It gives tips on where and how to begin learning about roadkill and also includes a form for reporting findings to Knutson and a life list (better thought of as a dead list) for recording long-term observations. He is very wary about advising people to stop to examine their specimens in case they too become part of the roadkill fauna and this reminds me of an incident when I was cycling across the states and spotted a beautiful red cardinal (a thrush-sized bird)

---

[47]

https://www.amazon.com/s?i=stripbooks&rh=p_55%3ARoger+M.+Knutson&ref=si3_rd r_bb_author by the road. There were three lanes of traffic surging along the road at the time and as I stooped to pick it up a police highway patrol car stopped and the officer wound down his window and drawled, "*Do you mind stepping off the highway before you get killed*". One man, who often uses the book, is Moose Mutlow who travels regularly through Yosemite National Park and campaigns for the animals that are getting killed on the roads. He is known as the Roadkill Man.

The Seibert and Conover study in Ohio (1991) was carried out on foot and lasted 14 months. It covered each side of a 1.6 km (1 mile) stretch of dual lane highway (US 33) and provided 188 vertebrate and 1,162 invertebrate victims. They recorded some carcasses disappearing in 24 hours, while two groundhogs lasted 3 months, most took between 2 and 14 days to disappear.

It was Dickerson (1939) who first recommended that better planning of the highway environment be considered as a means of reducing the death toll.

As a result of the publicity surrounding the subject, I was visited by a reporter from Belgium who was working on an article on Roadkill. He introduced me to a book on a scientific study of roadkill in Flemish, '*Dieren onder onze wielen, Fauna en wegverkeer*', (Animals under our wheels, Fauna and road traffic) by J Rodts, L Holsbeek and S Muyldermans. Vubpress, 1998. a most interesting book with some really excellent pictures. In Belgium, volunteer observers send in records of beasts seen on the road and these are analysed and tabulated to shed light on any trend in populations of animals or birds; this book is erudite and informative

One recent study by Kerry Foresman of Montana University, '*How does the small mammal cross the road?*' featured in *Montana Outdoors* for July–August 2006. Construction and dualling of highways through wetlands results in serious fragmentation of habitat. Steel pipes, 4 ft in diameter are laid below the road to balance water movements. But these pipes are not used by small mammals if they contain any water. It was found that metal grid shelves and plastic piping above the water level were readily used by small mammals to avoid the hazardous crossing above. Fourteen species, from shrews and deer mice to raccoons and even porcupines were identified using the passages. The shelving is able to be fitted to existing culverts which should improve the lot of animals beside existing roads.

Statistics

Deer Collisions[48]

"*Road traffic accidents involving deer present a major problem in the UK as well as in many other countries in Europe. For example, in Germany over 220,000 traffic collisions occur annually involving deer, over 1000 of which lead to human injuries and around 20 to human fatalities.*

"*In the UK until recently there had been no system for central registration of road traffic accidents involving deer or other wildlife. Firm statistics on the scale of the problem in this country remain unavailable. However, a survey commissioned by the Highways Agency in 1997 estimated that even then toll of deer killed annually in traffic collisions in the UK was already likely to have been between 30,000 and 40,000.*"

Reducing roadkill[49]

As new figures reveal millions of animals die on our roads every year, motorists are being urged to drive more carefully

"*Every year an estimated one million animals, including deer, foxes, badgers, otters and squirrels, are killed on UK roads. It's not only animal lives which are at stake; it's estimated that deer accidents alone account for over 500 personal injuries, including over 100 serious or fatal injuries. And costs for repairs to motor vehicles involved in deer collisions are estimated at over £17m.*

"*The Spring season signals the start of a peak period for road accidents involving badgers and Roe Deer – road accidents account for an estimated 100,000 deaths of badgers and deer every year.*

"*It's not just country roads where drivers need to beware of wild animals crossing - each year an estimated 20,000 urban foxes are killed on roads in UK towns and cities.*

"*Birds are also at risk with an estimated ten million killed on the roads each year. Three million are pheasants and for increasingly rare species such as barn owls, a worrying 3,000 juvenile birds are killed by motor vehicles annually.*

---

[48] http://deercollisions.co.uk/pages/background.html
[49] https://postandparcel.info/20824/news/post-office-counts-the-cost-of-wild-animal-accidents/

"Conover et al (1991) estimated that nationally more than 1.5 million automobile collisions with deer occur annually. These collisions result in more than 29,000 human injuries and more than 200 deaths. Rue (1989) estimated that 0.029% of the collisions with deer result in human mortality. Romin and Bissonette (1996) concluded that collisions with deer are on the increase. Vehicular damage can be severe and this is especially the case in states with high deer populations. Conover et al (1991) estimated that annual damage to vehicles from deer collisions exceeds $1.1 billion. Another economic impact of animal mortality is the loss of the animal for hunting. Romin and Bissonette (1996) estimated that the value of a mule deer harvested in Utah was $1,313."

I found a very informative website *'Driving Animals To Their Graves'* by Mark Matthew Braunstein[50]. Parts of it are well worth quoting. It records that: *"Everyday in the U.S., 190 million motor vehicles hit the road, and one million animals get hit by motor vehicles. Every year our nation's experimenters kill 100 million lab animals, hunters kill 200 million 'game' animals, and motorists kill nearly 400 million road animals. Only America's meat-eaters take a larger toll than its motorists. For every dead animal counted, three or four more die unnoticed. During the late 1950s, in a roadside version of the Audubon's Christmas bird counts, the Humane Society of the United States conducted some Fourth of July body counts. During the 1970s, again groping for numbers, the Humane Society compiled data from isolated scientific studies of single roads or single species. Its secondary sources yielded the same national death toll as its field studies: one million animals a day. Two regional surveys during 1993 and 1994 offer updated species death counts. Called 'Dr. Splatt' and coordinated by the Pinkerton Academy, the project involves mostly pupils in from 40 schools throughout the Northeast U.S. Concerned readers of the monthly Animal People also participate.*

"The National Highway Traffic Safety Administration chronicles the 47,000 Americans who die each year in traffic accidents. But it neglects to collect data on the animals whose deaths it does not even define as accidents. In the American lexicon, humans are living flesh and traffic deaths. But animals are dead meat and roadkills. Few roads or highways are designed with consideration for animal traffic. Some, such as those with concrete 'Jersey barriers' along the medians, are so lethal they could not be any worse. (A Jersey barrier is a concrete wall designed to keep the traffic from one carriageway entering the other carriageway).

---

[50] https://www.culturechange.org/issue8/roadkill.htm

"The widening of a state road into an interstate highway through Michigan's northern peninsula resulted in a first year fivefold increase in deer kill. Even death tolls on old roads can be alarming. Pennsylvania's roads in 1985 underwent no new major construction, yet over 26,000 deer still were killed. In wintry northern states such as Michigan and Pennsylvania, sick or starved animals travel on plowed roads through deep snow. Weakened animals sometimes cannot jump or climb over icy snow banks formed by plowing. At critical meetings with automobiles, the animals slip on ice and into oblivion. In the West, roadsides are laced with barbed wire to prevent cattle and sheep from prematurely becoming dead meat. But barbed-wire fencing ranks second only to hunting as the leading cause of death to mule deer and pronghorn antelope. Every sunrise illuminates impaled or ensnared wildlife who reached neither the shorter road nor the greener grass on the other side of the fence.

"Woodland caribou survive as a single herd of 50 diehards in northern Idaho and southern British Columbia. The U.S. Forest Service blames roadkills, not habitat loss, as the greatest threat to their survival. Of our nation's large mammals, Florida panthers hover nearest extinction. During the early 1980s, the panthers suffered nine roadkills—half their entire population. According to the state Department of Fish and Game, southern California's scant 40 cougars, already decimated by poaching, are threatened even more by Interstate 15. During the 1970s and 1980s, at least 357 of Florida's threatened black bears blackened the blacktop. That's one-quarter of their present population. Fewer than 300 of Florida's miniature Key deer survive. The Nature Conservancy estimates one deerkill nearly every week. Despite a 15-m.p.h. speed limit, driving vacationers remain the Key deer's worst enemy.

"Not all deer species that confront cars also face extinction. Many regions of the U.S. suffer from overpopulation of two species of large mammals: deer and humans. No wonder our two paths cross so often, as each year 350,000 deer fatally collide with vehicles. An additional 50,000 collide and survive. From 1993 to 1994, Ohio's deer population rose five percent, as did its deer collisions. Among its total deer population of over 500,000, there were 25,636 reported cases of deer colliding with cars. That's 1 in 20—and that's only what's reported.

"Collisions with motorists are usually fatal for the deer. In 1992, New York state motorists reported killing 11,822 deer. Cornell University researchers found that, for every deerkill reported, four more died and one more was injured.

"Human casualties also occur. In 1994, Michigan reported 56,666 deer collisions, of which five resulted in human fatalities. According to the National Highway Traffic Safety Administration, every year 120 people are killed and 8,000 are injured in deer collisions. For all animal collisions, it's 150 people dead and 10,000 injured."

Emma Parker-Bowles (yes, niece of the Duchess of Cornwall) has written an article which was published in The Sun newspaper (28/11/2006) which stated that *300,000 cats and 100,000 dogs are killed on the roads every year and that in 2005, the RSPCA was called out to help 17,710 injured animals on UK roads. In America 26 million cats and six million dogs are killed every year by cars and that is out of 400 million animals killed on American roads a year. The UK's Mammal Society has launched a nationwide survey to collate information on road conditions and wildlife casualties. It is estimated 50,000 badgers, 100,000 foxes and 10 million birds are killed or maimed every year. A survey by the Highways Agency estimated 30,000 to 50,000 deer are killed annually. And that doesn't include the walking wounded that die far from the road.*

"There have been too many times to count when I haven't been sure, so I have pulled over at the next safe space and run back like a maniac to prod a badger, fox or rabbit. Retired civil servant Arthur Boyt does the same thing but he is not a one-woman wildlife ambulance like me. My last rescue mission was a raven in London that was hit by a car. I wrapped it in a blanket and took it to a Putney animal hospital. No, Arthur Boyt would have been licking his lips and rubbing his stomach. Because he's the dude who scrapes up roadkill, takes it home and cooks it for dinner with some fava beans and a nice Chianti. Over the years he has eaten otter, great horseshoe bat, pheasant, deer and fox. Clearly Arthur is not in my BT Friends And Family".

Her statistics are right but her raven was most likely a crow (the only ravens in London are in The Tower) and she misjudges me as I have picked up and cared for many stunned and half-dead birds and animals from beside the road.

In Germany over 120,000 traffic collisions occur annually involving deer, over 800 of which lead to human injuries and around 25 to human fatalities.

Jasper

Wildlife collisions with vehicles and trains have been examined in Jasper National Park, Alberta[51]. The database used in this research was one of the largest and most complete wildlife/collision databases in North America. *"Over 4,000 wildlife collisions from 1951 to 2002 have been documented. The main species examined were elk, bighorn sheep, mule deer, moose, white-tailed deer, coyotes, wolves, black bear and grizzly bear. Having zones with lower speed limits reduced the rate of collisions with elk and other wildlife but had a negligible affect on reducing bighorn sheep collisions."*

Roadkill stats

"There were over 3,300 deer/vehicle collisions reported in the Nutmeg State in 2000[52] - modest by Pennsylvania or Michigan standards but still representing a significant amount of trauma and damage. In contrast, the first moose collision on record in this state happened in 1995, and there have been fewer than 10 since then. There have been several motor vehicle collisions with black bears in Connecticut every year since the first record in 1991, and these are probably on the increase today.

"(US) Nationwide, an estimated 135,000 deer are killed in collisions with vehicles, resulting in over 100 human fatalities and at least 7,000 injuries. The economic costs, it should go without saying, are considerable."

Studies in Germany in the 1960s suggested 40,000 deer were killed by road traffic every year. A more recent study has suggested that that has risen to 140,000 DVCs on German roads by 2002. Records have been kept for decades in Switzerland and shew that DVCs have doubled from 5000 p.a. in the 1970s to over 10,000 by the end of the century. Figures for DVCs in other European countries are: Sweden - >55,000, Austria – 35,000, Denmark – 10,000, Norway – 3500. In Western Europe 30,000 people are injured and close to 300 killed as a result of collisions with nearly half a million deer with damage to property in excess of £1billion[3].

The following statistic have been reported for the USA in 'High Country News':

253,000	Animal-vehicle accidents annually
50	Estimated percentage of vehicle-large animal collisions that go unreported.

[51] https://trid.trb.org/view/688296
[52] https://greensleeves.typepad.com/berkshires/2006/05/you_have_the_ri.html

90	Percentage of animal-vehicle collisions that involve deer
$2,000	Average minimum cost for repairing a vehicle after a collision with a deer
1 million	Vertebrates run over each day in the United States (a rate of one every 11.5 seconds).
200	Human deaths annually resulting from vehicle-wildlife collisions.
6	Bears killed last year by vehicles in Yellowstone National Park.
1,559	Animals killed on Yellowstone National Park roads from 1989-2003. Figure includes 556 elk, 192 bison, 135 coyotes, 112 moose, 24 antelope and 3 bobcats.
2,349	Large animals killed on New Mexico roads in 2001. Figure includes 30 black bears, 160 elk and 600 deer.
51,000	Vertebrates killed in and around Saguaro National Park by automobiles each year. Figure includes 1,400 birds, 6,500 mammals, 26,000 reptiles and 17,000 amphibians.

Breakdown of roadkill by species

In 1993, 25 schools throughout New England participated in a roadkill study involving 1,923 animal deaths. By category, the fatalities were:

mammals	81%
birds	15%
reptiles and amphibians	3%
undiscernible	1%

Extrapolating this data nationwide, Merritt Clifton, editor of Animal People Newspaper estimated that the following animals are being killed by motor vehicles in the United States annually:

squirrels	41 million
cats	26 million
rats	22 million
opossums	19 million
raccoons	15 million
dogs	6 million
deer	350,000

A one-year study of a two-mile length of U.S. Highway 441 (through Payne's Prairie State Park) in Florida, found a total of 3,356 dead animals:

snakes	1,291	mammals	72
Frogs	1,333	alligators	29
turtles	374	lizard	1
birds	265		

Australia

Wild kangaroos are a serious hazard at night in the Australian bush, accounting for 71% of animal-related insurance claims, followed by dogs (9%) and wombats (5%). Most vehicles in the bush are fitted with roo bars to minimize the risk of damage[53]. My question is, what kind of driver cannot avoid an animal of that size on a road that wide!

Roadkill kangaroo © Arthur Boyt

Eating meat isn't natural

In an article by Michael Bluejay titled 'Why humans are primarily plant-eaters by design'[54].

"Vegetarians live longer and have more stamina than meat eaters. We are not made to eat meat.

"In the course of my research I came across a website in which the author asserted that humans are not designed to eat meat and are better off being vegetarians. His grounds for this alarming attitude is that true carnivores'

---

[53] https://en.wikipedia.org/wiki/Roadkill_cuisine
[54] https://michaelbluejay.com/veg/natural.html

*teeth are designed for holding struggling prey, penetrating body coverings, slicing flesh and breaking bones; they cannot grind their teeth from side to side; they have acidic saliva for digesting meat (ours is alkaline); their stomach acid is 12x stronger than ours; their gut is only 3x body length and they are relatively short-lived. Whereas we are like herbivores with teeth that cannot grasp anything much bigger than a mouse or break into anything bigger than a rabbit; our teeth can grind from side to side like herbivores; we have alkaline saliva for digesting carbohydrates; our stomach acid is weak for dealing with vegetable protein; our gut is 10x body length like herbivores and we are long-lived like elephants and chimps. The Maasai tribe in Africa whose diet is mostly meat are the shortest-lived of the human race. Endurance tests on meat-eating athletes, vegetarian athletes and sedentary vegetarians gave the vegetarians a higher average performance than the meat-eating athletes. A group with a mixed diet were subjected to a cycle endurance test, and tested again after a meat diet and then a vegetarian diet. After the vegetarian diet they performed on average 3x as well as after the meat diet with a 150% average improvement on the initial performance. He asks the following question: 'Ask yourself: When you see dead animals on the side of the road, are you tempted to stop for a snack? Does the sight of a dead bird make you salivate? Do you daydream about killing cows with your bare hands and eating them raw? If you answered **no** to all of these questions, congratulations; you're a normal human herbivore; like it or not. Humans were simply not designed to eat meat. Humans lack both the physical characteristics of carnivores and the instinct that drives them to kill animals and devour their raw carcasses'.*" So there you have it!

Poems

Roadkill badger

As Arthur was driving home-bound in his car,
A badger he spied, it was freshly expired.
A lovely piece of roadkill is better he knew,
Than any shop meat that goes into his stew.
"To skin and disect with my scalpel's an art;
Leg meat and liver go well with the heart;
A puff ball diced, fried in garlic with oil;
A freegan cabbage brought up to the boil;
Will surely make me such a rustic repast;
So even in H90 I'll never be last!".

John Collier (© 2010)

Fleas

As upon my way I sped,
I saw a rabbit lying dead
And knowing I had nought for sup,
I stopped the car and picked it up.

The carcase, cooling, did not please
Its large community of fleas
Who thought that it would do no harm
To get themselves to somewhere warm.

So hopping round inside the car,
They hopped on me.

They bit me much below the waist,
But found I was not to their taste.
In fact, I tasted rather funny
And nothing like a good old bunny.

Arthur Boyt (© 2010)

A story

While I was writing this book, a cousin-in-law, Dean Robinson, said he had written a story for the book. It is worth including and is reproduced below.

The unfortunate influence of Arthur Boyt.

By Dean Robinson

Now I always felt a little sad whenever I saw dead wildlife by the side of the road. Not so much as feeling sorry for the sad loss of life, after all we are talking about dumb animals here, but more as a missed meal.

I have always loved game, and to see a dead cock pheasant or buck hare just lying by the side of the road always saddened my taste buds. Unfortunately, like most people, I was a little too inhibited to stop and put the corpse into the boot of my car, and so left it to other carrion collectors. With Arthur Boyt as my wife's cousin, and a frequent visitor to our family home, it was inevitable that my attitude to road kill would change. Arthur would come to stay for the weekend and arrive with a variety of dead animals and I would get out my cookery books. Badger Bourguignon, Squirrel au vallee d'Auge, and Sourris soufflé. We really know how to cook in the Robinson household.

One autumn morning, driving to work and passing by the Rockingham Forest in Northamptonshire, I eventually lost my road kill virginity. There by the side of the road was a very dead large roe deer. Someone had pulled it out off the road and onto the grass verge. Now what would Arthur think with this as my first road kill salvage? Not a little flat rabbit of the fields, but a royal animal of the forest. If you were found with it in bygone days, you could have been hung or at least shipped to the colonies for the rest of your life. It was still warm, the skin had not been broken, and there were no Michelin marks on the fine hide. I looked into a pair of very dead deer eyes – I'm sure I saw the letters ERF fading as residual images in those orbits - and told my new found friend it could come home with me.

However, I was on my way to work, and was due for an early morning meeting with my boss. If I left it there until returning home later in the day, there was a good chance that someone else would pick it up. No, it had to come to work with me and spend the day in the boot of my car. It was a big beast, and I struggled to push it into the boot. Modern cars are not designed for recovering large dead animals from roadsides. The best way was to stuff the back end in as far as possible, and leave the neck and head hanging over the edge. This did mean that I couldn't close the boot, so I had to wrap the head in a high visibility vest that was already in the boot. I thought it would would act as a good disguise. As I was doing the arrangement, a large clot followed by a thick flow of blood disgorged from the mouth of the dead beast. I wasn't quick enough and it landed on the trouser leg of my light grey work suit. I was getting really late for work now and didn't have time to return home and change. I thought there wouldn't be many people in work at this time in the morning, so I was sure I could strip off in the gents and rinse out the blood on my trousers. Arriving at work, the car and deer were parked at the rear of the car park, and I rushed past security and into the gents. Cold water is the best way of getting fresh blood out of cloth, and I was quite successful in getting the worse of it off. However, I now had the problem of a very damp trouser leg. After 5 minutes on the hand drier I had to put the on the very damp trousers and get into the meeting with the boss.

I sit down on one of his armchairs. The office is executive style. *"Dean, your leg is wet, have you had an accident?" "Well no, not exactly. Or at least it wasn't me that had the accident." "Then why the wet leg?" "Oh, that was the blood. I have just rinsed it off." "But you said you didn't have an accident. Was it someone else?" "Well no not a someone, I suppose you might say it was a something."*

At this point I did have a small regret that I had ever met Arthur. If it wasn't for him I wouldn't be in this very uncomfortable position, and the deer would have stayed by the side of the road for someone else to collect. Just then the phone rang. It was Frank from security letting the boss know that someone had dumped a dead deer in the boot of Mr Robinson's car. *"Must be someone out to get him"* said Frank. *"You know, as a warning, like that film the Godfather and the horse's head in the bed. I'll tell the lads to get rid of it."* My boss relayed the message on to me. This was getting out of hand. Not only was I suffering damage to my personal credibility and future career, there was now a risk of having my deer stolen by security. I took the phone. *"Frank. Call off your hyenas. That is my deer. You lay a hand on it and you will end up the same way as Bambi."* My boss senses potential conflict, and challenges me to sort it out immediately. *"You have one phone call, and 10 minutes, or security get the deer."* It is good to have friends at a time like this. A quick call to my chum Barry the Butcher in the village and I explain my predicament. *"No worry Dean, the lad and the van are on the way."* Exactly 10 minutes later the deer is in the butchers van and safely on its way to Barry's cool room. I had impressed my boss by my decisiveness and ability to recover the situation quickly and effectively. The rest of my workday was comparatively calm and uneventful.

We paunched the deer that night when I got home. Barry claimed he wasn't licensed for game so we had to do it in the shed in our garden. I buried the entrails in the compost heap and left the carcass to hang for a few days before calling on Barry to help butcher it. We had roast saddle the next weekend and I filled the freezer to overflowing with the remainder. Now that would have been the end of the story except for the way in which a game of badminton was interrupted by our dog Gemma. Two weeks later Barry and his family came round for a barbecue of venison sausages and a game of badminton on the lawn. Gemma had been begging for most of the afternoon and had consumed more than her fair share of sausages. Tiring of her attentions I chased the persistent pet away and we started the game. Badminton was in full swing when one of Barry's children suddenly shouted: *"Gemma has got a black hose pipe, and she is dragging it this way"* It certainly looked like a black hose pipe, but it wasn't. The foul dog had been digging in the compost heap and had found her own supply of venison. However these were not prime cuts, this was the offal I had buried two weeks previously. Barry's teenage daughter recognised the 'hose pipe' for what it was and screamed. I had to wrestle the intestine from Gemma, place it in a plastic bin liner, and put it on the roof of our bungalow out of sight and smell. We continued the game and had a very pleasant afternoon with Gemma trying unsuccessfully to climb onto the roof.

So my first introduction to road kill had been interesting to say the least. A mixture of embarrassment and amusement. The venison was delicious and we were still pulling it out of the freezer six months later. I presented the head to Arthur as a special Christmas gift for converting me to roadkill. Now 10 years later you may see a very respectable middle-aged gentleman stopping in the road and holding up the traffic to collect a rabbit, or pheasant, or even a squirrel from the roadside. I am that man, thanks to Arthur Boyt.

Bibliography

Sharp, H. S. 1930. Red-headed woodpeckers and automobiles. Bird-Lore, 32: 352.

Cottam, C. 1931. Birds and motor cars in South Dakota. Wilson Bull., 43: 313-314.

Gordon, K. 1932. Rabbits killed on an Idaho highway. J. Mammal., 13: 169.

Sperry, C.C. 1933. Highway mortality of rabbits in Idaho. J. Mammal., 14: 260.

Stoner, D. 1936. Wildlife casualties on the highways. Wilson Bull., 48: 276-283.

Simmons, J. R. 1938. Feathers and fur on the turnpike. Christopher Publishing House, Boston, MA. 148 p.

Scott, T.G. 1938. Wildlife mortality on Iowa highways. Amer. Midi. Nat., 20: 527-539.

Dickerson, L. M. 1939. The problem of wildlife destruction by automobile traffic. J. Wild. Manage., 3: 104-116.

Davis, W. B. 1940. Mortality of wildlife on a Texas highway. J. Wildl. Manage., 4: 90-91.

Bugbee, R. E. 1945. A note on the mortality of snakes on highways in western Kansas. Trans. Kansas Ac. Sci., 47: 373-374.

McClure, H. E. 1951. An analysis of animal victims on Nebraska's highways. J. Wildl. Manage., 15: 410-   420.

Jahn, L. R. 1959. Highway mortality as an index of deer population change. J. Wildl. Manage.. 20: 70-74.

Hodson N.L.,1966. A survey of road mortality in mammals. J. Zool., London, 148.

McCaffery, K. R. 1973. Road-kills show trends in Wisconsin deer populations. J. Wildl. Manage., 37: 212-216.

Pielou, E.C. 1974. Population and community ecology: principles and methods. Gordon and Breach, New York. 424 p.

Walro, J. M. 1976. Analysis of deer-vehicle accidents in southeastern Ohio. M.S. Thesis, Ohio University, Athens. 19 p.

Adams, C. E. 1983. Road-killed animals as resources for ecological studies. Amer. Bio. Teacher, 45: 256-261.

Garland, T., Jr. and Bradley, W. G. 1984. Effects of a highway on Mojave Desert rodent populations. Amer. Midi. Nat., Ill: 47-56.

Knutson, R. M. 1987. Flattened Fauna. A field guide to common animals of roads, streets, and highways. Ten Speed Press, Berkeley, CA.

Dodd, C. K.Jr, K.M.Enger and Stuart, J. N.1989. Reptiles on highways in north-central Alabama, USA. J. Herp., 23: 197-200.

Seibert, H.C. and Conover, J.H., 1991. Mortality of vertebrates and invertebrates on an Athens County, Ohio, highway. Ohio J. Sci., 91 (4): 163-166, [https://kb.osu.edu/handle/1811/23464]

Rodts, J. Holsbeek, L.and Muyldermans, S. Dieren onder onze wielen. 1998, Brussels, Vupress. 88 p.

Flattened fauna. Peter Hansard and Burton Silver. 2007

The roadkill cookbook. David Larcey, North Coast, 1990

Appendix

Report of an experimental burn of foot and mouth carcasses at South Arscott Farm, Holsworthy, 23 April 2001

by Arthur Boyt, BSc

Summary

The MAFF specification for the design of fires to burn animals slaughtered under the foot and mouth policy results in fires lasting for a week or more with prolonged high levels of atmospheric pollution. At the request of the army an experimental burn of sheep carcasses was carried out using a fire designed to reduce both the duration of the fire and the pollution of the atmosphere. The fire took place at South Arscott Farm near Holsworthy in Devon. Eight ewes and three lambs were burnt on a fire measuring 8ft x 8ft in area and consisting of a crib of timber sleepers. The fire was very hot, produced little smoke and no smell of burning flesh; it completely destroyed the carcasses in 3 hours and left minimal residue of ash and bone fragments. It is recommended that this design of fire be used in any future burns in order to speed up the destruction of carcasses and minimise atmospheric pollution.

Introduction

The outbreak of foot and mouth disease in Britain in February, 2001 resulted in many thousands of animal carcasses requiring disposal. The Ministry of Agriculture, Fisheries and Food became overwhelmed by the scale of the operation, so the army was called in to deal with the slaughter of animals and the disposal of carcasses in Devon and Cumbria. Public opposition to the mass burning of carcasses is fuelled by the vision of plumes of smoke billowing over the countryside to at least 5 miles downwind of fire sites and creating distress and a possible health hazard. Major Forsythe invited the author, a retired fire scientist, to demonstrate a design of fire that he claimed would greatly speed up the process of burning carcasses and cut down on the output of atmospheric pollutants. Any change in the process that would reduce the time to complete disposal and the perceived and actual harm from the process would help to reduce the overall impact of the disease throughout the country.

Fire design

An experimental fire was prepared at South Arscott Farm near Holsworthy in Devon using timber available on the site of a large pyre. The fire measured 8ft x 8ft in area and consisted of a crib of timber baulks (sleepers) 8ft long having a cross section of 9in x 5in. Two sleepers (bearers), 8ft apart, laid on their broad side formed the base of the crib. A sleeper was laid on its narrow side on both these bearers and the space between them filled with kindling. Over the kindling was placed 12 sleepers laid on their narrow side and spaced equidistantly (about 4in) save that the centre two sleepers were placed side by side to form a baulk (10in x 9in). Eleven more sleepers were laid across the others and spaced equidistantly. Four more sleepers were laid over these, two at the edge and two 2ft from the edge. Pallets were cut to fit between the four sleepers on the top of the crib.

Eight ewes (said to be Suffolk/Mule x) were laid in two rows on their sides over these last-mentioned sleepers with the heads of all but one in the centre and three lambs laid over the ewes' heads. Care was taken that the ewe carcasses did not touch each other so that flames could pass around each carcass.

A double layer of pallets was laid over the carcasses and two sheets of 8ft x 4ft particle board laid over the whole to deflect heat and flames onto the top of the pyre intensifying the burning of the carcasses. It was intended that adjustments to the burning rate could be achieved by addition of fuel beneath the crib and between the sleepers. The cover was expected to burn off fairly quickly, at which time it was intended to replace it with sheets of corrugated iron.

Ignition

The pyre had become somewhat wet from rain and fluids leaking out of the carcasses. The original intention to avoid the use of accelerants had to be abandoned and about 2 gallons of kerosine was eventually used to get the fire going.

Fire history

The burn was carried out on 23 April, 2001 starting at 1030 hrs. The weather was fine with a light to variable west wind. The crib was placed in the lee of a 12ft high spoil heap. A photographic record was made of the progress of the fire.

Sheep fire test before placing of covers and ignition © Arthur Boyt

10 min   Fire taking hold after burn-off of two applications of kerosine

Fire test at 10 mins © Arthur Boyt

20 min   Flames reaching through to cover and beginning to fan out over carcasses.

Fire test at 20 mins © Arthur Boyt

25 min   Crib fully involved driving a powerful column of flame and hot gas around the carcasses.

28 min   Upper surface of cover smoking.

30 min   Flame spreading to upper surface of cover.

35 min   Cover consumed, well oxygenated high-speed flames protruding above centre of pyre.

\Test burn at 35 mins © Arthur Boyt

40 min   Carcasses visibly reduced.

42 - 47   Layer of pallets put on top and a cover of sheets of corrugated
min   iron put in place.

60 min   Powerful fire continues unabated, carcasses greatly reduced.

75 min   Some timber 2in x 2in sections inserted between sleepers.
         Three sleepers collapsed.

90 min   Small lumps of carcase remaining, four more sleepers
         collapsed. More sections inserted.

95 min   Some carcass remains fallen through fire to hot fire bed.

100 min   Some carcass remains between sleepers.

120 min   Little carcass fragments remaining. Crib poked to cause
          collapse. Intense fire on the ground.

150 min   One small lump of burning carcass in fire bed.

Test burn at 150 mins © Arthur Boyt

180 min   Hot fire still burning on the ground. Fire raked through and no carcass remains seen. Some bone fragments.

Burn at 180 mins with MAFF burn after 24 hours © Arthur Boyt

At no stage was there any significant smoke production from the fire.

There was no smell of burning flesh. The column of hot gases was carried well up away from the ground once the fire was fully developed.

Residue

The two charred bottom bearers, wood ash and some bone fragments were all that remained on the fire site.

Conclusion

A fire involving a timber crib, 8ft x 8ft, comprised of thirty-one 9in x 5in softwood sleepers, loaded with the carcasses of eight sheep and three lambs and covered first with timber and then with corrugated iron, reduced the carcasses to ash in 3 hours with negligible production of smoke and no smell.

Recommendation

It is recommended that this design of fire be scaled up and tested using cattle as soon as possible. It could certainly be used in any future burns of sheep in order to speed up the destruction of carcasses and minimise atmospheric pollution.

Acknowledgement

The author wishes to thank Major Belinda Forsythe for the invitation and authorisation to demonstrate the design of fire and David Evans and staff of JDM Accord for assistance in provision of materials and help in constructing the crib

Index